Teaching Philosophy

Also available from Continuum

Doing Philosophy by Clare Saunders, David Mossley, George MacDonald Ross and Danielle Lamb

Teaching Philosophy

Edited by
Andrea Kenkmann

continuum

Continuum International Publishing Group

The Tower Building   80 Maiden Lane
11 York Road   Suite 704
London SE1 7NX   New York NY 10038

www.continuumbooks.com

British Library Cataloguing-in-Publication Data
A catalogue record for this book is available from the British Library.

ISBN-10: HB: 1-8470-6243-1
          PB: 1-8470-6244-X

ISBN-13: HB: 978-1-8470-6243-7
          PB: 978-1-8470-6244-4

Library of Congress Cataloging-in-Publication Data
Teaching philosophy / edited by Andrea Kenkmann.
   p. cm.
  Includes bibliographical references (p.   ) and index.
  ISBN 978-1-84706-243-7 – ISBN 978-1-84706-244-4
 1. Philosophy – Study and teaching. I. Kenkmann, Andrea. II. Title.

 B52.T38 2009
 107.1'1–dc22   2008028122

Typeset by Newgen Imaging Systems Pvt Ltd, Chennai, India
Printed and bound in Great Britain by CPI Antony Rowe, Chippenham, Wiltshire

Contents

Contributors

William Edelglass is Professor of Philosophy at Marlboro College, Vermont, US.

Maughn Gregory is Associate Professor at Montclair State University, US and the Director of the Institute for the Advancement of Philosophy for Children.

Finn T. Hansen is Associate Professor at the Danish School of Education at Aarhus University, Denmark.

Gillian Howie is Senior Lecturer and Head of Philosophy at the University of Liverpool, UK.

Phil Hutchinson is Senior Lecturer at Manchester Metropolitan University, UK.

Andrea Kenkmann is a freelance philosopher who taught philosophy at the University of Hertfordshire and the University of East Anglia, UK.

Matt Lavery is a Ph.D. student at the University of East Anglia, UK and currently working at St. Joseph's College, New York, US.

Megan Laverty is Associate Professor in Philosophy and Education at Teachers College, Columbia University, New York, US.

Brendan Larvor is Principal Lecturer and Subject Leader of Philosophy at the University of Hertfordshire, UK.

Drew Leder is Professor of Philosophy at Loyola College in Maryland, US.

Maya Levanon is Assistant Professor at National Louis University, Wisconsin, US.

Michael Loughlin is Reader at Manchester Metropolitan University, UK.

Michael McGhee is Senior Lecturer at the University of Liverpool, UK.

Rupert Read is Reader at the University of East Anglia, UK.

Richard Shusterman is Dorothy F. Schmidt Eminent Scholar in the Humanities and Professor of Philosophy at Florida Atlantic University, US.

Panayiota Vassilopoulou is Lecturer at the University of Liverpool, UK and currently holds a Research Fellowship with the Academy of Finland.

Acknowledgements

I would like to thank all the contributors who supported this project and provided me with encouragement and showed patience and tolerance with my editorial inexperience. Thanks also to all those who contacted me in relation to this project and shared their views and papers with me. I'm grateful to George Yancy for making me realize how prejudiced my conception of philosophy really is and that I have yet to discover the treasures of philosophy that lie outside the boundaries of the Western canon and that these boundaries need reflection.

Thanks also to Chris Webb, Tim Dant and Brendan Larvor for providing advice on matters regarding the English language; in case of any remaining inaccuracies they are of course my responsibility. Last but not least I would like to thank Sarah Campbell and Tom Crick at Continuum for their support and trust at all stages of the project.

Introduction

Andrea Kenkmann

When I had to give my first lecture, I was only worried about the content of what I was going to say. Surely, some smart student was bound to come up with a fiendishly difficult question on Husserl which would reveal my ignorance and leave me utterly embarrassed. I was soon to discover that my students were not quite as smart as I had feared or hoped for, that my ability to present phenomenology in fairly accessible terms gave little reason for concern and I gradually remembered that revealing one's ignorance was no cause for embarrassment anyway.

However, the more I relaxed about the content of my course, the more I wondered about the whole process of teaching philosophy. What was I meant to do? Was I simply preparing my students to pass their exams, or was I taking them along a path of wisdom and inspiring them to think beyond the basics of phenomenology in this case? What is a philosopher trying to achieve when s/he teaches? Yet as well as those fundamental questions regarding the value and meaning of my philosophy teaching, practical questions emerged. Why was the atmosphere in the seminar room so different from what I experienced in my adult education classes? Was it simply the window-less, tennis-court-shaped lecture hall on a Friday morning that prevented us from having vibrant and inspirational discussions or was I, as the lecturer, doing something wrong? Would I need to teach differently in order to achieve a more engaged response from students?

This book is in many ways the result of a personal quest to find answers to these questions. Although there is vast literature on the philosophy of education, there is remarkable little by philosophers reflecting on their own teaching. I wanted to know how colleagues saw their own teaching and find out what they actually did in their classes in practical terms. However, I also hoped to discover how students wished or how they hated to be taught. What would be a philosophy session that provides inspiration to all involved and leave an impact beyond the end-of-course exam? A session that makes us wiser – because is philosophy not after all the love of and desire for wisdom?

Editing this book soon became a tremendous pleasure and privilege as it brought me into contact with many inspirational people. The support and enthusiasm that I received for this project on all fronts was very encouraging; it felt as if this book was long overdue and much needed.

The contributions both from academics as well as students show a shared sense of frustration with the current situation in higher education. As Gillian Howie argues in her introductory paper education has become a commodity in the global economy, where measurability and comparability are paramount. How does the 'love of wisdom' fit into the context of current higher education? Is philosophy not a practice rather than a fixed and measurable entity? Is it not more like poetry rather than merely a set of easily teachable analytic skills, as Michael McGhee suggests?

However, the frustration is coupled with a shared sense of the value and need for philosophy in our times. Exactly because philosophy does not exist in a vacuum, but is embedded in society, it always has political and ethical implications, implications for the future of our society as a whole. Philosophy provides us with the tools of critical thinking, which Phil Hutchinson and Michael Loughlin see as an 'extraordinary opportunity in any society'. A tool that in our consumer society is not only vital to avoid total brainwash and uncritical acceptance of the status quo, but also to create and sustain meaningful communities that shape our future.

Most philosophers in this book see philosophy as a holistic activity that allows us not only to understand ourselves better but that also informs our relations with the world around us. Philosophy is by many of the philosophers here seen as a creative and transformative power. Teaching philosophy thus cannot be separated from ethics and politics; it reveals how and where we stand.

The contributors reflect on their own teaching from different perspectives. Whereas the first three papers provide an overview and introduction to the theme, the following papers deal with embodied and situated teaching. Richard Shusterman shows how his ground-breaking work on somaesthetics could be integrated into philosophy classes. William Edelweiss and Drew Leder both partly leave the traditional seminar room behind to allow students to philosophize in their community and natural surroundings.

In the third part contributors' emphasis is on language. Matt Lavery and Rupert Read argue that language provides a frame for our thinking and thus a critical engagement with language, as philosophy fosters it, will enable us to de-frame and re-frame, i.e. shift paradigms that we have long taken for granted. Whereas the focus on language is here aimed at political transformations, Panayiota Vassilopoulou's interest is to explore and thus also to encourage creativity. She teaches philosophy through metaphors and suggests that metaphors and myths which are often dismissed as mere embellishments of philosophy texts can actually help us explore and understand philosophical arguments at a greater depth. In contrast, Brendan Larvor discusses logic and mathematics and explores how the aesthetic and emotive aspects of learning are usually ignored in philosophy teaching and learning.

The final part brings together philosophers who also work with other groups as well as undergraduates. Megan Laverty and Maughn Gregory are experts on philosophy with children, yet their demand for a wisdom-orientated education is relevant for philosophy teaching irrespective at what level and in what context. Their description of a session with children provides food for thought for university teaching, as it is a community of wonder – as several of the philosophers in this volume suggest – that many of us aim to create in the classroom. Maya Levanon transforms the atmosphere of the classroom through community-of-inquiry pedagogy. Shared spiritual growth rather than knowledge transfer is the aim of learning circles. Finn Hansen draws on his experience of philosophical counselling with professionals to argue that 'to become good philosophical counsellors demands first of all that the philosophical counsellor has a "philosophical musicality", an ability to take his or her departure from the lived experiences of the professionals and a readiness to participate in a Community of Wonder with the professional practitioner'.

The mix of frustration about and passionate belief in philosophy is also echoed in the students' contributions. It is clear that the tuition that students receive provides a major influence on their appreciation of philosophy. As Sam Penman says 'it only takes a passionate lecturer, a lecturer that promotes independent thought, to snap me out of the philosophical doldrums'.

The students also draw our attention to how narrow our conceptions of philosophy are at times in academia. The Western canon remains fairly unchallenged as the core of any philosophy education. Maybe it's time indeed as Chris Rawls suggests that we begin to transcend borders and boundaries; time that we understand philosophy as philo-sophia, the love of and desire for wisdom, rather than as a selection of set texts.

Yet, as the academics, the students also provide some practical advice at times. The classroom tips, as Brendan Larvor calls them, are interspersed in the volume, but they do not provide us with any ultimate way of teaching philosophy, what they show us is that we, as philosophers, need courage to go beyond what is traditionally expected and done in philosophy classes; courage to explore new ways of teaching, not for the sake of a cheap round of applause from our students, but in order to revive philosophy as a praxis, a praxis that enriches our own lives as well as that of our community.

Editing the volume has on the one hand made me acutely aware of all the pressures on academic philosophers (the expectation to churn our publication after publication, acquire grants and deal with increasing amounts of paperwork), but on the other hand it has also shown me that many philosophers are still passionate about their subject and have courage to wander off the beaten track in order to provide inspiration to their students and beyond. My hope for this book is not that it is seen as a guidebook to teaching philosophy, but that it encourages those who are teachers of philosophy to be reflective, open, creative and responsible in their teaching, that it helps us to create communities of learning that are meaningful and that bring us closer to ourselves as well as the world around us.

Chapter 1

Teaching Philosophy in Context: Or Knowledge Does Not Keep Any Better Than Fish

Gillian Howie

Introduction

The term 'mass education' certainly has a populist overtone and for some it indicates an opening of educational borders and an assault on privilege. For others, though, it marks the introduction of 'quasi-academic courses' and 'vocational skills training' into the research-focused university sector. John Patten, as Conservative Secretary of State for Education, rang the first alarmist bells when he warned that to open doors to all and sundry was one way of growing the sector but risked the very excellence on which the sector was built.[1] This concern over the 'self-destruction of one of the nation's assets' chimed with Chris Woodhead's warning that standards would fall with an introduction of 'quasi-academic courses' into the research culture. The point of contention was whether or not the values which define the idea of a university, accepted in the Robbins report and the academic community more generally, were compatible with the provision of a mass higher education. Motivating this argument was the prosaic sentiment that more would mean less and so increased numbers would inevitably lead to a fall in standards.

The account of the development of education from elite to mass and then to universal was first developed by Martin Trow in the early 1970s.[2] Although initially introduced within an American, specifically Californian, context the term accrued political currency in the UK when Tony Blair announced an aspirational 50 per cent participation target at the Labour Party conference in 1999. As our participation rates reach levels which would suggest mass, even universal, education we might expect to see a convergence between US and UK higher education provision. But this is not the case. Peter Scott outlines four principal differences between the two: low failure rates in the UK; policy initiatives in the UK which tend towards uniformity; a cohesive academic culture, and a similarity of mission between institutions.[3] Indeed, these characteristics strain at the very definition of what would count as 'massified' education provision in the US. There are various possible explanations for this tension and, although I draw different conclusions, I find the explanation offered by Scott to be most suggestive. Although Trow's model of mass higher education presumed that a key role of higher education was to train professional workers and to offer vocational training its main role was democratic entitlement.[4] Instead, in the UK twenty years later, expansion was driven by the predicted challenges of globalization foreseen in the labour market.[5]

In this paper I shall be arguing that the cramped debate around 'mass education' as either a tool for social inclusion – and so a good thing – or as 'dumbing down' – and so a bad thing – misses the point. Globalization, which is as Scott notes the driver behind expansion, presents the UK with two well documented and relevant problems. First, the workforce has to be keenly attuned to the new demands of changing productive practice, in some quarters described as 'post-industrialization' or the 'knowledge economy.' Secondly, education itself has found a new global market. These two challenges intersect and provide the context within which universities function and 'grow'. The current political climate encourages education to be represented and treated as a private consumer good and as the public site for the production of skills thought exchangeable to advantage (public and private) in the global economy.[6]

For Scott, this new form of 'mass' education is more flexible in structure, breaks down traditional distinctions – such as that between core and widening participation student – and is less hierarchical. In this paper I shall be suggesting that Scott's rather favourable account of 'postmodern forms of knowledge production' leads him to underestimate the effects of the market on the process and content of learning. The real problem with 'mass' higher education arises not from accommodating greater student numbers, nor in adapting to flexible provision but in the impact of commericalization. This same argument was made by Theodor Adorno about the commercialization of culture in the US around the second-world-war. Mass, or better 'a commercialized', system - of either culture or education – requires there to be a product to distribute. It requires standards of calculable uniformity and multiple copies of a product that can be distributed to numerous – already presupposed – consumers. The purpose of quality mechanisms, procedures and audits was never to 'enhance the learning experience' for more students but to introduce the uniformity identified by Scott required to prepare higher education for the market: in effect to commercialize the sector. It is my contention that the transformation of learning into such an educational product affects not only how and what we teach but also, at a deeper level, learning and even reason itself. The commercialization of the sector requires and produces a form of reason appropriately described as instrumental. The term 'mass' acts as a 'cover-concept'; it disguises underlying tensions by directing attention to intended social benefit; indeed to democratic entitlement. But the underlying tensions are caused by the transformation of learning from a process into a product.

Philosophy in context

As a numbers game there is a superficial case to be made that the UK is now operating with a system geared towards mass provision. However, cutting across all the differences identified by Scott between mass education in the early 1970s in California and mass education in the UK in the 1990s are two definitions of the value and purpose of a university. The purpose of a university is fully exhausted for New Labour in the articulation of extrinsic value: a university's contribution to the knowledge economy and social benefit that thereby accrues. According to Michael Apple the integration of any service, including education, into the market requires four main obstacles to be overcome.[7] First, the service or process has to be transformed into something that can be bought and sold. Secondly, consumer demand has to be created. Thirdly, the working conditions and outlook of employees have to be modified from an idea of collective public service to profit delivery. Lastly, business risks have to be minimized through state support. I shall leave aside the last of these conditions and concentrate on the first three.

Just as the term 'the culture industry' should not be taken too literally, as sections of the cultural media do not resemble traditional production lines, the term 'educational industry' does not conform in a straightforward way to an industrial model. However, if the integration of education into the market required a 'something' that could be bought and sold, the conditions for more systematic delivery had to be created. The 1988 and 1992 Acts gave corporate status and independence from local education authorities to polytechnics and colleges, with the latter abolishing the binary between universities and polytechnics. In-itself this is of course not a bad thing. But, following the auditing effects of the

QAA (Quality Assurance Agency), all universities and colleges - even continuing education and the workers education association - have been brought into line. University central administrations predict a future and unveil their vision in mission statements according to which good practice can be measured. Teaching has become delivery, the learning process has become something that can be delivered, students (or their future employers) have become customers and research is an activity that can be measured in outputs. Despite all talk of diversity of provision, we can now say that pre- and post '92 universities, continuing education departments and the workers education association make up a system uniform as a whole and in every part: we have witnessed the birth of 'the education industry'.[8]

This formation of a uniform higher education system was perfectly in tune with the Bologna declaration (1992) which first introduced the idea of a European Higher Education Area and a European system of quality assured education – both to be established by 2010.[9] The systematization of diverse sectors was noted as a priority in the Berlin Communiqué (2003) which promoted the idea of quality assurance at institutional, national and international levels, as well as a coherent European system of 'mutually shared criteria' relating to quality assurance, peer review and accreditation'. The European systematization of diverse provision created the conditions for a European market and a European product. It could have been otherwise, but the product was articulated in terms of skills. Indeed, educational purpose was commonly articulated as the mission to contribute to the public good by providing new skills demanded by the transformed labour market. In this global economy, with the particular distribution of labour-intensive industries, the less-than-hidden hand has concentrated on funding high technology and biotechnology industries and on equipping workers with skills for employment within those fields.

Behind this skills-based product placement, was the political principle expressed in Lisbon (2000) to make Europe the most competitive and dynamic knowledge-based economy in the world. Commenting that our natural resource is 'our people', the recent Leitch Report argues that unless we become a world leader in skills we will condemn ourselves to a decline in competitiveness, diminishing economic growth and a bleaker future. Quite explicitly, the purpose and value of education is how it enables people to 'participate' more effectively in the labour market throughout the course of their working lives: to contribute fully to global 'knowledge-economies' from a European perspective. Arguments for the private funding of universities need to be placed within the context of a GATS motivated argument for liberalizing the market, where state support is seen as economic protectionism.

Uniform product-based delivery of market-driven skills is only one aspect of the commercialization of the sector. As a major earner of income from abroad – overseas fees were reported to be 2.7 billion in 1999/2000 – universities have become a market 'growth area'. Indeed, the annual global demand for educational services has been estimated at over two trillion dollars.[10] Pursuing a Fordist rather than Maserati production model, UK universities have attempted to exploit global attractiveness by circulating a recognizable product and perhaps it is the case that a good can only be exchanged on the internationalized 'liberalized market' if it is standardized. But the peculiarity of the system is that the product is the difference between the student – who is also the customer – on entry and the student on exit. This 'value-added' is measured by degree classification and employability (destination).

The growth in participation, described above, has been driven by demographics, rising levels of education attainment and enhanced prospects for those with degrees.[11] The cost of this was transferred in part to the home student first through reducing, then abolishing, grants and secondly, in England and Wales, through the introduction of fees. Although class demography barely altered, participation figures remained high as students were convinced that there would be a positive 'rate-of-return'.[12] However, such calculations depended on previous numbers and types of students graduating and to a different labour market context. According to Richard Pearson the number of graduates entering managerial and professional occupations has not only *not* kept pace with expansion but proportions have actually started falling. Numbers entering employment previously described as non-graduate have risen with many such jobs re-describing themselves as graduate positions.[13] Like a diet that increases weight, the increased supply of students has meant that to enter the workplace individuals need to be graduates which increases the supply and then demand of graduates. The consumer market has been secured. Given that students and universities play a major part in the regeneration of local economies it could be argued that we are witness to a brilliant economic strategy of regeneration built on the provision of service funded by undergraduate credit. But the triumph of the policy is that individuals as 'consumers' feel compelled to buy our educational products even though they see right through them.

Philosophy as social practice

The third obstacle to the marketization of education is, according to Apple, the outlook of employees which, he claims, needs to be adapted from an idea of collective public service to profit delivery. The term conservative modernization, adopted from Mark Olssen to explain neo-liberalism in the US, enables us to determine a process which brings 'free-market economics' together with an increase in micromanagement. It is this intrusive 'evidence-based' micromanagement which effects the greatest change in behaviour, if not outlook. In this section I shall explore how the teaching of philosophy could be subject to this process of conservative modernization. My primary interest is why it has become so difficult to articulate the value of education, especially of philosophy, as an end in-itself. In order to address this question, we must first consider our pedagogical model.

To be a teacher of philosophy is not simply to adopt an intention to teach but to occupy a social role in a social institution of an appropriate kind. A university is a set of relatively stable arrangements for regulating activities of academic and related staff, including their relations with each other and those they teach. The form of the relations, and what is taught, will depend on the idea of what the university is for and what it means to be educated. In order to consider this latter question, Glen Langford contrasts an educational model he develops from the art critic Ernst Gomrich with the more dominant empiricist Lockean model.[14] While the first suggests a horizontal or teacher-teacher model the second concentrates on a vertical relation between teacher and pupil. The vertical model indicates a transaction between teacher and student. Accepting that the vertical model complements the horizontal, Langford frames the question of teaching in terms of the horizontal model. Pivotal to this horizontal model is the idea that teaching is a social practice carried on in accordance with a social tradition. The philosophical problem that follows is not 'what counts as educational content?' but how to characterize that social tradition.

To teach in a university then requires an individual to be part of a social practice, to occupy a role, with duties and rights, and to intend to convey knowledge inherited from the past which may provide the grounds for future knowledge. The teacher of philosophy is such because s/he participates in a social practice which has identifiable values. The value or purpose of education is to educate, to bring about education, and for Langford to become educated means learning to become a person.[15] It is to be initiated into things of value, treasures, which may enrich our lives: a process of self-development as Whitehead might say. Each educational practice has an idea as to what a person ought to be, and this guides the practice. Central to the liberal humanist educational tradition is the understanding of a person as someone able to grasp their situation and the possibilities for change inherent within it; learning to be a moral agent in a moral community.

The ethic of the liberal university, the precursor to the modern, was for those working in it to bear responsibility for initiating and entrusting the next generation with the intellectual and cultural tradition. The idea of the university then includes the ideas of individual moral responsibility and responsibility for purpose. It could be argued that responsibility for purpose is what is meant by the characterization of academia as a profession. Any practice though can be organized bureaucratically: by a small number of individuals who may not be involved in the day-to-day vertical encounters and may be involved only in an administrative capacity. But even bureaucrats need to refer back to the principles of the tradition in order to explain and justify their actions. This may explain why the commercialization of the education system was presented in terms of widening participation and social inclusion; terms which resonated with liberal and humanistic principles of equality and social justice embedded within the tradition of the university.

There can be no coherent practice without the practitioners sharing a coherent conception of it. To change a practice, therefore, one must change the practitioners' conception of that practice. There is no way more effective to do this than by altering the mode of behaviour of the individuals concerned. This is why Margaret Thatcher once declared 'the task is not just to change the economy, but to change the soul' and why recommendations of good practice and benchmarking have been rolled out through the nations. The subject provision reviews, followed by institutional audits, have proved remarkably effective in altering first patterns of behaviour, the way in which we articulate what we do and finally the conception of the practice. All of which mark a fracturing, according to Scott, of the academic community itself. Once bound by a common culture, academic life is now 'wired together by management information systems, by the procedural protocols they demand, and by an informational superstructure of strategic targets and performance measures'.[16]

An initial characterization of the horizontal model suggested by Langford is that a tradition communicates a way of seeing the world. If a way of seeing the world is given by a tradition and traditions change, then it must be possible to see the world in different ways: creativity and change are made possible by the tradition which they leave behind. As Plato points out in the first book of the *Republic*, the way of seeing which a practice provides is not neutral so far as possible action is concerned. 'It is a way of doing which guides and structures practice and therefore largely dictates the use to which skills and techniques which it also provides are to be put.'[17] A critical tradition is one which is able to question the guiding principles of the tradition without appealing to any external or a priori criteria. To criticize a social practice from within is to criticize the overall purpose of that practice by appealing, not to something external, but to the purpose itself.

By considering the activity of teaching philosophy as a social practice, it becomes possible to identify values inherent within the tradition and then to distinguish between values which are constitutive from those which are contextual. Constitutive values are those values which make the activity what it is, define it and give it shape. Contextual values are those values and beliefs which although incidental to the activity in question are nonetheless carried by the individuals involved in the activity. These values do not map cleanly onto intrinsic and extrinsic values. Intrinsic values are those values which would define the activity as an end in itself, whilst its extrinsic value would suggests that the activity's value lies in the purpose or usefulness it serves. Constitutive values of the social practice of philosophy have always included an extrinsic or purposive feature. Indeed vocational training and skills provision have always featured as part of a university's function.

The constitutive values of our practice however are much more than this. Philosophers have in the past taken advantage of contemporary knowledge and expertise, often themselves innovators in new disciplines.[18] Although discipline distinction is rather a modern invention and all university disciplines share a wish to convey their tradition, intellectual pathways and the benefit of critical thought, philosophy is peculiarly concerned with critical thought. Learning to think critically is, according to Stephen Clark, learning to discover, order, verbalize, remember and present good argument. Discovery of good argument is itself a craft that requires arts of disposition, style, memory and presentation.[19] Learning to think provides necessary if not sufficient conditions for being genuinely virtuous; for learning to be a person. Learning to be a person is intimately bound to the idea of self-reflection, moral agency and responsibility. The test of a decent moralist, says Clark drawing on Chesterton, as of a decent scientist, is that she recognizes that her knowledge is incomplete, her theories tentative, and yet does not despair.

The gauntlet thrown by Plato in the Gorgias is to articulate the values intrinsic to 'a life of the mind'. Taking up Callicles' challenge, Raimond Gaita argues for a confluence between the idea of the university and the intrinsic values of (a philosophical) education, of the 'life of the mind'.[20]

While the cloistered origins of the university system could provide content to this idea, a secular and modern university system struggles to express the value of education as an end-in-itself.[21] If each discipline preserves and passes on treasures then perhaps the treasures to be preserved by philosophers concern the value of the 'life of the mind'; a space in which we can think about thought itself and develop an aptitude for critical reflection.

If academic philosophy has anything at all to do with 'learning to think' then the first question is whether or not it is possible to teach philosophy at all and, secondly whether it is possible to teach philosophy under the current conditions. I shall assume that under certain conditions it is indeed possible. But, if the treasure that philosophers pass to future generations is the idea of a learned and imaginative life then the pressing question is whether such a life can ever be an article of commerce. The contextual values of the contemporary social practice of teaching philosophy are infecting the practice of philosophy, becoming constitutive of the 'philosophical life' itself. It is my concern that without realizing it, we are teaching students not to tease apart the tangled web of doctrine, habit, mood and inspiration[22] but to think in a fashion that is antithetical to critical enquiry. The question I am pursuing is whether mass (commercialized) education eliminates the very possibility of critical and imaginative thought or whether still, within the dim recesses of properly modularized philosophical content, we can detect and then animate arcane philosophical practice.

The schema of mass education

Often accused of cultural elitism, Theodor Adorno introduced a distinction between works that could be described as 'high art' and those which he designated examples of 'mass culture'. 'High art', not to be confused with the cultural heritage of the elite, provides a refuge for individuality and critical knowledge whilst the latter reproduces the status quo and the personality structures that would accept it.[23] If the term 'mass' operates as a synonym it is not for 'popular culture' but for 'cultural commodity'. Acknowledging that there had always been a market in art he believed that something had happened such that artistic endeavours became commodities through and through. Extrapolating from this we can say that when the profit motive is transferred onto more and more cultural forms, artistic endeavours are transformed into a species of commodity 'marketable and interchangeable like an industrial product'.[24] At the same time, new reproductive processes are introduced into culture on the grounds that if millions participate in culture, culture has to 'modernize'; it has to be able to satisfy increased needs by delivering identical goods.[25] The customer should be shown that all his needs are capable of fulfilment but those needs are so predetermined that s/he finds himself the eternal consumer.

In mass education, 'educational industries' are a central part of the reconfiguration of the economic and industrial landscape. The transformation of learning into an educational product with providers, consumers and a market is not achieved when a student pays fees. Nor is it achieved when employers are defined as the new customers. The commodification of learning is achieved when the learning process is packaged as a uniform and interchangeable (standardized) good with numerous – *already presupposed* - recipients. It is this standardization of an educational product that distinguishes mass education from 'high' education.[26] The stratification of the sector into distinct providers and a range of educational goods, gives only the appearance of variety. For all talk of selectivity, or bespoke education, higher education institutions in England are funded according to a standard formula which only differentiates according to price group intended to reflect the higher cost of teaching those subjects.[27] Structural similarities arise in education as the result of distribution and mechanical reproduction: so that all students can be guaranteed 'the same learning experience' and standardization must aim at a standard response.

For Plato education is the attempt to ignite fire in a child's soul and certainly has nothing to do with scraps of information. Rob Brecher draws our attention to the derivation of the term 'modular'. Originally meaning a small measure (*modulus*), it came to mean, in the context of Henry Ford's production line 'a length chosen as the basis for the dimension of parts of a building, car etc to facilitate their co-ordination'. It is as a production unit or component part that the module reveals the current political and economic context of higher education. With the process of learning segmented into parcelled-up weeks, each with learning objectives, outcomes and assessment appropriate to task, the module has become mechanically reproducible. Each part is a tasty morsel of philosophical delight: a light sprinkling of logic, a dash of 'the spiritual', a blast of scepticism. 'The result of teaching small parts of a large number of subjects is the passive reception of disconnected ideas, not illuminated by any spark of vitality'.[28]

Reproducing the structure of the module, each lecture is supposed to introduce three main points and conclude with the same, as though learning were predictable and without surprise. With highlights appearing in the virtual learning environment, and handouts reflecting the perfectly-honed circle, students are acclimatized to philosophical argument as climax and repetition: a neurotic and desolate return of sameness over and over.[29] As lecturers struggle with podcasting and discussion fora, new technologies merely contribute an aura of innovation and spontaneity which are calculated in advance. To be user-friendly, content has to be reduced and each part sliced from the whole. In such cases, the organization of the whole makes no impression whatsoever except as an extrinsic demand which determines the range of what is permitted. Even these parts are given a pedagogic shine as though ease of consumption were unproblematically in the interests of students. An impression bolstered by reading lists which include innumerable 'idiot guides'. A similar phenomenon in the music industry was described by Adorno as 'quotation listening'.

Contributing to the wooden futility in education, for most the rhythm and character of mental growth is forced into a twelve week pattern of note-taking and assessment. A successful course is attuned to the students' instrumental fixation on assessment and delivers the right contribution to the 'degree classification ratio'. This is all the better for league tables if student feedback reflects that a few hits were played along the way. Far from being a democratization of learning, this tends to amount to a three minute sound-bite that stands a chance of arresting the students' wavering attention; 'the easy yet catchy, the skilful yet simple; the object is to overpower the customer who is conceived as absent-minded or resistant'.[30] As pleasure turns into boredom, philosophical conversation regresses to mere reaction with familiar and standardized formulas.

In the rush to assessment, students require cognitive adroitness and powers of observation but sustained thought is impossible if they are not to miss the relentless outpouring of facts. The most adroit among them will note that all s/he has to do is complete the assessment according to the criteria that are specified in the course description.[31] Because 'failure' is marked as failure of product delivery and counted against a department, we maintain progression rates at all costs.[32] In this closed economy, the student is assured that his needs will be satisfied, the 2:1 guaranteed, if he only delivers according to the pre-specified criteria. Lecture content passes through the student without mastication, regurgitated without thought. Here, values are collapsed into one basic value: survival or successful self-assertion.[33]

Professional concern for students, which was implicit in the practice of academic philosophy, has been exploited so that staff adopt 'new learning strategies' in order to accommodate 'new learning needs'. For all talk about self-reflective learning, we excise from students' vocabulary their own experience and responses to that experience; except, of course, in the most reduced sensory fashion. The student will find herself rewarded for internalizing pre-formed assessment criteria. Reflecting on herself according to external criteria linked to course outcome, the student's process of self-reflection is infected and she will only be able to understand herself as a series of performative projects whose aims neatly coincide with the status quo. This increasing tendency to define practical problems in such an instrumental way is what Habermas would describe as technocratic consciousness.

The recent alliance between neo-liberalism and 'universal welfarism' is most marked in the government policy to drive out the slothful and indolent, to clear out the dead wood and to make sure that staff are 'kept up to the mark'. Under the auspices of professionalism, the university has been soaked in the language of productivity. We can see the crude positivism once again in the publishing frenzy, engendered by the research assessment exercise. A frenzy described by Louise Morley as 'coercive creativity'. For Whitehead it seemed obvious that a university's output, in the form of original ideas, could not be measured solely by printed papers and books labelled with the names of the authors. Nor by citations, we could add. But the academic community, abstracted from – but in hock to – the hurdy-gurdy of commerce, has been unable to respond with any conviction.

In the disenchanted cloisters, the concept of vocation has given way to career development and 'professionalism'. Estranged from the intrinsic values that animated the academic practice in the first place, staff are encouraged to reflect on their intellectual life and, in their annual reviews, they find that the new telos is performance rather than enlightenment. The appropriate criteria suited to promoted roles are articulated in terms of skills and measurable outputs and soon it will appear to be irritatingly – rather than quaintly – anachronistic to consider the value, rather than values, of scholarship. Each of us is encouraged to 'make a continual enterprise of ourselves', to demonstrate 'excellence' and 'innovation'. In the Kantian cosmopolitan tradition roles may have a function, but those filling the roles do not. The recent higher education role analysis makes a virtue of the fact that a role possesses objective reality in that it is independent from any individual who happens to occupy it. But, just as it is not always clear how Kant's public man of critical letters could maintain a distance from the role he occupies, so individual members of staff – who are asked to quantify that which is most intimately their own – may find it more difficult to think against the grain.

Even those of us sceptical of the neo-conservative alliance find ourselves extolling the virtues of transparency, efficiency and enterprise: 'all the better to manage you with, my dear'. We encourage, chivvy and harass staff into behaving in ways that conform to the mission, keeping quiet as to how this enables us to convert cultural into economic capital. In the process, quantity takes the hue of quality and the weight of an idea depends on the amount of copies sold. Peer exploitation is in some cases an unintended consequence of distancing strategies adopted to cope with the pressure of bureaucracy but in others it can be a conscious strategy 'enacted through tactical micro-political manoeuvring by certain individuals to enable them to pursue their own particular research and career interests'.[34] Where the appropriation of labour takes place by senior faculty, the actual conditions for academic labour are revealed and it seems laughable that we may ever have had the experience of a living, courteous, analytical community of collegial discourse.

The proliferation of auditing, from subject provision reviews to internal undergraduate and graduate periodic reviews, from module questionnaires to national student satisfaction surveys and league tables, is an over-excited and shrill demand for measure and system. In this world of Taylorism and crude positivism, the means have become the ends and reason has become instrumental. The homogeneity of the learning experience betrays the product placement of 'bespoke education' as all activities are gathered together in a uniform, quantifiable and standardized manner. This unifying function – abstraction, quantification, standardization – brings about a mass rather than open education, conformism rather than enlightenment. Education is precisely the very condition that excludes a mentality that would wish to measure it and mass education is 'counter-enlightenment'.

Mass education then reproduces the status quo and helps to produce the personality structures which affirm the world as it is. It reinforces a state of dependence, anxiety and ego-weakness. The work of philosophy is not to line up alternatives along a shelf of possible utopias but it surely is 'to resist by its form alone the course of the world, which permanently puts a pistol to men's heads'.[35] Yet this seems to be in tension with the opposing demand for liberty and autonomy or its academic equivalent 'the life of the mind'. Without such political autonomy, as Isaiah Berlin and Bertrand Russell warned, cognitive reflection is assimilated into political function. But by already claiming such autonomy academics insist on a rupture between the content of philosophy and political and social reality. Despite the post-Kantian tenor of most philosophy, there is an a priori commitment to the distinction between transcendental and empirical subjectivity. The latter for the most part is without interest, being the material for psychologists and sociologists. Only the former provides the substance of philosophical discussion, even if just to eliminate such talk. In his account of philosophy 'as part of a flesh and blood human life', Colin McGinn for instance describes the philosopher as one who has a proclivity for the general, not the particular, the abstract, not the concrete. The rupture leaves reason conducting its own appeal and setting its own limits. The very values that would make sense of the 'life of the mind' are already exorcized along with spirits, hobgoblins and sprites.

Jay Bernstein's insightful analysis of instrumental rationality draws our attention to the broad consequences of this when he explains how the convergence of scientific rationality in intellectual life with bureaucratic rationality has resulted in a disenchanted world. Such a world finds itself drained of sources of meaning and significance that traditionally anchored not only ethical practice but also all meaningful goal-directed action.[36] Rigid concepts, immune to development, actually prevent thought grasping the object. Similarly, the 'administrative apparatus of thought' and its laws lose flexibility, become rigid and impair reason.[37] Not unlike the bureaucratic mode of thought, the administrative principles of reason come to dominate thought.

Conclusion

Each profession guards a particular range of values, described by Gaita as treasures, and makes its own contribution to the community. The description of education as the 'engine of the economy' seemed to place the university system on centre stage, under the full glare of the lights of administration. But in adopting the coveted role, universities – encouraged by the government – concentrated on extrinsic social and economic values. Professions make a contribution to the life of the community because the values they reflect in their practice are those more generally held as social values.[38] The curious blend of financial rewards and penalties with pedagogical directives from the quality assurance agency has brought the ends of education in line with particular political ends. This is indeed Apple's account of conservative modernism: an identity of values between what were public services and the economy and a modification of individual practice appropriate to delivering the ends.

Yet from within our philosophical tradition can be drawn the resources to recognize and appraise a dissonance between the new social values of teaching and those critical values which are constitutive of reflective philosophical practice. How can we keep ideas alive so that they do not become inert, merely replicated by students in an examination hall? Human minds are not dead matter:

> The evocation of curiosity, of judgment, of the power of mastering a complicated tangle of circumstances, the use of theory as foresight in special cases – all these powers are not to be imparted by a set rule embodied in one schedule of examination subjects.[39]

Academics may well impart information but can do so in such a way that the imagination is engaged, which in turn transforms knowledge.

Of course, I have been considering tendencies, social critique must after all begin in exaggeration, and there are important counter-tendencies. The language of productivity may be totalising but it is not-yet-total. We can exalt those learning spaces which have resisted pick-and-mix modularization. Where there is modularization, we can begin by unpicking pre-specified modular intended-learning-outcomes so that we may reintroduce some spontaneity into the learning process. By reminding students of the virtues of depth and complexity, we can begin the struggle against the cognitive closures of the PSP generation. By failing students we can break through the administered and closed circle of 'product delivery'.

As Whitehead appositely notes, imagination cannot be measured by the yard or weighed by the pound and then delivered to the students by members of the faculty. The intellectual dishonesty of the league tables should no longer be our secret. The justification for a university is that it preserves the connection between knowledge and the zest of life in an imaginative consideration of learning. It is because of this connection to the imagination that Whitehead declares that 'knowledge does not keep any better than fish'.[40]

The connection to the imagination, and incidental benefits brought to commerce, has not gone unnoticed and Advanced Institutes make it their mission. In a closed space, protected from the sector's quantification of quality, Advanced Institutes settle within their institutional privilege and replicate patterns of condescension.[41] Just as the distribution of research funding predictably relates back to neatly structured hierarchies, in which the position of elite universities is strengthened, star academics, in quasi-autonomous Advanced Institutes, are able to recover an 'other-worldliness'.[42] But from this, our tradition can remember and recover the intrinsic value of the scholarly, creative and intellectual life.

During the first period of modernization, Humboldt argued that the State should protect universities from social imperatives and that it is in the State's interest to guarantee unlimited internal freedom. Hannah Arendt echoes this when she describes education as the preparation of the next generation for the task of renewing a common world, in a way unforeseen by the current generation. 'Other-worldliness' is precisely the opportunity to consider the future anew, in light of the past, according to values which may – or may not – accord with the values of the present. Just as the employability agenda saturates the imagination of the student by eliminating any autonomy of the learning process, so too the bureaucratic procedures and processes overwrite critical reason with instrumental reason for the academic. Peter Scott encourages the academic community to develop new definitions of general education appropriate to future global learning economies.[43] To do so, we need to retrieve the imaginative ideal of the university and liberal-humanist ideal of person-hood: wishing for the right thing may be the most difficult art of all.[44] As Adorno said of art, this may not be the time for philosophy that is political but politics has certainly migrated into the autonomous sphere of the academy and into academic philosophy and sometimes universities must resist their times if they are not to betray their students.[45]

Notes

[1] Quoted in Morley, L. (2003), *Quality and Power in Higher Education*. Berkshire: SHRE and Open University Press. p. 130.

[2] Trow, M. (1974), 'Problems in the Transition from Elite to Mass Education'. *Policies for Higher Education from the General Report on the Conference on Future Structures of Post-Secondary Education*. Paris: OECD.

[3] Scott, P. (2005), 'Mass Higher Education – Ten Years On', *Perspectives* 9 (3), pp. 68–73, p. 70.

[4] Ibid, p. 71.

[5] David Blunkett's speech on higher education at Greenwich University (February 2000).

[6] Jonathan, R. (1997), 'Illusory Freedoms: Liberalism, Education and the Market', *Journal of Philosophy of Education* 31 (1).

[7] Apple, M. (2005), 'Education, Markets and an Audit Culture' in G. Howie (ed.) 'Universities in the UK: Drowning by Numbers'. *Critical Quarterly* 47 (1–2), pp. 11–29, p. 12.

[8] Adorno, T. and Horkheimer, M. ([1944]1986), *Dialectic of Enlightenment*. London: Verso. Adorno describes the formation of the culture industry p. 120. I refer to Adorno rather than Adorno and Horkheimer because this essay complements other essays on the culture industry.

[9] See Howie, G. (2005), pp. 1–10.

[10] Merrill Lynch estimated this demand to be in excess of US$2 trillion per year (figure quoted Alex Nunn, *The General Agreement on Trade in Services*; briefing

document, June 2004). US college students spend $105 billion annually. Globally the numbers of degree students are estimated to rise from 42 million in 1990 to 97 million in 2010 and 159 million in 2025 (quoted Wende, M. (2002) 'The Role of US Higher Education in the Global E-Learning Market' *CSHE* 1.02, p. 2). This would suggest that the UK and US experience will converge, although the European market might tend away from 'luxury' goods such as that provided by the Ivy League. I would expect the Russell Group to try to position its own goods against Ivy League bespoke production. This would require government policy to be less invasive.

[11] The percentage rise has been from 39.2% (2000) to 39.8% (2007) quoted Gill, J. 'Labour concedes that it won't deliver its 50% target on time'. *THES* no 1,841, 17–23 April 2008.

[12] This would support the argument that 'mass education' like 'mass culture' ensures hierarchical stability despite promising otherwise.

[13] Pearson, R. (2005), 'The Demise of the Graduate Labour Market' in Ian McNay (ed.) *Beyond Mass Education: Building on Experience.* Berkshire: McGraw-Hill, pp. 68–78, p. 71.

[14] Langford, G. (1985), *Education, Persons and Society: A Philosophical Enquiry.* London: Macmillan.

[15] As a consequence of this association, Langford argues that education is connected to the youth. Although learning might continue, education in this sense could be complete. Such an analysis would provide the grounds for saying that the idea of 'life-long learning' conflates education and learning absorbing into learning those activities more properly suited to education, such as forms of assessment. Continuing education classes that have found themselves submerged by the new regime of rigorous assessment might find relief in Langford's argument.

[16] Scott, P. (2002), 'The Future of General Education in Mass Higher Education Systems,' *Higher Education Policy* 15 (1), pp. 61–75, p. 64.

[17] Plato, *Republic.* p. 18.

[18] See here Clark, S. (2000), 'Have Biologists Wrapped Up Philosophy', *Inquiry* 145.

[19] Clark, S. (1996), 'Thinking about How and Why to Think', *Philosophy* 71, pp. 385–403, p. 390.

[20] Gaita, R. (2005), 'Callicles' Challenge', *Critical Quarterly* 47 (1–2), pp. 40–52.

[21] For an account of the gendered quality of this cloistered characteristic see Howie, G. and Tauchert A. (2002), 'Institutional Discrimination and the Cloistered Academic Ideal', in Howie, G. and Tauchert A. (eds) *Gender, Teaching and research: Challenges for the 21st Century.* London: Ashgate, pp. 59–72.

[22] Clark, S. (1989) 'How to Reason about Value Judgments' in A. Phillips-Griffiths (ed.) *Key Themes in Philosophy.* Cambridge University Press, pp. 173–190.

[23] Kellner, D. (2002), 'Adorno and the Dialectics of Mass Culture' in N. Gibson and A. Ruben. *Adorno: A Critical Reader.* Oxford: Blackwell, pp. 86–109, p. 92.

[24] Adorno, T. And Horkheimer, M. *Dialectic of Enlightenment.* p. 158.

[25] Ibid, p. 121.

[26] Scott draws a distinction between 'old style' and 'new style' mass education which might be useful in this context, p. 72.

[27] Ibid, p. 70.

[28] Whitehead, A. (1962), *The Aims of Education and Other Essays*. London: Ernest Benn Limited, p. 2.

[29] Jameson, F. (1990) *Late Marxism, Adorno: Or The Persistence of the Dialectic*. London and New York: Verso, p. 16.

[30] Adorno, and Horkheimer *Dialectic of Enlightenment*. p. 163.

[31] In *Sociology, Equality, and Education* (1976), Anthony Flew argues that the notions of pursuing a course of instruction and of trying to master its contents without any kind of assessment are self-contradictory.

[32] Scott points out that our 'wastage' rate in the worst-performing institution in Britain would be average for a state university in the US. p. 70. See also Attwood, R. (2008) 'The Verdict: Universities are Failing Too Few People', *THES* no 1,841, 17–23 April 2008.

[33] This is the third level of rationalization pinpointed by Jurgen Habermas. It is followed by a fourth; automated decision-making which could be delegated to computers. It is pertinent here to note the new assessment software.

[34] Worthington, F. and Hodgson, J. (2005), 'Academic Labour and the Politics of Quality in Higher Education: A Critical Evaluation of the Conditions of Possibility of Resistance', *Critical Quarterly* 47, 1–2. pp. 96–110, p. 98.

[35] Adorno, T. ([1962]1978) 'Commitment', in Andrew Arato and Eike Gebhart (eds) *The Essential Frankfurt School Reader*. London: Blackwell, pp. 300–318, p. 304.

[36] Bernstein, J. (2001), *Adorno: Disenchantment and Ethics*. Cambridge: Cambridge University Press. p. 4–5

[37] Yvonne Sherratt (1999) 'Instrumental reason's unreason' in *Philosophy and Social Criticism* vol 25 no 4 pp. 23–42.

[38] Langford, *Education, Persons and Society*. p. 61.

[39] Whitehead, *The Aims of Education*. p. 8.

[40] Ibid, p. 147.

[41] 'What we continue to have is – very sadly – an untidy and rather volatile hierarchy of institutions distinguished not by different functions but patterns of condescension – in other words the good old British class system at its worst.' Scott, 'The Future of General Education', p. 73.

[42] Scott sees this in contradiction to the 'flat' and 'mobile' structures more closely associated with 'the knowledge-economy'. If, however, we do not view the 'knowledge-economy' as a distinct productive phase, a securing of the status quo would be quite predictable. Indeed, Scott's endorsement of the description of 'postmodern' knowledge production undermines his ability to make sense of the concentration of research selectivity, aggravated and casualized working conditions and the reformation of institutional hierarchy.

[43] Scott, 'The Future of General Education', p. 67.

[44] Adorno, quoted Horowitz, A. (2002), 'By a Hair's Breadth: Critique, Transcendence and the Ethical in Adorno and Levinas', *Philosophy and Social Criticism* 28 (2), pp. 213–248, p. 213.

[45] Gaita, p. 51.

Chapter 2

Wisdom and Virtue:
Or What Do Philosophers Teach?

Michael McGhee

A standard of comparison

Beneath the surface of these fragmented reflections on teaching philosophy
are personal images of scenes from the last 35 years, scenes of my success
and failure, courage and cowardice, as a teacher of philosophy. There is
more than one kind of success and failure in teaching, but my occasional
perplexity about teaching intertwines with a more chronic one about what
it is to do philosophy at all, or, since even that phrase carries a certain self-
distancing within it, about what it is to *be* a philosopher, and whether and
to what extent I have been *either* a philosopher *or* a teacher of philosophy,
questions grounded in an uncomfortable standard of comparison in the
tradition – that of Plato's Academy, the inauguration of which was a *creative
act* that sprang from the desire to protect and nourish the possibility of
wisdom rather than, say, 'knowledge transfer' – itself a laudable aim which
is, however, in the ascendant in our universities, trailing a methodology of
teaching which is entirely proper to its needs but applied thoughtlessly to
disciplines that requires quite different methods.[1]

What follows is impressionistic and as much about my own intellectual ambivalence and uncertainty as about the state of philosophy. In
any event I am sure that other philosophers have had a sense of empti-
ness when they have talked about what most matters to them, but without apparent reaction; or a sense of hollowness when they have given
the audience what it wants but not yet what it ought to have; or, and
marvellously, a sense of fulfilment when students are utterly absorbed
and engaged – and all this quite independently of the petty domestic
achievement of proper preparation, the PowerPoint presentation, the
e-learning and other initiatives commended with one (anxious) voice by
our Teaching and Learning Committees as 'good practice' or, and even

better, as 'innovative' in 'delivering' a module – though 'delivering' is a more significant metaphor than first appears . . .

Feeling and poetry

It seems to me that two related and half-submerged dichotomies have infected philosophy and the way we teach it – the first of these is between intellect and feeling, the second, to put it pointedly and controversially in these scientist times, is between philosophy and poetry. Now contemporary philosophers almost never talk of the 'love of wisdom' and if it is raised by their students as the true vocation, perhaps, of the philosopher they are likely to say, though, alas, without irony, that such a notion belongs to the distant history of the discipline and has little to do with our contemporary agenda. And yet, perhaps the embarrassment has something to do with the dichotomies.

We have a dichotomy, an a priori intellectual distortion that determines in advance the direction of conscious reflection, when two elements that belong together within an integrated whole, are forced apart and treated independently and out of all connection with each other. Overcoming the dichotomy is a matter of restoring the connections, though practice, and this is crucial and almost the main theme of this paper, may well lag behind the theoretical achievement. Thus, although it is now widely acknowledged that we have sometimes fatally split thought from feeling, the terms of their re-integration in our practice have hardly been considered, and this seems to me to be a failure of (collective) *wisdom*.

But my claim that there is a dichotomy between philosophy and *poetry* may seem more surprising, and even tendentious, so it may be helpful to call in aid here two rather different figures, John Stuart Mill and Ludwig Wittgenstein. But before I do so it is worth repeating that if there is indeed a genuine dichotomy to be overcome it should issue in a change in how we approach the teaching of philosophy, since our practice as philosophers, which I take to be continuous with our practice as teachers, is a function of our *conception* of the discipline: if literary art or poetry should be (re-)integrated into that conception then it must make a difference to how we teach – though this may not be to the liking of all teachers or all students because it will make on us a different set of demands (and the academy institutionalizes *a set of aptitudes* and the interests in both senses that go with it). This dissonance between theory and practice, though, is itself, again, an image of the distinction between knowledge and wisdom.

The young John Stuart Mill wrote in a letter to Thomas Carlyle that

> ... one thing not useless to do would be to ... make those who are not poets understand that poetry is higher than logic, and that the union of the two is philosophy.[2]

In his notebooks Wittgenstein wrote: Philosophie dürfte man eigentlich nur dichten.[3]

These remarks are striking, and if they put pressure on our conception of philosophy they also must put pressure on our conception of poetry. It must be more than 'the merely decorative word', as Pound said. So it is not 'what oft was thought', as Pope puts it – indeed must *not* be what oft was thought, but rather what we are by its means only now able to bring to thought at all – in the spirit of Shelley's 'marking the before unapprehended relations of things' – which poetry does just because it is, as he says, 'vitally metaphorical', where, in the same way, what is metaphorical is to be understood, not as an ornamental way of expressing what we already know or understand, but as the unexpected means to the startling disclosure of what we did not until then realize or understand.

But I said that the two dichotomies are related (and one can hardly articulate this without the absurdity becoming evident): philosophy is alleged to appeal to the intellect and poetry to feeling. One might recall here and against that thought Wordsworth's notion of 'feeling intellect', and there is no such dualism in Kant:

> *Poetry* ... expands the mind by giving freedom to the imagination and by offering, from among the boundless multiplicity of possible forms accordant with a given concept, to whose bounds it is restricted, that one which couples with the presentation of the concept a wealth of thought (*Gedankenfülle*) to which no verbal expression is completely adequate, and by thus rising aesthetically to ideas.[4]

This highly perceptive remark of Kant's hints at how the metaphorical content of an image works upon the imagination in a vivid present of experience, but such content also and crucially discloses itself and the realities it opens up *slowly* and over time, attracting a compelled attention before it is understood, where the compulsion is the unconscious recognition of significance.

Teachers of philosophy take themselves, on the whole, to have a responsibility to *train the intellect* and are all too likely to consider the *feelings* of their students, as indeed their own, to be a private and irrelevant[5] matter that is no one else's business – a 'defensive' attitude which shows that we know ourselves 'vulnerable' where feeling is concerned: indeed our resentment when our *ideas* are 'attacked' shows that unconsciously at least we all know very well that thought, feeling and our sense of identity are vitally related, and it shows that this 'embattled' and anxious self is in danger and that this is the real source of the unconscious martial imagery so much deplored in philosophy.

Many students of philosophy also seem to subscribe to this never quite explicit doctrine, that their feelings are not part of the contract, even though one knows very well that their feelings are involved in the very business of philosophy, in the unsettling experience of the *elenchus* and the emotional shock and disarray of *aporia*, in which the sense both of the world and one's identity within it seem threatened and undermined. Unfortunately, we no longer provide health warnings about such eventualities. Not all students are capable of the logical and conceptual dexterity that is demanded by philosophy and not all of those who possess that dexterity are able or willing to submit themselves to this ordeal of emotional shock and disarray.

But it is worth noting, by contrast, and as a possible future aid, that no such contract about feeling appears to be in place in Departments of Drama, where teachers almost routinely appeal to the *emotional intelligence* of their students, who implicitly consent to their emotional lives and resources being addressed and challenged. Part of their training is in the authentic representation of feeling in articulated thought, in speech, conduct and demeanour and this means that they must draw on, and are encouraged and goaded into drawing on, their own life-experience, their own perplexities, and must learn to rely on observation, imagination, memory and self-knowledge – and, also, of course, on each other.[6]

On knowing the main positions

Philosophers are famously reluctant to *define* philosophy – beyond saying, for instance, that it is an *activity* rather than a subject to be studied, that it is not a body of knowledge but a method and spirit of inquiry that depends upon conversation and dialogue, though this latter aspect becomes increasingly unavailable as student numbers rise and the basic conditions for the possibility of genuine conversation and dialogue – time and personal acquaintance – recede. The teacher of philosophy will tend to dismiss requests for definition and just get on and *do* philosophy – with the students in tow as it were – in the expectation that they will get the point and start to do on their own account what their teachers exemplify.

Although this approach is pedagogically sound as far as it goes, nevertheless what one *does*, how one teaches philosophy, is a function of one's conception of the discipline, and that conception will certainly and properly reflect the necessary tasks of one's time, which become as it were the 'normal science' of philosophy – and *may*, in a time of specialism and narrow focus, exemplify nothing else. The resident danger of this approach, then, lies in taking these tasks to be *the thing itself* – and in regarding the *history* of philosophy exclusively in the light of advances in the treatment of particular favoured problems, without further attention to what else might be found outside the narrow focus determined by these prior interests. And yet this amounts to an almost catastrophic failure to learn how to read – to learn just to read without this being a kind of search for proof texts as it were.

A philosophically well educated student in the mainstream Analytic tradition will answer more or less to the Aims and Objectives that have attached themselves to Programmes of Study, they will have good dialectical skills, will have an engaged acquaintance with the state of the discipline within their own tradition and a good grasp of the historical developments that led to that state. They will, however, share with many of their teachers an almost invincible ignorance of the other traditions whose progress helps to determine the larger and more fragmented state of the discipline in the wider world. In particular, to use an egregious example, they will be unaware of how a European philosophical dialogue which still seemed entirely possible, not to say normal, in the eighteenth and nineteenth centuries had become unavailable in the twentieth.[7] So they will disdain (and quite rightly in some cases) styles of thinking and philosophical idioms with which in truth they are ill-equipped to engage – styles and idioms that have grown out of close attention precisely to what is 'vitally metaphorical'. But they will know a good argument when they see it, and a bad one, though perhaps if they favour an argument the premises may be granted too easily without the patient sifting of distinctions that is prior to argument, and they are likely to see the history and contemporary condition of philosophy in terms of a set of 'positions' which can be defended or refuted thus and so.

It would be mad to *deny* that philosophy deals in positions and problems and arguments – but it is not mad to complain that we come to them too quickly, without reflecting on the conditions of inquiry that eventually give rise to them. The virtue of negative capability that sustains a person through the unpleasant experience of disorientation and loss of bearings is not on the curriculum; the 'not knowing one's way about' that Wittgenstein said was the form of a philosophical problem, is hardly referred to. And so our students seek impatiently and indignantly for release into the clearly defined terrain of positions, problems and arguments . . . which will allow them to finish an assignment before the deadline or pass an exam: in this environment the creative condition of philosophical confusion and tension before release is not permitted – or will at least be penalized for lateness on the grounds that otherwise it is unfair on those whose time-management is allegedly more efficient.

What troubles me about this kind of otherwise admirable philosophical education is that it can leave one's life and sense of identity intact, as in 'untouched' and unaffected. In some cases philosophers simply shore up by minute and ingenious argument their prior sense of world and identity. There is no inwardness in it, no loss of the sense through *elenchus* and *aporia* of self and world, but rather a self image built up around a carapace of *expertise* and *competence*, no gestation or bringing forth – and therefore no wisdom and what Socrates says to Agathon seems little to do with the case:

> It would be very nice, Agathon, if wisdom were like water, and flowed by contact out of a person who has more into one who has less, just as water can be made to flow through a thread of wool out of the fuller of two cups into the emptier.[8] (*Symposium* 175d)[9]

Now we have to make compromises in the face of difficult political and social realities, we have to negotiate with an inimical instrumentalism in our institutions of higher education which suffer systemic anxiety in the face of the need to deliver and so defend like out-voted cabinet ministers policies not within their control or of their making, and of course it is possible to identify the knowledge and skills that are developed in a philosophy degree, transferable skills that render students (highly) employable, and if the ethos demands that we factor employability into our module specifications, then no doubt that can be done. But the compromise can also be corrupting since it encourages us to emphasize in our teaching what is *most teachable* and to wave vaguely and perhaps ironically in the direction of what is more hardly won in philosophy. But even what is most teachable is relative to the aptitudes of the taught and as our intake targets are further pushed up by external forces we knowingly admit students who will not benefit from their programmes.

Nevertheless, if we talk of 'compromise' in the face of political imperatives, it is well to remind ourselves of the standards and principles which
we have had to compromise, and from which we have therefore fallen:
philosophers desire to be wise, philosophy is a disguised form of *eros*, better therefore thought of as a passion – at least according to the priestess,
Diotima, who makes an interesting claim about the term *eros*:

> . . . 'the truth is that we isolate a particular kind of *eros* and appropriate
> for *it* the name of *eros*, which really belongs to a wider whole, while we
> employ a different name for the other kinds of *eros*.' (205b)

Eros, in other words, has been arbitrarily assigned to just one form of
desire, viz sexual desire, even though it takes other forms whose inter-
connections are concealed by language: one of these forms is philosophy. As Robin Waterfield, the translator of the Oxford World Classics
edition of *The Symposium*, points out (p. 85) *Eros* and philosophy become
increasingly identified in the dialogue and become so in the figure of
Socrates himself as the *Erastes* who is born of Poverty and Contrivance.

But Diotima immediately makes a similar point about *poiesis* – after the
young Socrates is made to ask a conveniently artless question:

> 'Can you give me another example of such a usage?' . . . 'Yes, here it is.
> By its original meaning poetry means simply creation, and creation, as
> you know, can take very various forms. Any action which is the cause of a
> thing emerging from non-existence to existence might be called poetry,
> and all the processes in all the crafts are kinds of poetry, and all those
> who engage in them poets . . . but yet they are not called poets, but have
> other names, and out of the whole field of poetry or creation one part,
> which deals with music and metre, is isolated and called by the name of
> the whole. This part alone is called poetry, and those whose province is
> this part of poetry are called poets.' (205c)

Although Diotima wants to include philosophy as a form of *eros* and
although the comments about *poiesis* are juxtaposed to that discussion, the
connection between philosophy and poetry is not obvious. But if we recall
that the philosopher is one who desires to be wise, then the connection is
mediated by what she says about the 'best' kind of poetry:

> there are some whose creative instinct is of the soul, and who long to
> beget spiritually, not physically, the progeny which it is the nature of the

soul to create and bring to birth. If you ask what that progeny is, it is wisdom and virtue in general; of this all poets and such craftsmen as have found out some new thing may be said to be begetters. (209a)

Thus Diotima identifies the *poets* as among those who generate wisdom and virtue.[10] The point is emphasized later when she mentions Homer and Hesiod:

Take Homer, for example, and Hesiod, and the other good poets; who would not envy them the children that they left behind them, children whose qualities have won immortal fame and glory for their parents? (209c)

But this is not just the poets in the sense of those who write in metre and verse: *poiesis* is to be understood in terms of human creativity more generally ('Any action which is the cause of a thing emerging from non-existence to existence might be called poetry') though Diotima's particular interest is in those 'poets' who are the cause of bringing into existence 'wisdom and virtue', where 'bringing into existence' is mediated by the metaphors of begetting and bringing forth, metaphors which remain entrenched within our thinking about creativity, though what are omitted here are conception and gestation – 'begetting' is somewhat different from 'conceiving' and both from gestation and bringing forth. The imagery is essential to how we understand creativity, of course, but it gives a particular content also to the idea of transmission and the kind of relationships upon which this depends.

Re-conceiving philosophy

Now one way to connect the idea that philosophers are those who desire wisdom with the idea that philosophy is, like poetry, a form of creativity, is through the further thought that the 'best' poets are creative in their begetting and bringing forth precisely of wisdom and virtue – and this is just what those who desire wisdom, the philosophers, also desire. Philosophy and poetry converge in being creative of wisdom and virtue, in bringing wisdom and virtue forth in oneself, and in begetting it in others.

Here it would be reasonable to object that philosophers and poets *may* at least sometimes have a common end, but that is all – poetry and philosophy are different kinds of activity. Indeed it is significant that one translator of the *Symposium*, Robin Waterfield, refers in his Preface to what he calls 'the balance' in the dialogue 'between philosophy and literary art'. But to talk in this way is to assume that we know the quantities that rest on the scales, that we know where and what the philosophy is and how it is to be distinguished from the 'literary art'. The objection relies on the dichotomy I mentioned at the beginning, and one move towards its overcoming is to deny that it is *philosophy* and *poetry* that have a common end, and to assert, by contrast, that *certain* activities associated with what we now call 'philosophy' and *other* activities that we now associate with 'poetry' are unified by a philosophical *telos* by which they are constituted together as *philosophy*.

If I might make a suggestion inspired by Diotima's comments on *eros* and *poiesis*, what we now tend to think of as 'philosophy' refers only to a subset of the activities that can properly be called 'philosophical'. What happened to *eros* and *poiesis*, in other words, has happened in a damaging way to philosophy. Just as *eros* and *poiesis* have both been appropriated for one form of *eros* and *poiesis* whose connection with other forms is thus concealed by the surface appearance of language, so 'philosophy' is now a term that applies to just one part of philosophy, which is then distinguished from other activities that really belong to it. So, very crudely, we tend to think of philosophy as a matter of analysis and argument, as part of *dialectic*, and explicitly distinguish it as a discipline from other forms of reflection.

I should prefer to talk rather of a *convergence* of methods and tropes, a range of forms of reflection, all of which are philosophical – story-telling, allegory, theatre, metaphor, dialectic, analysis, in combination and mutual dependence, and what makes them 'philosophical', to come to the point at last, is their tendency to emancipate us from error and ignorance or delusion and to lead us towards self-knowledge and wisdom. So, for instance the *elenchus* is not 'the philosophy' but only one of its activities, a particular procedure which has a role within the whole philosophical enterprise, viz to undermine attachment to such beliefs and attitudes as conceal from us what can be shown only by other means – in a way that depends upon the imagination. All the aspects in combination have the function of investigating and revealing realities that were previously concealed from view because we stand in our own light. At the beginning such realities may be only dimly discerned, and we proceed feelingly by means of images and metaphors that attract our attention before we are able to draw out their meaning. But this slow process precisely invokes the metaphor of gestation that precedes the bringing forth. In other words the term 'philosophical' names a function or *telos* rather than a subset of the methods by which this *telos* or function might be achieved.

But this enterprise is *already* a moral endeavour which depends upon a moral response and it envisages a philosophical community (an Academy) composed of teachers and their pupils, though who the teachers are and who the pupils will not always coincide with their social role. But who would dare to be a teacher if these are the terms?

The Cave

The image of the Cave exerts power before we are aware of what it reveals, which is strange because we must know the truth before we realize that we do and while it is still apparently concealed. The released prisoner looks back and sees for the first time the mechanisms which had determined the form of his whole previous experience, and that of his fellow prisoners. Even this moment of looking back and observing the absorption of the others in the shadows is an image of 'wisdom'. It is an image of seeing the constrictions of a previous perspective, and represents a form of self-knowledge and *freedom* constituted by the revelation of possibilities that had been hidden, including that of *movement* from the one condition to the other, both in the sense that there is a path that others can follow and in the sense that one can fall back and lose perspective again.

The 'wisdom' lies in the revelation of things as they *really* are as opposed to how they had seemed to be, though perhaps it is better to say that the extent of someone's wisdom lies in the *applications* of such a phrase, in the many contexts in which one learns the hard way that such distinctions obtain, and that if one knew . . . one would behave differently. So there is a further, 'virtue' aspect to wisdom: being able to comport oneself and order one's desires in the light of that knowledge of how things really are. This is the force of the Platonic connection between knowledge and virtue–one only 'really' *knows* when one is able to act in the light of one's knowledge: it is then that one knows in one's body or in one's heart, it is a criterion of a degree of knowledge determined by how much of the person acknowledges it. The Cave is also an image of Kierkegaardian indirection: you cannot simply announce to the prisoners that this is their real condition, because they will make no sense of what you tell them – unless you want to get yourself killed, because the murderous response envisaged in the narrative indicates that what the prisoners represent is not so much engulfment in their perspective as bad faith.[11] Where does the murderous impulse come from then? Well, they are at least aware that they are *restless* even if they do not realize that their energies exceed their condition, and they suffer from an unexplained frustration. In other words they have feelings which they are not yet able to articulate.

The gods and the ignorant

In her account of *eros* Diotima says that there is something that the gods and the ignorant have in common: they do not desire wisdom. The gods do not desire it because they are already wise and you cannot desire to have what you do not lack – and the ignorant precisely do not know that they lack it:

> The tiresome thing about ignorance is precisely this, that a man who possesses neither beauty nor goodness nor intelligence is perfectly well satisfied with himself, and no one who does not believe that he lacks a thing desires what he does not believe he lacks. (204a)

In fact Diotima's description is ambiguous, at least in the translation. It may be true that an *ignorant* person 'does not believe' that they lack wisdom, but this is consistent with their having no beliefs in the matter at all, and in this they are to be distinguished from the *deluded* who believe positively that they do not lack wisdom. The purely ignorant will be entirely unaware that there is anything that they lack.

So it is one thing to lack something and another to know that you lack it. It is this latter condition which is described in Diotima's answer to Socrates' next question, what kind of person *can* be said to love or desire wisdom? – it is 'those who fall between wisdom and ignorance'. They are not entirely ignorant because they know that they lack wisdom, and they know this because they feel their lack because they are victims of the dissonance between what they now know and the state of their passions and desires, which is precisely the condition of *akrasia*.

But what is it to feel the lack of wisdom? This condition is personified precisely in the figure of *Eros*, that weather-beaten, shoeless, homeless person who exemplifies the felt lack at the heart of desire, most crucially at the heart of the desire to be wise, and it includes *Eros* because

> wisdom is one of the most beautiful things, and Love is love of beauty, so it follows that Love must be a lover of wisdom and consequently in a state half-way between wisdom and ignorance. (204b)

But really we need a better objective correlative to render intelligible this unkempt and passionate condition of 'homelessness' – and 'wisdom is one

of the most beautiful things' sounds too pious and effete, at least in translation, and does not give us what we need if we are to capture the ordeal
of the *erastes*. It does not, for instance, give us any clear idea of the nature
of the spur that impels the philosopher forward in a state of felt lack. We
also have to acknowledge that the conclusion is dubious. A lover or *erastes*
of (any kind of) beauty could only 'love wisdom' if they were in a position
to perceive it as 'one of the most beautiful things' and even then we can
admire something beautiful without desiring it. There is a general comment to be made here on Plato's account of *eros* and beauty. Beauty is something that we admire and we can admire a person or a beautiful object
without conceiving a desire for them or suffering that sense of lack which
belongs to desire. Indeed the whole Kantian aesthetic rather depends on
this point.

But there is a further objection. Surely one needs to know *what wisdom
is* if one is to desire it. But there is more than one reason for rejecting
this objection. If we make a distinction between knowledge and wisdom
we need to specify a difference. As I have already implied, the difference
lies in the fact that wisdom is a condition in which one *not only* knows how
things really are as opposed to how they had seemed to be, but in which
one can *also* comport oneself and order ones desires in the light of that
knowledge. Indeed it might be said that the intermediate state between
ignorance and wisdom is precisely that of knowledge in advance of the
re-ordering of desire. One way of lacking wisdom and feeling and thus
suffering its lack is just in this experience of *dissonance* between what one
knows and how one feels and acts. One can have the knowledge without
the capacity to act so, in that sense, one knows what wisdom is and suffers
its absence. More mundanely, and to talk perhaps more specifically of *phronesis*, our ordinary human follies and stupidities are precisely failures to
learn from experience, defined by our inability to act in the light of knowledge of the causal chains that characterize the human condition, and the
wisdom consists not just in knowing but also in the power to act in the light
of that knowledge.

In any event, Diotima crucially represents the philosopher as a lover,
an *erastes*. But at this point we surely need to get more personal. If one
really wants to represent Socrates, the figure of the philosopher, as to that
extent an *erastes* one surely needs an *eromenos*, a corresponding 'beloved'.
Wisdom and Beauty have indeed both been personified in the traditions
as a goddess. Even so, although Diotima might resist this because she
does want to talk about an *eros* directed towards ideas and institutions,
as well as towards 'beauty itself', there is some point in staying with the

idea that the *eromenos* of the one who desires wisdom, is a *person*. There are two related possibilities here: it can be someone who is 'beautiful' in their wisdom or in their capacity for wisdom. Thus someone who is further along the path of wisdom would see the attractiveness of someone who is capable of the same wisdom, and someone at an earlier stage will be attracted to those who are wiser. This latter distinction also allows us to see the reciprocity of desire between *erastes* and *eromenos* as well as the switching of roles from one to the other. However, to bring a little primness in to this wonderful *locus* of self-deception (which is surely anyway one of the notions over against which wisdom is defined) – if we recall Diotima's comment that *eros* has been assigned exclusively to sexual desire when really it applies to other forms of desire as well, then the relationship we are talking about is not a sexual one even though it appears to use erotic language. However, one has to recall Nietzsche's good-humoured remarks in *Twilight of the Idols*:

> Plato . . . says with an innocence for which one must be Greek and not 'Christian', that there would be no Platonic philosophy at all if Athens had not possessed such beautiful youths; it was the sight of them which first plunged the philosopher's soul into an erotic whirl and allowed it no rest until it had implanted the seed of all high things into so beautiful a soil. Another singular saint! – one doesn't believe one's ears, even supposing one believes Plato. One sees at least that philosophizing was *different* in Athens, above all public . . . Philosophy in the manner of Plato should rather be defined as an erotic contest . . . What finally emerged from this philosophical eroticism of Plato? A new artistic form of the Greek *agon*, dialectics. (*Twilight* §23 pp. 80–81)

. . . Or at least the *form* of the relationship we are talking about is not a sexual one. But the central comedy of the *Symposium* turns on Alcibiades's sexual and philosophical faux pas in seeking to offer sexual favours in exchange for wisdom. The dialogue almost centres on this comedy. The point about the figures of Alcibiades and Socrates is the admiration of the former and the attractiveness or moral beauty of the latter. Alcibiades is *also* a figure of the philosopher, but a figure who shows the parlousness of that precarious condition poised between ignorance and wisdom. If Socrates is, for all that, also a figure of one who desires wisdom he is also the figure of one who is attractive just because he exemplifies it, who embodies what is desired. He can be both of these things just because one person can be wiser than another and there is such a thing as increase in wisdom.

The reciprocity of *erastes* and *eromenos* must work something like this: even
the Silenus figure of Socrates who is physically ugly can be an *eromenos* to
one who desires wisdom but just to the extent that the latter does indeed
desire wisdom they themselves are attractive to one who is already wise
because they exemplify some degree of moral beauty. To make sense of
any of this one needs to accept that these various states of *eros* are precisely
embodied and have a characteristic presence.

However, what we are shown is the *failure* of Alcibiades to comprehend
what he is attracted towards and that failure is also embodied and has a
characteristic and palpable presence that makes him unattractive to one
who thus discerns his condition and whose desires are in any case differently ordered and at a higher stage of the Ascent. There is a further
aspect of the comedy which has a Wittgensteinian flavour. If we think
abstractly of the attractiveness of wisdom – as opposed to the attractiveness of what we see embodied in one who is wise – then one may be led
into the error of thinking of wisdom as a possession, even a commodity with an exchange value. But this is just the mistake that Alcibiades
makes in proposing his exchange. Diotima pointedly remarks that the
aim of *eros* is not 'possession' of the beautiful but 'procreation in the
beautiful':

> 'The object of love, Socrates, is not, as you think, beauty'. 'What is it
> then?' 'Its object is to procreate and bring forth in beauty.' (206e)

The talk here is of begetting and bringing forth, though what is obviously missing from the metaphorics is the equally important conception
and gestation. However, it brings us to a point where philosophy as *eros*
coincides with philosophy as *poiesis*. What the philosopher seeks to do is
to bring forth as well as to procreate and the capacity for both depends
upon a prior conception and gestation. What the one who desires wisdom does is to bring forth in themselves as well as beget in others. But if
what is brought forth is wisdom and virtue then we can also say that what
is brought to articulate expression is insight and the realization of how
things really are as opposed to how they had only seemed to be – which is
the common revelatory function of what we call philosophy and what we
call poetry. It is one reason at least why it might be true that philosophy
should really only be written as poetry because that writing is a bringing forth and into existence a sense of how things are that was before
unapprehended.

Notes

1 But my comments are about the state of the discipline of philosophy rather than about our institutions of higher education, though see my colleague, Gillian Howie's, contribution elsewhere in this volume for an account of what higher education policy is doing to the discipline and the way it is now being taught.
2 Quoted in Reeves, 2007, p. 68.
3 Philosophy should really only be written as poetry. Wittgenstein, 1980, p. 24e.
4 *Critique of Judgment*, §53 p. 191.
5 To some parts of philosophy 'feeling' is indeed largely irrelevant and in these days of specialization some philosophers never stray from that confined space.
6 A Joint Degree in Philosophy and Drama, in which a dedicated, jointly taught module dealt with just these issues, would provide an illuminating experimental forum.
7 Obviously there is a much larger debate to be had here. As I have already indicated, many philosophers would be genuinely baffled by this talk of feeling and poetry and they would not think that what they wrote about could make a difference to how a person *lived*, for instance. But this is partly a matter of personnel and self-selection prolonging the life of particular philosophical movements. What is on offer in our philosophy departments will attract or repel according to temperament and aptitude, and those who share neither have migrated to other, neighbouring disciplines, who might have made a difference to philosophy if they had found there a congenial space for themselves. *Caveat emptor* makes melancholy sense now that our students pay for their education.
8 I have used the Hamilton translation throughout.
9 A friend remarked that this is a nice image of 'knowledge transfer' and thus precisely not an image of philosophy.
10 This is an entirely unexpected thought if we think of Plato as the philosopher who wished to banish the artists.
11 See my 'In the Beginning was the Deed: Philosophers, Reality and the World'.

References

Kant, I. (1952), *Critique of Judgment*. Oxford: Oxford University Press (trans. Meredith).

McGhee, M. (2007), 'In the Beginning was the Deed: Philosophers, Reality and the World'. *Practical Philosophy* 8 (2).

Nietzsche, F. (1969), *The Twilight of the Idols: Or, How to Philosophise with the Hammer*. Harmondsworth: Penguin (trans. Hollingdale).

Plato (1951), *Symposium*. Harmondsworth: Penguin (trans. Hamilton).

Plato (1994), *Symposium*. Oxford: Oxford University Press (trans. Waterfield).

Reeves, R. (2007), *John Stuart Mill: Victorian Firebrand*. London: Atlantic Books.

Wittgenstein, L. (1980), *Culture and Value*. Oxford: Basil Blackwell. (ed. Von Wright, trans. Winch).

Chapter 3

Why Teach Philosophy?

Phil Hutchinson and Michael Loughlin

A critical citizenry is a society's one sure defence against tyranny.

J. S. Mill, On Liberty

The reasonable man adapts himself to the world; the unreasonable one persists in trying to adapt the world to himself. Therefore all progress depends on the unreasonable man.

G. B. Shaw, Man and Superman

There are of course many possible answers to the question that comprises our title. Some philosophers might even answer that they could think of little else to do other than teach after completing their Ph.D. We, here, want to answer this question as if it were put to us, now, and with the thought that we could choose to do something else, were we so minded. How would we answer this question? What is so important about teaching philosophy? As a discipline it is surely somewhat out-of-step with dominant trends within our culture, where to be effective is to be successful, and where what counts as success is some combination of fame and material wealth. The person who devotes a life to the pursuit of excellence within a particular practice, a practice the mastery of which does not confer upon its master material wealth or fame, is seen as eccentric.[1] 'Why spend so much time and effort working on that when you stand to gain so little?' seems to be the question that informs the judgement of eccentricity. Of course, the use of the word 'gain' in the question is one that has a specific meaning in the culture of which the questioner is a product, a culture that not exclusively but certainly predominantly measures success in terms of material wealth (or the power to control material resources). Teaching philosophy simply does not fulfil such criteria for success. We work for so little gain, according to most (or at least many) of our peers.

An alternative title, therefore, might have been 'In Defence of Eccentricity: A Polemic in Favour of the Pursuit of Wisdom and Instruction in the Arts that Might Aid Others in that Pursuit'. This title has, we feel, a certain precision, not to mention a pleasingly unmodern tone likely to enhance our reputation as eccentrics wholly out of step with 'the current realities'. Despite such advantages to this title change, we stick with our original. What we want to defend is the non-instrumental value of the pursuit of wisdom and the passing on of those things that we have found crucial to that pursuit to others, our students. Not only do we want to defend this, our eccentricity, but we want to recommend it to others. Furthermore, if we are not at risk of overstretching ourselves in the tasks we set, we want to argue that it is something that is needed here (in the West or the Economic North) and now (in the early twenty-first century) if not more than ever, then certainly no less than at any time in history.

The contemporary condition

There is one decent line in an otherwise thoroughly unpleasant Tarantino film.[2] A minister unfortunate enough to have been kidnapped by gangsters, and soon to suffer the further misfortune of being attacked and ultimately devoured by vampires, asks his macho captor: 'Are you such a loser that you don't know when you've won?'

The charge implicit in this question could be levelled at many employed to teach philosophy at institutions throughout the developed world. Millions of our fellow citizens spend the bulk of their working lives earning profits for others by processing forms, promoting products they do not believe in, engaging in centrally monitored telephone conversations with people whose legitimate complaints they know they may not concede for fear of the sack, and generally participating in corrupting, de-humanising exercises that leave them fit for little more than the mind-numbing, 'reality-based' entertainment the mass media provides before bedtime.[3] In contrast, professional philosophers get a rather good deal. Despite the well documented 'advances' of 'management science' in the university sector over the last thirty or so years, we still manage to engage in largely unmonitored dialogue with our students, in encounters that are just about as varied and stimulating as we care to make them. Fortunate inheritors of a tradition of open enquiry and debate dating back to the pre-Socratics, we are allowed to earn our keep by engaging in a quintessentially human occupation. We get to talk to our students about all the stuff that really matters in life, to develop our own thinking and re-learn our subject again and again through our engagement with them, and in so doing to teach them what we believe to be the most important, personally challenging and intellectually exciting academic discipline this species has.

We get to pass on methods of reasoning that we have found and which we consider to be of enormous personal value to our students and may well even make them more valuable to the people around them, helping them to think more clearly about any problem which confronts them and to understand the world they face with greater clarity than before. We help them to distinguish sense from nonsense, good arguments from bad. Most importantly, we help to foster the disposition to think critically. A student qualifying in philosophy should have come to expect, as a matter of routine, those who make assertions and issue instructions to be able to produce good reasons in support of what they say. She should similarly expect her peers to hold her to account for the claims she makes and positions she espouses. She should have been trained to expose and question assumptions, even ones presented as too obvious or too widely shared to be worth questioning; even those so fundamental that they have slipped out of sight, making their presence felt in a line of reasoning only when someone notices that they may indeed be questioned, and that without them an otherwise sound argument collapses. She should have learnt the difference between pertinent and impertinent questions;[4] also between questions for which there can be an answer that makes sense and ones for which there cannot.

To make one's living in such a fashion is an extraordinary opportunity in any society. We submit that in one such as this, it represents much more. In the intellectual climate of the early twenty-first century, to be both blessed and cursed with the disposition to think philosophically is to be outstanding in the most straightforward sense of the word. It is to stand out as contrary to the norms of life and discourse in a way that marks one out as peculiar, petty and 'unreasonable' to some, while simultaneously (and for the same reasons) being seen as exciting, serious and a 'breath of fresh' air to others.

We live in an era when governments, employers and corporations invest more time and intellectual energy than ever in the non-rational manipulation of the populace. Propaganda has always been a crucial component of communication. Indeed, the word did not always have its current negative connotations. However, propaganda has now been elevated to the status of a significant and very well resourced science, with applications to almost any area of human activity regarded as sufficiently important to require 'management'[5] A key postulate of this science is the existence of a population whose beliefs and behaviour are susceptible to modification with reference to the various presentational and motivational strategies that exponents of the science strive to perfect. The very last thing the new science requires if it is to flourish is the presence of 'Socrates-types' within the populations it proposes to manage – persons who insist on questioning the basis for decisions and assertions and even the categories and assumptions in terms of which issues, situations and problems are presented and which subsequently frame their discussion.[6] Hence the vast literature 'diagnosing' the 'psychological needs' of such 'commitment-averse' individuals, advising 'leaders' on how to minimize the damage they do and even, where possible, to 'help' them learn better how to 'move with the tide' rather than 'resist' it.[7] We are now so used to governments and corporations engaging in what used to be called 'brainwashing' that terms like 'spin', 'on-message' and even 'opinion management' and 'perception management' have passed, quite uncontroversially, into common usage (Loughlin 2004).

The alternative to thinking critically about one's fundamental assumptions is to allow one's ideas and attitudes, and consequently one's behaviour, to be shaped and directed by forces which one fails even to perceive, let alone control. If that is my condition, it makes very little sense to speak of me as a person who 'thinks for himself' or who makes his own decisions (Loughlin 2002a). A political culture which derides critical reflection is, as Mill noted, fertile soil for tyranny. As practitioners/teachers of philosophy[8] we are like the makers of the most effective wooden stakes in an environment dominated by vampires, and we also do an excellent line in therapies for those victims of the blood-suckers not already too far gone to want them.[9] Yet many of us spend our time either apologising for the lack of practical applications of our skills, or asserting that they should have no practical application, or groping around for some way to stretch or alter what we do to *give* it some application, assuming the discipline, in and of itself, to have none.

It would seem that many philosophers, explicitly or implicitly, endorse a conception of 'the practical' that renders their own discipline practically useless. Each contributor to this article has attempted to promote applied philosophy in a range of contexts. While we have met with enthusiastic receptions from audiences of non-philosophers, we have found that the audiences most disdainful of the idea that the subject has any relevance to the 'real world' are those made up largely of professional philosophers. Yet they, of all people, should know that nothing is useful or relevant *per se*: things are useful or relevant in the context of particular purposes or projects. It does not strike us as difficult to defend the value of a discipline crucial to one's status as a person who thinks for herself, as someone in control of her own beliefs and the conduct predicated upon them. In the current environment, philosophy is the paradigm case of a practice valuable for its own sake as well as for its consequences.

The 'real world' for the vast majority of people is one in genuine need of the sort of clarity of thought and reflection upon fundamentals that is philosophy's concern. In the workplace people are increasingly bombarded by the most audacious abuses of rhetoric to bolster periodic revisions of their practices on the basis of the unexplained 'innovations' and 'visions' of their managers. Senior figures in such major 'service industries' as education and health see themselves as locked in a struggle against shop-floor 'cynics' to win the 'hearts and minds' of their staff and 'customers'.[10] We learn repeatedly that the 'innovators' in this 'culture of perpetual change' (Peters 1989) operate with conceptions of the nature and value of their practices that members of the workforce typically regard as alien, bizarre, sometimes barely recognizable. In many institutions, including many contemporary universities, it is regarded as unreasonable to expect one's senior managers to demonstrate the most rudimentary forms of reasoning in public communication. In the context of the same conversation, one can be labelled a 'cynic'[11] for asking one's managers to explain the reasons behind their declarations and overwhelmingly 'naïve' for actually expecting them to provide you with any. Point out the apparent inconsistency and you are now being 'petty', 'difficult' or 'belligerent'. No level of sanctimony is excessive when managers and politicians pronounce upon the need for high standards in professional practice. Yet anyone who thinks that the people who make such pronunciations should be judged by similar standards is somehow being foolish or 'unrealistic' (Loughlin 2002b).

Business schools teach 'opinion-management', 'perception-management' and 'culture-management' as essential components of 'leadership skills' and offer to supply would-be 'leaders' with 'management technologies' capable of 'delivering support' (of working populations and the public) for almost any policy – of being capable of persuading the 'turkeys' to 'vote for Christmas' (Taylor 2003, Charlton 2000, and cf. Spiers 1994 discussed in Loughlin 2002a). Such 'technologies' typically consist of well documented fallacies and the exploitation of the rhetorical properties of evaluative terms, in a manner that has been grist for the linguistic philosophy mill since the work of people like Austin (1955) and Stevenson (1944). They tend to be effective only for as long as no-one with the requisite analytical training to challenge them actually does so.

A political system that accords the spin-doctor the status of an essential worker is one that sanctions routine assaults on the intelligence and integrity of its citizens, since the acknowledged expertise of such a person is the manipulation of an intellectually disempowered populace. In such an environment philosophical analysis is a necessary form of intellectual and moral self-defence (Loughlin 2002a). Even in the serious media, debates are typically framed with reference to assumptions that are clearly intellectually contested, and have indeed been subjected to extensive critical analysis and controversy, yet their acceptance becomes the de facto criterion of a 'reasonable' and 'relevant' contribution.[12] Intelligent people want to think for themselves. They increasingly (and wisely) do not trust many official sources of information. Indeed, it is hardly over-stating the matter to label perplexity about which sources of information to trust 'the contemporary condition'. Philosophy addresses this perplexity more immediately and consistently than any other subject. We would argue that one legitimate way of construing the fundamental questions of both epistemology and ethics is in terms of this condition, since the question of which sources of information to trust (and why) is of first importance in determining one's conception of the world and one's place within it, how to conduct one's life and negotiate the world that faces each one of us.

Some respond to this condition with radical scepticism, bordering on paranoia – 'trust nothing and no-one'. We have seen this response in a number of our students over the years. Some embrace extreme forms of epistemic and moral subjectivism, which reassure them that whatever 'opinions' they now hold are as good as any possible alternatives – 'I can think what I like'. Both these responses strike us as unsustainable – though facilitating the realization that such 'positions' are unsustainable will be achieved through dialogue and/or therapy. Some recoil in the opposite direction and seem to simply select sources in which to place their faith, apparently (from our perspective) at random, which is just to say the selection appears to us somewhat arbitrary and, again, rationally unsustainable – again facilitating the realization as to the arbitrariness and unsustainability of their 'secure footing' might be achieved through therapeutic dialogue.

But the best students, and certainly the ones most satisfying to teach, eschew such escape routes in favour of a direct confrontation with the problem – and many of these express frustration at an education system which they say has thus far failed to encourage them, and has frequently actively discouraged them from pursuing the most serious and fundamental questions they have about what they should believe and why. The majority of intelligent students come to philosophy looking for methods of distinguishing plausible from implausible claims, valid from invalid ways of establishing conclusions, and seeking a more penetrating understanding of the world than they can find elsewhere. All these can be brought under the heading of 'clarity'. What they feel is confusion, what they seek is clarity or understanding. From our encounters with professionals in a number of areas, there is a growing hunger for philosophy in precisely this sense. Those who practice opinion-management have, no doubt unintentionally, created a 'market' for the very subject whose methods and spirit are the antithesis of their own.

How to stop being losers

Philosophy can be construed as therapy to relieve the distress and confusion engendered by the contemporary condition, as characterized above. Philosophical clarity is achieved through gaining clarity about the language we use, and this means how that language frames our world and our relationship to that world. If philosophical problems have a distinct identity – distinct from scientific questions, for example – it is in that they cannot be answered empirically, through the employment of experimental methods. As Peter Winch (following Wittgenstein) pointed out fifty years ago in his now classic *The Idea of a Social Science*, to try to answer a philosophical question through employment of experimental methods, to try to answer it empirically, is to simply beg the question.

A question is a philosophical question if that which is in question involves, has intrinsic to it, a further question as to the question's subject's criteria for identity. For example the question, 'What's the meaning of life?' has intrinsic to it a further question as to what counts as (what are the criteria of identity for) 'meaning'. The question, 'Does God exist?' has intrinsic to it the further question as to what counts as (what are the criteria of identity for) 'God'. The same can be said of the question 'what is consciousness?', and so on. These questions – the questions of the criteria for 'meaning' and 'God' in our examples and many others[13] – are conceptual questions and cannot be bypassed in the name of experimental methods. Philosophy is the attempt to gain clarity regarding such conceptual questions. Therapy is the label – though we are happy to give it up – we give to the practice of trying to achieve such clarity through calm reflection, dialogue and discussion.

For reasons indicated in the previous section, we believe there is not only a need but increasingly, from the more intelligent members of the community, a demand for this form of therapy. Despite being constantly encouraged to regard questions of policy in the political, economic and organizational spheres as scientific or technical, as concerning the most effective means to secure some shared ends against a background whose nature is understood and agreed by all[14], reflective members of the populace find that 'we' do not have a shared, unproblematic conception of the nature, 'values', goals nor even (in anything but the sketchiest form) the identity-conditions of 'our' societies, practices and organizations. People don't need to know 'how' to achieve 'our' goals so much as they need to think about *why* they should regard certain projects as 'ours' (Loughlin 2002a). Philosophy really does seem to be more needed than ever.

Why then do philosophers act like the 'losers' alluded to above, habitually apologetic for the practical uselessness of their ancient discipline? Currently in the UK, philosophers are joining the swelling ranks of academics keen to learn more about 'flexible learning strategies' whose stated purpose is to save academics' time – invariably by enabling them to spend less and less time with their students. Teaching in the Socratic sense of dialogue, and even in the sense of providing regular, formal lectures has been discouraged by university managements dedicated to discovering more 'efficient' methods of delivering the educational 'product' to the (paying) 'customer'. If we can just put our lectures on the web, we can save so much time to do our own writing, and of course to meet the ever-expanding requirements of administrative exercises designed (with no sense of irony) to 'assure' 'teaching quality'.[15] The turkeys may indeed be voting for Christmas, since academics show as little awareness of the recent industrial past as Russell's naïve inductivist chicken (Russell 1982) has of the fate of his unfortunate fellows. Like the people one used to find behind the counter in the local branch of one's bank (way back when there was a local branch) who dutifully persuaded customers to shift to online and telephone banking, thus beating the ground for their own cull, we seem determined to show our primary 'customers' (formally known as 'students') that our contribution to their 'learning experience', though currently peripheral, is making strides, with the help of advanced technology, towards becoming wholly redundant.

In this new context, the idea of what a university is becomes transformed, and income-generation via mechanisms other than teaching becomes the way to demonstrate one's value to the employer. It is here that philosophy struggles to find a role, and it is in terms of this concept of 'practical relevance' that the subject is typically judged to be of no use in the 'real world'.

We have allowed ourselves to be judged practically worthless in terms of conceptions of value that we have good reason to reject. We have at hand a weapon that we could employ in our own defence, the analytical skill to defend ourselves against the tide of nonsense that currently assaults us. But we don't even use it in the context of our own institutions to defend practices central to the real value of our work, let alone attempt to export this skill to others who could make good use of it. What message does this send to our students about the importance of the discipline we teach them in class – that is, for those of us who do still teach our students? How, then, do we stop being losers?

We have to begin by eliminating the performative contradictions high-lighted in the preceding comments. We need to reject the conception of practical value that renders our activities in philosophising valueless. We do not need to make philosophy 'relevant' to the preconceived ideas of a soci-ety that increasingly sees no intrinsic value to intellectual pursuit. We need to be more like Shaw's 'unreasonable man', to explain to our students what their conception of relevance must be like if they are to function as worthy citizens of a free society, if they are to determine their own thinking about the world and their place within it, and the decisions they base upon that thinking, if they are truly to be in charge of their own ideas and their own lives. We need to teach by example, to promote (critical) thinking and dis-course by engaging in it. There are many ways to do this.

First, we must challenge nonsense in our own institutions, working with colleagues to defend *our* conception of what we do and to resist processes that rob us of the time and energy required to do our job to the satisfac-tion of *our* standards. If this means partaking in organized activities to challenge the internal politics of our institutions then this is what we must do.[16] We owe it to our students and the students of the future as much as we owe it to ourselves in the here and now. We are educators, first and foremost. That is the core value of what we do, it is where philosophy has its origins and it should be just as central to the identity of the subject now as it was when Plato took on the Sophists and the distinction between teaching philosophy and teaching the art of rhetoric emerged. We need to fight to make sure that it continues to be resourced. Philosophy without teaching is not philosophy. Take away that aspect and you have destroyed the form of our core activity, taken away its soul. Clearly we cannot expect our students to take philosophical methods of thinking and arguing away with them, and to use them to take charge of their own lives, if we do not even attempt to take charge of our own lives and the processes that effect us most directly.

Furthermore, we would do well to make links and engage in debate with professionals doing serious work outside of the academy, who (as noted above) have found their own conceptions of the value of their work under attack, and have come to respect and value the reflection upon fundamentals that a training in philosophical dialogue makes possible. It is testimony to the shocking arrogance of some colleagues in philosophy that they assume such dialogue necessarily entails a 'dumbing down' of the subject. When we consider some of the extremely serious work currently going on in medical epistemology, where debates about evidence, (Cartwright 2007) tacit knowing (Henry 2006) and the nature of clinical reasoning (Upshur 1997, Upshur and Colak 2003) are of profound practical and intellectual import, it is just plain obvious that the challenge of a new context can provide the opportunity for exciting developments of the discipline.

Far from 'dumbing down' the discipline, we enhance our abilities as teachers, thinkers and communicators in being required to apply the discipline, do philosophical work, in new contexts. It is always a good exercise to look at something at once difficult and not specifically written with the goal of being relevant to oneself.[17] We should require our students to do this as a matter of course, and they should see that this is something we also do – that it is simply part and parcel of being a proper philosopher.

The same arguments apply to doing our civic duties as intellectuals by contributing to general public debate. Where public dialogue is infested with unreason, dogma and cynical manipulation – where appeal to arbitrary or unexplained distinctions, shameless inconsistencies and unexamined assumptions are the norm in discussions of all matters of profound importance, we need to point out the shocking stupidity of a society which chooses to make all of its most serious decisions in terms of mechanisms whose irrationality the vast majority of its members freely recognize. The specific perspective we bring to such debate as philosophers – in particular our sense of the history of ideas and the consequent ability to see contemporary fads in context and to appreciate their historical contingency, contributes value to the debate and enhances the status of our subject in terms of its contemporary relevance.

We should indeed be proud of our subject, and promote it far and wide. We would do well to adopt the attitude expressed by some of the philosophy undergraduates at MMU Cheshire – an anecdote we recount with some satisfaction. When we told them about the possibility of developing a cross-campus unit with a substantial philosophy component their instant response was 'all well and good – the more philosophy at this place, the better; it bloody needs it'. They knew that the proposal would not affect them, since it would only come into effect for future cohorts following a review event to take place after their graduation. Yet all present were ideologically committed to the idea that the proliferation of philosophy is an inherent good, and could only improve the general environment within the institution.

Implications for teaching philosophy

While there are some versions of 'applied philosophy' (including some deeply regrettable versions of 'applied ethics': cf. Loughlin 2002a) whose exponents maintain that we should promote the contemporary relevance of philosophy *at the expense* of traditional approaches to the subject, all that we have said so far indicates that any such opposition represents a false dichotomy. The distinction between the subject and its applications, like the dichotomy between practitioners and teachers of the discipline, is ultimately unsustainable. Dogmatic, unsystematic discussion of content that has frequently been the subject of philosophical discussion in the subject's history (such as the nature of the mind or of science) is not philosophy. The subject's identity and value are carried by its methods, not its typical content. It is a discipline, a form of activity. It is taught by demonstration, by practice, and the tutor needs to work with her students to understand their specific assumptions and to assist in their development as critical thinkers. (cf. our discussion of therapy above) This is why she has to be able to meet them, get to know them, engage in dialogue with them. This is why the traditional idea of the university, as a place where practitioners of a discipline do their work and where students learn the discipline by their engagement with these same practitioners, needs to be defended if philosophy is still to have a home within such institutions.

This is why the 'old-fashioned' linkages – between research and teaching, and between teaching and people actually learning anything – need explaining and defending, against the onslaught of crude market thinking advocating a division of labour in the 'provision' of these various 'outcomes' of the university sector. While we are yet to see the formal establishment of 'research only' and 'teaching only' universities, a de facto division between individual academics in terms of these categories was accepted by the profession long ago. Young academics, many on short term and/or part time contracts, invariably lacking the 'right' connections, increasingly find they have no time to write, while in some philosophy departments a professor who humbles himself to teach a boring old class thereby acquires Christ-like status for the sacrifice of precious time and energies, that could otherwise have been spent either writing or meeting people who actually matter. Far from regarding the opportunity to teach philosophy as a privilege, some of the most prestigious representatives of our subject confess (or, depending on the context, boast) that they cannot stand being around students and do all they can to minimize the time they spend teaching. Such processes need to be reversed if the subject is to thrive. Like many living things, it does not do well when separated into its component parts.

Philosophy as we know it began with dialogue and this is still the best way for it to survive. It is through dialogue that students can best see why the subject addresses concerns relevant to them. When we teach epistemology to our undergraduate students, we begin by asking them to comment on a number of propositions. The propositions represent a range of different types of claim, some that we would usually classify as straightforwardly empirical, others moral, aesthetic, scientific, psychological, phenomenological, religious, and some that are less easy to classify, including a quotation from *He-Man and the Masters of the Universe* to the effect that so long as there is love within the human heart, the forces of darkness will never triumph. We ask the students whether or not they believe each specific claim, and whether or not they would say they 'know' it to be true. We then ask them whether or not they would characterize the claim as 'subjective' or 'objective'.

In the ensuing discussions, students will stridently defend certain responses, and we will frequently try, always unsuccessfully, to persuade them to alter some of those responses. In the class following the discussion we take on briefly the posture of pseudo-social scientists, providing a detailed written analysis of the patterns of students' responses and what they reveal about the group's conceptions of belief, knowledge, subjectivity, objectivity, rationality and reality. We go through the summary in class, noting that even where there are disagreements about specific claims, there are underlying assumptions about the meanings of key terms that are shared by both parties to the disagreement, and this explains why there are certain detectable patterns to the disagreements (people who read proposition 1 as 'subjective' also categorized propositions 3 and 5 in the same way, while people who read 1 differently invariably read 3 and 5 differently also; no-one who thought 6 was 'objective' also thought it could be 'known', and so on). Students are given the chance to recommend changes to our summary if they think it fails to reflect the true nature of their responses.

Once they have agreed the summary to be an accurate account of their responses, we reveal (when possible, with the help of a witness who did the unit in the previous year) that the slide we have talked them through, summarizing 'their' responses, is precisely the same one we used in the previous year, and in the year before that, and for as long as this unit has been taught. This is an interesting experience for the students and really does take them by surprise, since they have just had the experience of *making their minds up* about how to respond to these propositions: yet these philosophy tutors seemed to know, in advance, what answers they would give. How is that possible? Are they psychic or what?

The answer, of course, is that we know something of the history of ideas, and so we know where most of our students are located in intellectual history. While the answers they gave were in no sense necessary, given who they are and the intellectual culture that has shaped their thinking to date, it was overwhelmingly likely that certain underlying conceptions would be in evidence in dictating their responses to claims that were of course carefully selected in the first place. Our ability to predict their responses to such a wide range of propositions, gives our students a lively conception of the relevance of the subject to who they are, to the way they think about the world and their place within it. They realize that they can learn to understand their own thought processes better by studying this subject, since in advance of the exercise, they could *not* have predicted the answers they and their fellow students would give as well as we could. When we go on to deliver lectures and conduct seminars on the history of modern epistemology, they have a good sense that they are learning about processes that have helped to make them the people they are now, they learn the sources of their selves, for better or worse. And what is exciting for us is that they also acquire the desire not only to understand how they got here, but to determine where they go in future.

Notes

[1] Here we invoke Alasdair MacIntyre's distinction between the pursuit of excellence (the pursuit of goods internal to a practice) and the pursuit of effectiveness (goods external to a practice). MacIntyre discusses the distinction in *Whose Justice? Which Rationality?* (MacIntyre 1986), though it appeared in a different guise in his earlier *After Virtue* (MacIntyre 1985). It is telling that the distinction entered the language via management theory. Thus one now often finds 'excellence' used to mean the opposite of that which it meant for MacIntyre in his drawing a contrast between excellence and effectiveness. In this sense management rhetoric has strong affinities with the linguistic innovation one finds one's students employing, where 'bad' means 'good', 'sick' describes a well performed (if risky) action and to be up-to-date with the current linguistic innovations is to be 'down' with them.

2 *From Dusk till Dawn*, a wilfully quirky effort to merge the horror genre with a gangster movie, that in fact amounts to little more than the now expected attempt by Tarantino to portray a grotesquely violent sociopath (the George Clooney character) as heroic.

3 And here we refer only to our own cultural context. Reflecting on the average person's life globally it is hard not to feel very, very fortunate, and maybe a degree of shame. In this regard see Chapter 4 of Hutchinson's *Shame and Philosophy* (2008).

4 This does not mean that the impertinent question ought to be proscribed, but just that the ability to recognize a particular question in a particular context as impertinent is one indication of a good philosopher. All those who have taught the subject must have experienced at one time or other the first year student who just repeatedly asks impertinent questions. You might be discussing the issue of torture and its de facto sanctioning by countries whose own laws forbid the practice, by their engaging in what has come to be called 'extraordinary rendition' or by their attempt to redefine 'torture' so as to claim that the practice of 'waterboarding' no longer falls within the class of practices picked out by that term. Your student at the back of the class blithely and somewhat smugly raises his hand and says 'yeah, but do any of us exist; are we not just living in the Matrix? None of this is real, man'. Now there is a context in which 'brain-in-a-vat' type qualms about the reality of the external world are clearly pertinent. A discussion of the practice of 'extraordinary rendition' is not one of them, neither is Prime Minister's Questions in the House of Commons. Gordon Brown responding to a question from David Cameron by saying 'well, as we know, none of that which is apparent really exists' would be seen as indication of his having 'lost the plot' (or as a 'cry for help'), not indication of a philosophical training which he now employs to cunning effect. One thing we should try to teach our students therefore is how to judge when certain questions are pertinent or not. That there will always be a grey area between pertinent and impertinent detracts not a jot from the importance of such a task.

5 Some evidence for this claim is presented in the paragraphs which follow it, but for a fuller account of the various forms of intellectual manipulation employed in the work place, government policy and popular media, and an account of the real and present threat to our status as free agents that such processes embody, see Loughlin (2002a), Chapter 5 of Bakan (2004), and Poole (2006). See, also, the latter's website/blog: *http://unspeak.net/*, last viewed on 03/03/2008.

6 It is revealing to consider the anger directed at Dave Edwards and Dave Cromwell by certain prominent representatives of the mainstream media for their excellent work on the website: *www.MediaLens.org.*, last viewed on 03/03/2008 (Sign-up for their alerts and see also their book, *Guardians of Power*). The desire to silence questions about the assumptions that frame popular debate is as strong amongst today's self-proclaimed defenders of democratic dialogue as it was in ancient Athens.

7 The literature is indeed vast. The 'classics' include Peters (1989) and Crosby (1980) but to get a flavour of the casual Orwellianism of contributors it is instructive to look at the contributions of Merry, Al-Assaf, Curtis and Berwick

to Al-Assaf and Schemele (1993), or to look at some of the papers cited in Lough-lin (2004) on the application of this brand of organizational science to the university sector.

8   And as we will argue, in line with a very long tradition some of our colleagues seem in danger of forgetting, in our subject the distinction between a teacher and a practitioner is somewhat contrived.

9   For more on philosophy as therapy, see the comments immediately underneath the next sub-heading. For a more detailed exposition and defence of this con-ception of philosophy, see Hutchinson (2007) 'What's the Point of Elucidation'; Hutchinson and Read (2008) 'A Perspicuous Presentation of "Perspicuous Pres-entation"'; and Hutchinson and Read (forthcoming) *A Radically Therapeutic Vision of Philosophy.*

10   Cf. Williams (2002), discussed in Loughlin (2004) and Halligan et al. (2001), discussed in Loughlin (2002b). It is interesting to consider the growing similar-ities between the management vocabulary in both business and the public sector and the vocabulary of the CIA's 'covert operations', and what this reveals of the 'mind-set' of contemporary management.

11   Of course the contemporary meaning of 'cynic' has little to do with the Cynic movement – the ideas of Diogenes of Synope, for example. To be labelled a cynic now is to be labelled as one who responds irrationally in the negative – negatively on principle – to any proposed change or one who reads in to every suggestion for change an ulterior and malicious motive and on that basis rejects the suggestion. The Cynics of antiquity saw social norms, and the shame con-veyed on one by such, as constraints on one's freedom, and their actions – at least what we know of some of the actions of Diogenes of Synope – were con-ducted in an attempt to demonstrate this. See Chapter 3, section 2.3.1 of Hutchinson (2008).

12   Again, we cannot recommend highly enough in this regard the media alerts found at *www.medialens.org.* But, for now, consider one example: the presump-tion that economic growth is a good thing and an economic 'downturn' (!) a bad thing. There is a wealth of economic literature, which draws this in to ques-tion. Indeed, broadly speaking, one could say that in light of what we now know about anthropogenic climate change, economic growth is incontrovertibly bad. Needless to say we need not argue either way on this matter here. Our point is that economic-growth-as-a-good-thing shouldn't be but is assumed by the main-stream media and thus frames any debates about such things as the mitigation of climate change, and so on.

13   Of course Winch argued that the questions asked in social studies – questions asked/answered by sociologists, anthropologists and psychologists, etc – have much closer affinity with philosophical questions than with scientific questions, *pace* what many of their practitioners thought. See Hutchinson et al.(2008).

14   At least, by anyone not too eccentric to be included in the category of the 'rea-sonable': for numerous examples of this strategy – the construction of the spurious consensus – see Loughlin (2002a,b).

15   For a fuller account of the application of 'management technologies' to the whole-sale destruction of the traditional university education, see Loughlin (2004).

[16] As a friend of ours notes from time-to-time, most academics' answer to the question 'will you join us in the struggle' is 'of course . . . so long as suitable sabbatical arrangements can be made'.

[17] There are notable prominent philosophical figures that bucked this trend. Paul Feyerabend has a reputation for being the most insatiable of readers. He was even known to read much management literature, frequently recommending it to his graduate students as crucial reading material.

References

Al-Assaf, A. F. and Schmele, J. A. (eds) (1993) *The Textbook of Total Quality in Healthcare*. Delray Beach: St Lucie Press.

Austin, J. L. (1955) *How to do things with words*. Oxford: Oxford University Press.

Bakan, J. (2004) *The Corporation*. London: Constable.

Cartwright, N. (2007) 'Are RCTs the gold standard?' *BioSocieties*. 2, 11–20.

Charlton, B. (2000) 'The new management of scientific knowledge' in A. Miles, J. R. Hampton and B Hurwitz (eds). *NICE, CHI and the NHS Reforms: Enabling Excellence or Imposing Control?* London: Aesculapius Medical Press. 13–31.

Cromwell, D. and Edwards, D. (2005) *Guardians of Power: The Myth of the Liberal Media*. London: Pluto Press.

Crosby, P.B. (1980) *Quality is Free: The Art of Making Quality Certain*. New York: McGraw-Hill.

Halligan, A., Nicholls. S. and O'Neill, S. (2001) 'Clinical governance: developing organisational capability' in Miles et al. (2001) 129–154.

Henry, S. (2006) 'Recognising tacit knowledge in medical epistemology' *Theoretical Medicine and Bioethics*. 27, 187–213.

Hutchinson, P. (2007) 'What's the point of elucidation' *Metaphilosophy*. 38 (5), 691–713.

—(2008) *Shame and Philosophy: An Investigation in the Philosophy of Emotions and Ethics*. Basingstoke: Palgrave.

Hutchinson, P. and Read, R. (2008) 'A perspicuous presentation of "Perspicuous Presentation" '*Philosophical Investigations*. 31 (2), 141–160.

Hutchinson, P., Read, R. and Sharrock, W. (2008) *There is No Such Thing as a Social Science: In Defence of Peter Winch*. London: Ashgate.

Loughlin, M. (2002a) *Ethics, Management and Mythology*. Oxon.: Radcliffe Medical Press.

—(2002b) 'On the buzzword approach to policy formation' *Journal of Evaluation in Clinical Practice*. 8 (2), 229–242.

—(2004) 'Quality, control and complicity' *International Journal of the Humanities*. 2, 717–724.

MacIntyre, A. (1985) *After Virtue* (2nd edition). London: Duckworth.

—(1986) *Whose Justice? Which Rationality?* London: Duckworth.

Miles, A., Hill, P. and Hurwitz, B (eds) (2001) *Clinical Governance and the NHS Reforms*. London: Aesculapius Medical Press.

Mill, J. S. (1991) *On Liberty* (eds Gray, J. and Smith, G. W.) London: Routledge.

Peters, T. (1989) *Thriving on Chaos: Handbook for a Managerial Revolution.* London: Pan.

Poole, S. (2006) *Unspeak.* London: Little Brown Books.

Russell, B. (1982) *The Problems of Philosophy.* Oxford: Oxford University Press.

Shaw, G. B. (1946) *Man and Superman.* Edinburgh: Penguin books.

Stevenson, C. L. (1944) *Ethics and Language.* London: Gollancz.

Taylor, P (2003) 'Waiting for the barbarians' *Higher Education Review.* 34(2), 5–24.

Williams, P. (2002) 'Define "quality" then we'll talk "assurance"' *Times Higher Education Supplement.* 11 January, 14.

Winch, P. (1958 [2007]) *The Idea of a Social Science and its Relation to Philosophy.* London: Routledge.

Upshur, R. (1997) 'Certainty, probability and abduction: why we should look to CS Pierce rather than Godel for a theory of clinical reasoning' *Journal of Evaluation in Clinical Practice.* 3 (3), 201–206.

Upshur, R. and Colak, E. (2003) 'Evidence and argumentation' *Theoretical Medicine and Bioethics.* 24, 283–299.

Student Interlude I

The most demoralising aspect of studying a philosophy degree is the fact that ultimately all you ever study, quote and analyse is the history of other people's ideas. True 'philosophy' is an action, and requires no such degree and certainly no such examinations, yet at the same time, one could never imagine studying anything else. It is inherently a contradiction.

Mark Moreau,
University of Liverpool, UK

What I see as a limitation of philosophy studies at our faculty is a narrow analytical-philosophical curriculum with little or no emphasis on history of philosophy and older philosophers (except Plato and Aristotle briefly, British empiricists, Descartes and Kant), continental philosophy and other philosophical traditions.

The central problem for me is the way analytic philosophy is taught and studied here, a way that resembles acquiring a predetermined set of skills with little or no critical reflection on (analytic) philosophy itself. There lacks cultivation of that which has since Plato been called 'philosophical wonder' and considered to be a generative and constitutive source of any and all philosophy.

Not taking into account the attitude that is presented to us as predominant in analytic philosophy, the one that claims philosophy is no longer a 'queen of sciences' nor a 'systematic reflection of the world', I believe that it is impossible to achieve fruitfulness and real relevance even in a philosophy understood in this restricted way without any cultivation of philosophical wonder.

If we have on our path of philosophical education lost that primal human wonder, we will never become philosophers. Only artisans of a linguistic skill. I feel that, unfortunately, through my education at this faculty I have received mostly the kind of tuition that sharpens analysis but numbs philosophy.

Aleksandar V. Božić,
University of Rijeka, Croatia

In light of the apparent victory of mathematics and science as immovable forces in intellectual progress, philosophy seems somewhat sterile, a barren wasteland where one is reduced to studying the history of thinking rather than thinking for oneself. In fact, the very notion of thinking for thinking's sake seems useless, even absurd, to those that have been raised amidst a goal-orientated society drowned in its own production, a society that looks at the philosophy student askance as if he is wandering in the wilderness of pointless endeavour, searching for something the rest of us believe technology has already provided; or worse, just wondering aimlessly.

Maybe a true philosopher will not be fazed by the derisions heaped at his door, but the philosophy student may become disenchanted with philosophy because of its apparent failure to produce results. I myself have met with this disenchantment; it is as if philosophy has provided the tools for its own dismantling.

However, it only takes a passionate lecturer, a lecturer that promotes independent thought, to snap me out of the philosophical doldrums.

Sam Penman,
Greenwich University, UK

Chapter 4

Teaching Philosophy:
A Somaesthetic Approach

Richard Shusterman

'Please take off your shoes and lie down on your back. Keep your legs long, lengthened, if that is not uncomfortable. But if it is, just put something under the backs of your knees or lie with your knees bent and your soles on the floor. Close your eyes so that you can concentrate on feeling your body and notice that you don't really need to see your legs (or to remember what they looked like) in order to know that your legs are long or instead bent sharply at the knee. We can sense this directly through proprioception (our inner bodily sense) and our tactile sense of the body's contact with the floor. What we're going to do in this lesson is to come to know ourselves better somatically by examining how our body feels through such proprioception and bodily tactile feeling. We're going to do it in an organized way that will take about 10 minutes, proceeding systematically from one body area to another, comparing and contrasting felt positions, angles, weights, volumes, etc.

'In following my instructions and my questions – for example, about which side, arm, leg, shoulder (left or right) feels heavier or lighter – you should not worry about the responses of others. You should just answer on the basis of your own experience and to yourself – not answer aloud so as not to interfere with the experience and replies of others. Different people have different bodies and different habits of bodily posture and use, and those differences will be reflected in their experience of self-examination in this prostrate position. Always make sure you're breathing comfortably, lying comfortably, and are not straining. If you feel you are getting sore or stiff, find a more comfortable position. The purpose of this lesson is not to embarrass, shock, provoke, or give you the giggles, but to instruct you in a method that can contribute to the realization of one of philosophy's central goals – that of self-knowledge, here somatic self-knowledge. Philosophy has traditionally linked its central goal of self-knowledge with the goal of self-cultivation or self-care, on the grounds that we can care for something better if we know more about it; that to effectively cultivate or improve the self and its behavior, we need to know at least the aspects of that self and behavior we wish to improve or cultivate. So please relax with your eyes closed (eyes probably tired from too much reading or video viewing) and follow my instructions . . .'

I won't continue here this body scan protocol. But that is how I would like to begin a philosophy lesson in the field of somaesthetics, a field whose name I first proposed in 1997 but whose content and agenda can be traced back to the beginnings of philosophy. Briefly defined, somaesthetics is the study of one's experience and use of the body as site of sensory appreciation (aesthesis) and creative self-fashioning. A field of theory and practice, it aims to improve our somatic experience and self-fashioning, not just examine it in the abstract. Somaesthetics comprises not only critical study of the external body norms and images that pervade our culture but offers alternative models and an alternative focus on the pleasures of inner somatic perception and on the methods to increase the acuity and power of such perception.[1] But the value of lessons like the one I started to sketch above is not confined to somaesthetics. They can be useful more generally in teaching philosophy because they relate to the central issue of self-knowledge that has so powerfully shaped philosophy.

Though convinced of the philosophical relevance of such lessons in somatic self-awareness, I've never really dared to use them systematically to teach philosophy in the standard undergraduate academic philosophy course for two kinds of reasons.[2] First, because of the implicit norms and concrete physical conditions of academic philosophy instruction: that the students' philosophical thinking in the classroom is expected to be done in the sitting position with their eyes open, that such instruction is to be essentially conceptual rather than experiential, and that the floors of philosophy classrooms are totally unsuited for lying down – the floors are typically hard, cold and dirty with no available mats in the classroom to make lying down a comfortable possibility for learning. All these reasons could be designated as practical or external reasons against such somatic teaching of philosophy. But there is also another type of reason that discourages the use of such somatic study of philosophy – one that is internal to our dominant philosophical tradition: Namely, the presumption that attentive consciousness of one's body is either not proper self-knowledge or is rather an inferior and dangerous form of self-knowledge; that rather than contributing positively to self-cultivation it tends to promote forms of self-damage or weakness.

After briefly considering the key internal or theoretical arguments against cultivating body awareness as a valuable philosophical goal, this paper turns to the more practical task of showing how exercises of body awareness could indeed be productively taught in an academic philosophical classroom – by giving the reader an example of one such exercise, the body scan, whose preparatory instructions opened this paper. I then demonstrate how the body scan can be adapted to conditions more acceptable to the classroom, conditions that do not require lying on the floor but instead permit a seated position for performance; and then I conclude by analyzing the logical principles of consciousness that underlie the body scan. By combining such analysis with the experiential learning of the scan itself, one can provide an interesting way to combine theory and practice in the classroom.

Since its ancient inscription on Apollo's Temple at Delphi and its Socratic advocacy, the maxim 'know thyself' has been long and widely affirmed as a central quest in Western philosophy. Yet reflectively examining one's somatic self has found little favour among its most influential philosophers. By defining the self as 'the soul', Platonism and much of the ensuing idealist philosophical tradition have concluded that 'the command that we should know ourselves means that we should know our souls' and make them the object of our self-cultivation. Hence, a man's knowing or caring for his body is merely knowing or 'caring for something that belongs to him, and not [knowing or caring] for himself'. Despite affirming the value of bodily training in some other dialogues, Plato, in *Phaedo*, most influentially argued that the philosopher should not concern himself at all 'with the body' but rather turn attention away from it 'as much as possible,' 'because the body confuses the soul,' distorts perception and distracts from the pursuit of truth.[3]

Though Descartes was an expert in anatomy, his enormously influential *Meditations* insist that the substance of self is mind not body, since one could (he alleged) know one's mind by direct introspection while knowledge of one's body is inherently flawed and limited. Immanuel Kant famously took meticulous care in bodily matters such as diet and exercise, but he sternly warned against paying attention to one's somatic state and feelings. When claiming that 'the First Command of All Duties to Oneself' is to 'know (scrutinize, fathom) yourself,' he emphasizes that this is 'not in terms of your physical perfection (your fitness or unfitness for all sorts of . . . ends) but rather in terms of your moral perfection in relation to your duty.'[4] Kant instead repudiates the project of reflecting on bodily feelings, claiming that it leads to the madness of hypochondria and morbid despondence. Somatic introspection, he elsewhere warns, 'weakens the body and diverts it from animal functions'. Hence: 'Turning reflection away from the body leads to health'. In short, introspective somatic self-study is harmful to both mind and body, and the best way to treat one's body is to ignore, as much as possible, the self-knowledge of how it feels, while using it actively in work and exercise.[5]

Even William James, one of the most body-friendly of modern philosophers and one of the great masters of somatic introspection in psychology, similarly warned against its use in practical and moral life because of 'the inhibitive influence of reflection.' He urged that we should instead 'trust [our] spontaneity and fling away all further care' in our sensorimotor performance of action. 'We fail of accuracy and certainty in our attainment of the end whenever we are preoccupied with much ideal consciousness of the [bodily] means' and the internal (or 'resident') feelings they involve, he argued in his masterpiece *The Principles of Psychology*. 'We walk a beam the better the less we think of the position of our feet upon it. We pitch or catch, we shoot or chop the better the less tactile and muscular (the less resident), and the more exclusively optical (the more remote), our consciousness is. Keep your eye on the place aimed at, and your hand will fetch it; think of your hand and you will very likely miss your aim.' Moreover, like Kant, James feared that somatic introspection would lead to melancholia.[6]

Merleau-Ponty is another philosophical champion of the body who nonetheless rejects the value of somaesthetic reflection. Like James, he contends that spontaneity and unreflective perceptual awareness will always serve us best in everyday life, while somatic reflection and representational images are (for normal people) unnecessary and even get in the way of smooth functioning. Insisting that the body 'guides us among things only on condition that we stop analyzing it . . . only on the condition that [we] do not reflect expressly on it'.[7] Merleau-Ponty even suggests we cannot really observe the body in a proper way. It 'defies exploration and is always presented to me from the same angle . . . To say that it is always near me, always there for me, is to say that it is never really in front of me, that I cannot array it before my eyes, that it remains marginal to all my perceptions, that it is *with* me.' I cannot change my perspective with respect to my body as I can with external objects. 'I observe external objects with my body, I handle them, examine them, walk around them, but my body itself is a thing that I do not observe; in order to be able to do so, I should need the use of a second body.'[8]

In my book *Body Consciousness: A Philosophy of Mindfulness and Somaesthetics*, I challenge these claims not only by refuting their specific arguments but by enlisting the insights of philosophers and theorists who recognize the value of somaesthetic reflection for improving the quality and efficacy of our self-use and even our capacities for greater pleasure. The body is our

tool of tools; even more, it forms our primal perspective or mode of engagement with the world; it is the medium of all perception, thought and action.
It is therefore crucial to self-knowledge and self-cultivation.

John Dewey is rare among philosophers for recognizing the value of
reflective somatic attention and its training for the effective performance
of our activities, including intellectual ones. A long-time student and advocate of the Alexander Technique of somatic education, Dewey recognized
the horrible power that bad habits have over our action, thought and will.
Spontaneous action is the product of habit, not of a pure, free will; and
habit typically incorporates aspects of the conditions of its acquisition,
which are often unfavourable. Spontaneous, unreflective action will simply reinforce our habits, even if they are bad habits. Initial nervousness
about working on a computer, for example, tends to generate postures of
self-use that have too much muscular contraction and strain but that get
habituated as the normal spontaneous way of sitting, despite the discomfort they involve, which typically is not noticed because our somatic awareness is deficient. Improved, reflective body consciousness, Dewey argued,
after Alexander, is therefore necessary for correcting such bad habits and
achieving 'better control of the use of ourselves'. We have to know what
we are doing with our bodies, in order to know how to correct what we are
doing so that we can more effectively do what we wish to do with them.
'True spontaneity, Dewey concludes, is henceforth not a birth-right but the
last term, the consummated conquest, of an art – the art of conscious control' through an enhanced, reflective awareness of our bodies.[9]

Moreover, there is now scientific evidence that a number of body-mind
disciplines involving systematically enhanced somatic awareness (such as
yoga, zen meditation and body scanning) are not only not harmful to
mental and physical health but can actually improve it. And such evidence
confirms the more basic empirical evidence that if ancient practices like
yoga and *zazen* were harmful, they would not have flourished for so long
and in so many different cultures. Finally, as a matter of practical fact, we
can observe our bodies, since the body is both subjective intentionality
and an object of that intentionality. I both am a body and have a body that
I can feel and identify as mine but not as all that I am.[10]

In what remains, let us see more quickly how we can learn to feel (and
experientially know) our bodies with greater perceptual acuity and awareness by going more deeply into the discipline of somaesthetic observation
with which I introduced this paper – the body scan. Because it is not associated with any religious tradition and especially with those of Asian exoti-
cism, the body scan might be easier to introduce into academic contexts

of philosophical instruction, which are most often secular and dominantly Western (and sometimes ferociously so). Deployed by numerous body-mind disciplines (including the Feldenkrais Method developed by a twentieth-century scientist trained in Israel and France), the body scan involves systematically scanning or surveying one's own body, not by regarding or touching it from the outside but instead by introspectively, proprioceptively feeling ourselves as we rest motionless, typically on our backs with our eyes closed.

The advantage of lying down for developing acute body awareness is that this position not only relieves the habitually more intense stress of gravity that we feel in holding ourselves erect in standing or sitting, but by being a non-habitual position for awareness, it enables one's awareness to be freer from, hence less distracted by, the habitual associations of action we have in our more habitual and active positions. Similarly, the closing of the eyes is aimed at avoiding visual stimuli that would distract from our proprioceptive attention and awareness. But the self-examining discipline of the body scan can be adapted to other postures. If lying down is very embarrassing or uncomfortable, then it will not be a good position to do the body scan, because one's attention will be on one's embarrassment or one's discomfort rather than on the more subtle dimensions of one's bodily state and feelings. Because my essay aims to offer a practical orientation to teaching somatic philosophy, I now will provide a very brief experiential demonstration of a body scan that I have adapted to the sitting position, which is the position that could be most easily used in a philosophy classroom, where students typically feel most comfortable sitting. I have condensed the scan to its most basic elements because of this paper's editorial limits and have deleted the sort of introductory remarks about breathing, comfort, etc. with which this paper opened. Those remarks are worth adding in giving this lesson in the classroom.

Seated body scan© Richard Shusterman

Remove your shoes. Sit comfortably toward the edge of the chair, with your feet flat on the floor. Place your hands on your thighs where they are comfortable. If you wish, close your eyes as it may help you to do the following.

Starting with your left foot, notice how your heel makes contact with the floor. Does most of the weight go to the centre of the heel, or to the right, or left, of the heel? We do not want to change anything, or to judge how it should be. We simply want to feel where the heel contacts the floor.

Does your left foot carry most of its weight on the heel or on the ball of the foot? Is there more weight on the inside of the foot or the outside? Do all your toes make contact with the ground? Which of the toes make clear contact with the ground and which do not? Notice how your left foot is turned in or turned out, or is does it point straight ahead?

Now move your attention from your left foot, up your lower leg, to your left knee. Where is your left knee in relation to your heel? Is it in front of it, behind it, or right above your heel?

As you continue to move your attention up your left leg, notice the angle at which your left leg turns out or in. If you drew a line from your belly button straight out in front of you, how far would your knee be from this centre line?

Now notice your right foot. How does your right heel make contact with the ground, at what point on the heel, at the centre of the heel, to the right or to the left? How does it compare with the left heel? Which heel seems to make more contact with the ground?

Where does the right foot carry most of its weight, on the heel or on the ball of the foot? Does the foot make more contact with the floor on the inside of the foot or the outside? Which toes are making contact with the floor and which are not? How does the right foot compare with the left foot? How much does the right foot turn in or turn out? How does it compare with the left foot?

Move your attention up your right lower leg, and find the relationship between your right knee and right heel. Is the knee over the heel, or is one in front or behind the other?

As you bring your attention higher up your right leg, notice the angle at which your leg turns out. How far is your right knee from the centre line that you drew straight out from your belly button? Which knee, the right or the left, is further away from this centre line?

Now notice your pelvis and how it rests on the chair. Does the right side or the left side feel heavier? Which side feels that it makes more contact with the chair? Do you feel your entire buttocks on the chair? Is there more pressure felt on the left or right cheek? Do you find the contact also on your upper thighs? Which thigh has more? Do you feel any changes of pressure as your awareness is directed to the left or right buttock, left or right thigh?

Move your attention to your lower back. Which side, the right side or the left side, feels longer? Which side feels wider?

As you move your attention to your middle back, do you feel it as clearly as you do your lower back? Which side feels longer, the right side or the left side? Which side feels wider?

Feel now the width of your upper back. Which side feels as if it takes up more space? Which side feels longer? Which side feels wider?

Move your attention to your neck. Does the right side or the left side feel longer? Does your head feel that it is sitting on top of your neck, or is it to the front or to the back of it? Is there any tension in your neck from holding your head above it? Notice whether your head feels as if it is tilting right or left. Notice the space between your chin and your throat.

Check in with your mouth. Is it open or shut? How wide or how tight?

Sense your shoulders. Which shoulder seems higher, the left or the right? If you were to draw a line between your right shoulder and your ear, and another line between your left shoulder and your left ear, which line would be longer?

Now move your attention to your arms. Which feels longer? Which feels heavier? Notice how far your right arm is from your body. Then notice how far your left arm is from your body. Are your hands resting face up on your legs or do they face down?

Sense how you feel overall. Do you feel that one side of you is lighter than the other? Is one side of you wider than the other? Taller? Stand up for a minute or two to give yourself a feeling of how you feel standing? Do you still feel any difference in the two sides? Do you feel different from what you remember you felt when you were standing earlier in the day? If so, how?

The logic of somaesthetic introspection

Having performed a body scan, we can now inquire more deeply into the logic of its method. What strategies help us, in practical terms, to make our somaesthetic introspection more effective? One crucial way is to make it more attentive; and certain techniques of heightening attentiveness emerge from considering two key principles of attention: change and interest. As human consciousness evolved to help us survive in an ever changing world, so our attention is habituated to change and requires it. One cannot attend continuously for very long to an object that does not change, which suggests the paradoxical argument that in order to keep attention unchangingly fixed on the very same object of thought, one must somehow insure that some kind of change is introduced in the object attended, even if it is only a difference of the perspective from which it is examined as an object of thought. Similarly, as consciousness evolved to serve our interests, so continued interest is required to sustain attention. We cannot focus for long on things that do not interest us, and even our interest in the thought of something we care about (say, our right hand) can soon be exhausted unless we find some way of reviving that interest and introducing some change of consciousness. From these basic features of change and interest, five distinct introspective strategies of the body scan (and of somaesthetic reflection more generally) can be elaborated.

a. Questions: We can better sustain attention to a given topic of thought, including a somatic object or perception by considering different aspects and relations of it in turn to avoid monotony that destroys attention. One useful technique of doing this is by asking a variety of questions about the object on which we want to fix continued attention. Such questions provoke renewed interest in the object by prompting us to reconsider the object in order to answer the questions. Moreover, the very effort of considering the questions effectively changes the way or aspect in which the object is perceived. It is hard, for example, to keep our attention focused on the feeling of our breathing. But if we ask ourselves a series of questions about it – is our breath deep or shallow, rapid or slow? Is it felt more in the chest or in the diaphragm? What does it feel like in the mouth or in the nose? Does the inhalation or exhalation feel longer? – then we will be able so sustain attention much longer and introspect our feelings more carefully.

b. Division into parts: As William James notes, if we try to examine our 'corporeal sensations . . . as we lie or sit motionless, we find it difficult to feel distinctly the length of our back or the direction of our feet from our shoulders'. Even if we succeed 'by a strong effort' to feel our whole self at once, such perception is remarkably 'vague and ambiguous', and 'only a few parts are strongly emphasized to consciousness' (PP 788). The key to a more precise bodily introspection is therefore to systematically scan the body by subdividing it in our awareness, directing our focused attention first to one part then to another, so that each part can be given proper attention, and a clearer sense of the relations of parts to whole can be obtained. The *transition of focus* not only provides the sense of change that continued attention requires; it also provides renewed interest with each newly examined part presenting a new challenge.

c. Moreover, this transition of introspective probing from one body part to another helps in providing successive contrasts of feeling, and such contrasts help sharpen the discrimination of what we feel. Enhancing discrimination is another crucial strategy for more effective introspection, and we readily see how questions and divisions into parts also encourage discrimination by discriminating foci of interest. But let me now focus on how this works through contrast of feelings. If asked to assess the felt heaviness of one of our shoulders as we lie on the floor, we are not likely to get a clear impression of this feeling. But if we first focus on one shoulder and then on the other, we can more easily get a clearer impression of each by noticing which feels heavier and rests firmer on the floor. Contrast makes feelings easier to discriminate, and we can distinguish contrasts in terms of two different contrasting kinds.

First, we can distinguish between 'existential' and 'differential' contrasts. The first is the simple contrast between whether the feeling (or, more generally, element) in question is actually there or is absent, without considering the specific nature of that element. Differential contrast is a matter of contrasting the nature of the existing feelings (or elements). Both kinds of contrast can be helpful in somaesthetic introspection. We can, for example, learn to discriminate a previously unnoticed feeling of chronic muscular contraction in our antigravity extensors by suddenly feeling what it is like to have those muscles relaxed (say, through the work of a somatic therapist who supports our weight) and thus to have a momentary absence of the contraction. But we can also learn to discriminate the degree of felt tension in, say, a clenched fist by the contrast of intensifying the fist's muscular contraction through one's own greater effort of flexion or through the therapist's squeezing of that fist (or indeed the other fist). We can also (with respect to both existential and differential contrasts) distinguish between contrasts of succession and simultaneous contrasts. Empirical research suggests that at least with respect to differential contrasts, successive contrasts are more precisely discriminating. So focusing first on one shoulder and then the other is usually far more effective for noticing how our shoulders feel than the method of trying to combine our attention on the feeling of both shoulders in one simultaneous perception. When it comes to more global discriminations of body experience, as when trying to feel which parts of the body feel the heaviest or densest or tensest, it is even clearer that we cannot rely on a simultaneous comparative grasp of the feelings of all our body parts, but must instead proceed by successive examination and comparison of parts. That is what a body scan is all about.

d. Associative interest: Besides the use of focusing questions and the transitions, subdivisions and contrasts of the body scan, there are other principles to sustain the interest necessary for effective somaesthetic introspection. One is *associative interest*. Just as the faint knock of an expected lover will be heard over louder sounds because the listener is interested in hearing it (PP 395), so we can stimulate attention to a bodily feeling by making its recognition a key to something we care about: for example, the recognition of a certain feeling of muscle relaxation or rhythm of breathing whose presence and perception can sustain a feeling of repose that leads into desired sleep; or the associated interest of recognizing that attention to a particular body part or feeling in a body scan has had the capacity to induce a muscular readjustment associated with feelings of somatic ease and cognitive empowerment.

e. Avoiding distracting interests: Another strategy for enhancing introspective attention to bodily feelings is by taking steps to ward off competing interests, since any form of attention constitutes a focalization of consciousness that implies ignoring other things in order to concentrate on the object in focus. That is why introspective body scans and other forms of meditation are performed with the eyes closed (or half closed) so that our minds will not be stimulated by perceptions from the external world of sight that would distract our interest. Internal perception is thus indirectly improved by blunting external perception.

f. Still another technique for sharpening our attention to a feeling we are trying to discriminate is by preparing for or anticipating its perception, since 'preperception . . . is half of the perception of the looked-for thing' (PP 419). With respect to the body scan or other forms of somaesthetic introspection, such preparation (which in itself heightens interest) can take different forms. One can prepare oneself to discriminate a feeling by conceptualizing where in one's felt body to look for it or by imagining how it will be induced and felt there. Such conceptualization and imagining clearly involves linguistic thought, which means that language can be an aid to somaesthetic insight, though it can also be a distracting obstacle when the range of language is assumed to exhaust the entire range of experience. While emphasizing the limits of language and the importance of nameless feelings, we must also recognize that language can improve our perception of what we feel.

For such reasons, the use of language to guide and sharpen somaesthetic introspection – through preparatory instructions, focusing questions, anticipatory imaginative descriptions of what will be experienced and how it will feel, and contrasting descriptions or names of feelings – is crucial even to those disciplines of body consciousness that regard the range and meaning of our feelings as going well beyond the limits of language. Body and language, so often posed as oppositional forces competing for primacy or all-subsuming privilege, are both essential for somaesthetics. The key is not to rank them in importance but, to coordinate them better. The body scan

I gave you required linguistic instructions but it also required from you more than mere conceptual understanding. Philosophy and life demand a multiplicity of tools, and so does the teaching of philosophy.

Notes

1   The most complete account of somaesthetics can be found in Richard Shusterman (2008), *Body Consciousness: A Philosophy of Mindfulness and Somaesthetics*. Cambridge: Cambridge University Press.
2   I have, however, used it frequently in special workshops, conferences and advanced seminars.
3   I quote from *Alcibiades and Phaedo*, in John Cooper (1997) (ed.), *The Complete Works of Plato*. Indianapolis: Hackett, pp. 56–58, 589. Plato offers a much more balanced account in *Timaeus* and the *Laws*, where certain forms of somatic cultivation are recommended.
4   Immanuel Kant (1991), *The Metaphysics of Morals*. Cambridge: Cambridge University Press, p. 191.
5   (1992), *Reflexionen Kants zur Kritischen Philosophie*. Stuttgart: Frommann-Holzboog, 68–9. See also Kant's (1996) *Anthropology from a Pragmatic Point of View*. Carbondale: Southern Illinois University Press.
6   William James (1962), *Talks To Teachers on Psychology and To Students on Some of Life's Ideals*. New York: Dover, pp. 99, 109; and (1983), *The Principles of Psychology*. Cambridge: Harvard University Press, p. 1128; hereafter referred to as PP.
7   Maurice Merleau-Ponty (1964), *Signs*, (trans. Richard C. McCleary) Evanston: Northwestern University Press, pp. 78, 89.
8   Maurice Merleau-Ponty (1962), *Phenomenology of Perception*, (trans. Colin Smith) London: Routledge, 90–91.
9   I refer to the authorized edition of John Dewey's collected works, published by Southern Illinois University Press between 1969–1990, respectively *Later Works*, volume 6, p. 13, and *Middle Works*, volume 11, p. 352.
10 For more on all these points, see *Body Consciousness*.

Chapter 5

Philosophy and Place-Based Pedagogies

William Edelglass

Introduction

In 'Of Other Spaces,' Michel Foucault suggests that 'our own era . . . seems to be that of space. We are,' he argues, 'in the age of the simultaneous, of juxtaposition, the near and the far, the side by side, and the scattered'.[1] Foucault's analysis is echoed in prominent discussions of space and place across the humanities and social sciences.[2] Along with explorations of the body, the local, the regional and the global, there is considerable inquiry into gendered spaces, embodied spaces, subaltern spaces, political spaces, cultural topographies, cyberspace, architecture and social action, nomadism, contested spaces, spaces of desire, monumental spaces, forgotten spaces, the production, practice and performance of space, etc. The overturning of the temporocentrism associated with several centuries of European thought has been broadly termed the 'spatial turn'.[3] Questions of space and place are also at the heart of much recent educational theory and practice, which has seen its own spatial turn.[4]

The spatial turn in education is manifest in the research on how learning and school communities are conditioned by architecture, local social structures and the natural environment. But the spatial turn is perhaps most evident in the growth of place-based pedagogies – also known as 'community based' learning, which includes 'service-learning'[5] – that have entered the mainstream of North American educational theory and practice.[6] According to David Sobel, place-based education is

> the process of using the local community and environment as a starting point to teach concepts in language arts, mathematics, social studies, science, and other subjects across the curriculum. Emphasizing hands-on, real-world learning experiences, this approach to education increases

academic achievement, helps students develop stronger ties to their community, enhances students' appreciation for the natural world, and creates a heightened commitment to serving as active, contributing citizens.
Community vitality and environmental quality are improved through
the active engagement of local citizens, community organizations, and
environmental resources in the life of the school.[7]

While place-based pedagogies have seen significant growth across the
humanities, as well as the social and natural sciences, philosophers have
been exceptionally slow to explore the pedagogical resources of local
places. Perhaps this is because philosophy has often been regarded as
an attempt to transcend the limitations of embodiment and the particular places that nourish us. Novalis suggested that philosophy is a kind of
homesickness; according to this model, the pursuit of wisdom is motivated by a desire to be everywhere at home. This cosmopolitan desire, to
be free from the prejudice and bonds of particular places, makes philosophy an unlikely candidate for place-based pedagogy. One might wonder,
then, is there any value to place-based pedagogy when teaching philosophy? What does philosophy have to offer place-based learning? And
what are the possibilities of place-based pedagogies for teaching philosophy? My purpose in this chapter is to address each of these questions.
I will begin with a brief introduction to place-based education. Then
I will turn to the ways in which philosophy courses can contribute to a
deeper understanding of place. Finally, I will explore the possibilities of
place-based pedagogy for critical reflection on significant philosophical
questions, drawing on my own teaching experience as well as resources
that have inspired me. I do not intend this chapter to be a rejection of
philosophy's cosmopolitan aspirations – place-based education is simply
one of a variety of pedagogies that may be helpful when teaching philosophy. However, I do believe that place-based pedagogy in philosophy
courses can contribute to the ideal Kwame Anthony Appiah describes
as 'rooted cosmopolitanism': guided by critical reflection, a commitment to world citizenship – intellectually, morally and politically –
accompanied by a commitment to engaged living in singular places.[8]
While all my courses are grounded in textual analysis and discussion, it
has been my experience that assignments which engage students outside
the classroom, when appropriately employed, consistently deepen students' sensitivity to the nuance, complexity and value of the philosophical questions under consideration.

Place-based pedagogies

Place-based education seeks to overcome the divide marked by classroom walls through grounding learning in lived experience via the exploration of local cultural studies, nature studies, real-world problem solving in the community, internships and entrepreneurial opportunities and induction into community decision-making processes.[9] It has its roots in John Dewey's progressive education. According to Dewey, the dominant school model undermined the integration of students' experience outside the classroom into their education and made it difficult to apply what they learned in school to their daily life.[10] Place-based pedagogies are proposed to bridge this gap by contextualizing knowledge in students' lives: history students research the stories of local places and people, perhaps interviewing elders in the community; language arts students document people and events in their places; social studies and government students observe their local governments in operation and the communities and people government decisions impact; science classes monitor local environmental conditions etc.

Place-based education, however, is not just motivated by a desire to overcome the divide between conceptual knowledge and lived experience; it seeks to address some of the varied ways in which we are connected to our places and communities. Place-based education is often presented as one part of the solution to the problem, widely diagnosed, that too many of us in North America have lost the necessary knowledge and love of local places to nurture and sustain healthy human and natural communities. According to this diagnosis, disconnection from singular places constitutes a significant cultural condition of the dissolution of community fabric as well as the degradation of ecosystems. Moreover, because many of us are disconnected from the sources of our food, water, energy, entertainment and much else that sustains us, we fail to see the consequences of our actions that are inflicted on other places. As Wendell Berry writes,

Most people are now fed, clothed, and sheltered from sources toward which they feel no gratitude and exercise no responsibility . . . We are involved now in a profound failure of imagination. Most of us cannot imagine the wheat beyond the bread, or the farmer beyond the wheat, or the farm beyond the farmer, or the history beyond the farm. Most people cannot imagine the forest and the forest economy that produced their houses and furniture and paper; or the landscapes, the streams, and the weather that fill their pitchers and bathtubs and swimming pools with water. Most people appear to assume that when they have paid their money for these things they have entirely met their obligations.[11]

According to David Orr, our educational system bears significant responsibility for the failure of imagination Berry describes. Orr argues that 'a great deal of what passes for knowledge is little more than abstraction piled on top of abstraction, disconnected from tangible experience, real problems and the places where we live and work'.[12] The knowledge students acquire in college is generally unrelated to their place; it is a universal expertise of no-place. Place-based education, Orr suggests, with its emphasis on local knowledge, needs and communities, can teach us how to live well in place, how to nourish and sustain our human and natural communities.[13]

While Orr's account of place-based pedagogy generally emphasizes environmental sustainability, much contemporary community-based learning is also motivated by critical pedagogy, with its attention to structures of oppression based on race, class and gender.[14] Stephen Haymes, for example, in *Race, Culture, and the City: A Pedagogy for Black Urban Struggle*, draws on spatialized critical social theory to propose a pedagogy that enables Blacks to understand the ways in which power relations are inscribed in urban spaces and how to transform these relations.[15] Some recent theorists of place-based learning have resisted what they regard as a romantic nostalgia, an antimodernism in the discourse of 'connection to place'. As Claudia Ruitenberg notes, ' "place" means much more . . . than the natural environment alone. Each place has a history, often a contested history, of the people who inhabited it in past times. Each place has an aesthetics, offers a sensory environment of sound, movement and image that is open to multiple interpretations. And each (inhabited) place has a spatial configuration through which power and other socio-politico-cultural mechanisms are at play'.[16] A radical or critical pedagogy of place teaches students to attend to the conflicting interpretations of their places, and the multiplicity of meanings they have for others. It teaches students to attend to who lives, works and plays in which spaces, and why, and who benefits and who loses from the different modes of emplacement.

There is ample evidence of the benefits of place-based pedagogies, including engaged pedagogies such as service-learning.[17] These pedagogies enable students to play an active role in recognizing and analyzing phenomena, to draw on theories with which they are familiar, and also to gather evidence with which to critique theories they have studied.

For many students learning is more likely to take place when they are excited by their work and when they can connect it to real world challenges and their own lives. When students are able to choose which problems they will address, they are more likely to become emotionally invested and take responsibility both for their own learning and for the particular issue in their community that they are investigating.

While much of the early development of place-based pedagogy took place at the elementary and secondary level, many professors in post-secondary education are now employing place-based pedagogy as they recognize the ways in which it augments the relevance of their discipline as students are motivated to apply their conceptual learning to real-life problem solving, with all its nuance and complexity.[18] Today, Campus Compact, an organization of colleges and universities in the United States committed to 'campus based civic and community engagement,' has over 1,000 member institutions – private and public, large and small – committed to integrating service learning into the curriculum. Encouraged by school leadership, as well as the desire of many faculty to contribute constructively to the wider community through their research, teaching and service, service-learning and community-based research have become commonplace in colleges and universities.[19]

Philosophy and place

What role can philosophy play in place-based education that is engaged locally? Perhaps the first – and by no means inconsequential – contribution philosophy can make to place-based learning is a careful consideration of emplacement that allows students to become aware of the multiple ways in which human experience is embedded in and shaped by place.

Early in their career, philosophy students may not be inclined to recognize the philosophical significance of place. One of the seductions of philosophy is that it can be understood as an activity that is, or ought to be, free from local conditions. This view may very well be strengthened in an introductory course, where students read Plato's argument that knowledge is located outside the realm of becoming in a world beyond sensation, accessible only to reason. For Plato, the project of philosophy is to liberate the soul, to enable its escape to pure forms from the cave of shadows, the physical plane of singular places. Later in the semester they may read Descartes' arguments for considering the realm of knowledge wholly distinct from the realm of things and places.

Students who make it past their introductory course on Plato and Descartes, however, are likely to encounter philosophers who emphasize the ways in which we are always situated in local conditions, that there is, in Thomas Nagel's words, no possible 'view from nowhere.'[20] Indeed, one can argue that at the heart of much philosophy of the last two centuries is the insight that we are always *some place*, inescapably embedded in history, class, language, culture, nature and our own singular psychobiographies. In contrast to the view of philosophy that lifts us out of the particularity and singularity of place, philosophers have been devoted to understanding our emplaced condition, and how this situatedness influences the production of knowledge. More recently, philosophers working in epistemology, metaphysics and ontology, ethics and other fields have explicitly emphasized the significance of place.

Lorraine Code,[21] Evan Thompson,[22] Mark Johnson,[23] Andy Clark,[24] Christopher Preston,[25] Donna Haraway,[26] Sandra Harding[27] and others[28] have argued for the epistemic import of place. For some epistemologists, the project of naturalizing epistemology has meant rooting our understanding of knowledge in natural and cultural conditions that are embedded in particular places. As Preston argues in *Grounding Knowledge*, 'Thought, knowledge, and belief are not products of mind alone but expressions of its integration and participation with the physical world that lies around it. Recognition of this cooperative relationship brings knowledge firmly back down to earth.'[29]

Other contemporary thinkers, inspired most prominently, perhaps, by Martin Heidegger, have made place a central concern of metaphysics and ontology. According to Jeff Malpas, throughout his life Heidegger was concerned with understanding 'the "placed" character of being, and of our own being, so much that we may describe the thinking that is associated with the name "Heidegger" as a thinking that does indeed consist, as he himself claimed, in an attempt to "say" the place of being – as a *topology* of being'.[30] Heidegger understood his own philosophical thinking to be rooted in the Black Forest outside of Freiburg where he wrote; it was, he insisted, no less connected to his place than the work of the farmer and shepherd to their places.[31] Heidegger's emphasis on enrootedness has been problematized by some, for instance Emmanuel Levinas, as the embrace of an intimate relationship between 'blood and soil,' which ultimately leads to the distinction between the native and the foreign other who does not belong, who is excluded from the home place.[32] For Levinas, then, and many other thinkers, questions of place and dwelling are central concerns of ethics and political philosophy.

By disclosing the epistemic, metaphysical, ontological and ethical significance of our embeddedness in singular places, philosophy courses can provide a deeper understanding of our relation to the local. Moreover, philosophers can also offer place-based education a critical concern for the dangers of nativism, a wariness of all the ways in which connection to place can justify exclusionary violence. Unsurprisingly, however, it seems more challenging to actually practice place-based pedagogy when teaching philosophy than to philosophize, more generally, about place. In the spirit of sparking the imagination more than offering prescriptions, in the following section I share some examples of place-based pedagogies as elements of philosophy courses.

Philosophy and place-based pedagogies

Service learning, perhaps more than any other place-based pedagogy, has made some inroads in philosophy departments.[33] In my own forays into service-learning I have been inspired by *Beyond the Tower: Concepts and Models for Service-Learning in Philosophy*.[34] This collection begins with chapters on the philosophical frameworks and foundations of service learning, especially in the context of teaching philosophy. Part II consists of a series of ideas for courses and course narratives for ethics, political philosophy, critical thinking, philosophy of art, logic, philosophy of sport, feminist philosophy, environmental philosophy, philosophy of law, existentialism etc.[35]

As only a brief perusal of *Beyond the Tower* confirms, service learning in philosophy is most easily imagined in the various fields of applied ethics. Students in a medical ethics course, for example, can work with local medical care providers or advocacy groups, or even participate in a medical ethics discussion group at a hospital. Working with patients may deepen student engagement with philosophical theory, for this experience discloses the complexity and nuance that often complicate the seductive clarity of theoretical models. For students studying animal ethics, working at an animal shelter – which may be overwhelmed with unwanted dogs and cats – or a small organic farm – where chickens or cows may be treated with care – could complicate general rules against killing nonhuman animals, and will certainly give the theoretical questions discussed in class a sense of gravity rooted in experience. Similar arguments can be made for service learning as a component of courses in environmental ethics, legal ethics or philosophy of law, business ethics, human rights, political philosophy, etc, where working in the community can challenge and inspire students to deeper philosophical engagement.

Dan Lloyd, who teaches at Trinity College, in Hartford, Connecticut, describes what is perhaps the most creative course in *Beyond the Tower*. In Lloyd's philosophy of art course – 'Art/Hartford' – students work with and observe 'the artworld,' or rather 'artworlds,' in local institutions such as galleries, public arts organizations, a senior cultural centre, a prison arts program, etc. While also studying the usual suspects in the canon of philosophy of art, Lloyd's students are able to observe and participate in decisions about what is art, what distinguishes good from bad art, how aesthetic values are related to other values, and develop more nuanced understandings of the cultural and economic dimensions of artistic production and aesthetic experience. Lloyd echoes other contributors, and indeed many colleagues who have described their own service learning courses, writing that his 'experiments with service-learning in several philosophy courses, including Art/Hartford, suggest that service learning is inherently philosophical. While it does contribute to the welfare of the community and also increases the civic engagement of students, neither of these outcomes is what I value most. Rather, it is the reflective connection students make between what they read and what they experience. The encounter is inevitably Socratic, as students discover the incompleteness and falsity of their assumptions, and it is equally Aristotelian, in the sense that their encounters lead them to a richer, more articulated description of the world around them'.[36]

While service learning is growing in popularity, even in philosophy, I have also found simpler, and less logistically demanding engagements with local places to be philosophically significant for my students. For example, in my own philosophy of art courses, the students are assigned papers which require them to visit local galleries and museums, choose a particular work of art and write about it in the context of texts discussed in class. Does the work provide good evidence for a theory of art or is it a counter example? This assignment encourages students to look at artworks in a way that is informed by philosophical theory and also to draw on their aesthetic experience to evaluate different theories of art. Additionally, the students become more familiar with the art that is being shown – and sometimes produced – in their own community. They are often surprised at how accessible the art is, and how much they enjoy going to a gallery or museum they may have walked by – but not into – for several years. Because I generally teach some environmental aesthetics, I also have the students write about their experience of places on or near campus, experiences that can be analyzed in light of the readings, and serve as evidence for or against specific arguments. I show the Andy Goldsworthy film, *Rivers and Tides*, and then give the students an opportunity to create their own environmental art and reflect on their experience in writing. For the students, seriously considering the natural and built environment that surrounds them and engaging with local artwork has been philosophically fertile and deepened their relationship to place.

Courses in environmental ethics or environmental philosophy readily lend themselves to place-based pedagogies. No community has an equal distribution of environmental goods; thus every place offers fertile opportunities for reflecting on questions of environmental justice. And most communities have disagreements over how to use – or not use – lands and resources. These disagreements over policy and values invite philosophical analysis and reflection; they are ultimately grounded in the very metaphysical and ethical views that constitute the subject of most environmental philosophy courses.[37] It is sometimes tempting for students to make facile moral judgments concerning what is right and wrong in environmental contexts. Engaging with local efforts – for example the restoration of salmon or the reduction of campus carbon emissions – increases sensitivity to economic, political, cultural and ecological conditions that must be taken into account when making good arguments in environmental philosophy. Over the years students in my environmental philosophy courses have applied readings from class to a wide variety of local issues, and used these issues as examples to justify or critique one theoretical approach or another. And every student has considered their own life and practices – for example, the sources of their food, clothes and energy – and come to a new, more nuanced and still morally inflected, self-understanding.

To accompany readings on place I have sometimes assigned students to choose an accessible place to which they can regularly return and then reflect, in writing, on their own relationship to that place. Similar assignments that engage students with their local places may be appropriate to a wide variety of courses. When I teach Martin Buber's *I and Thou*, in which Buber argues that it is possible to have an I-Thou relationship with a tree, I assign students to spend fifteen minutes contemplating, in proximity, a tree. Again, my hope is twofold. I do want the students to engage, with attention, the trees around them. But I also hope that the students can have their own experience that can justify either agreement or disagreement with Buber's claim. And when I teach phenomenology I assign students various kinds of phenomenological descriptions, including descriptions of their experiences of familiar places.

As Edward Casey demonstrates in *The Fate of Place: A Philosophical History*, space has been an important, if not always primary, theme for much of the history of Western philosophy.[38] Nevertheless, it seems that there are numerous courses in the history of philosophy or contemporary thought that do not lend themselves to place-based education. My point, here, however, is that place-based pedagogy *can* be integrated into many courses, even if in a modest and small way. In my experience, students find even relatively small assignments that allow them to engage the texts under discussion with their own life-world, when approached with care and rigor, to be philosophically fruitful and personally enriching.

Success in philosophy courses generally depends on what Howard Gardner – whose model of multiple intelligences is widely employed in educational theory – calls 'verbal-linguistic' intelligence and 'logical-mathematical' intelligence. Engaged pedagogies may allow students who are not as strong in these particular kinds of intelligence but may have strengths in other areas, to flourish in philosophy courses.[39] For place-based learning engages students both cognitively and affectively.[40] This holistic engagement leads to deeper and stronger connections between knowledge and responsibility.[41] For these reasons place-based pedagogies have entered the discourse of cultivating a renewed 'sense of place' – what Gary Snyder refers to as 'the real work.'[42] This is the work of learning to live well in one's place, or, as Wes Jackson describes it, 'becoming native' to one's place.[43] Additionally, and perhaps most importantly for teachers of philosophy, place-based pedagogies, if used well, facilitate deeper, more nuanced engagement with philosophical questions.

Notes

[1] M. Foucault (1997), 'Of Other Spaces: Utopias and Heterotopias', in N. Leach (ed.), *Rethinking Architecture: A Reader in Cultural Theory*. London: Routledge, p. 350.

[2] For recent reviews of the literature on space in a variety of disciplines in the social sciences and the humanities, see B. Warf and S. Arias (2008), *The Spatial Turn: Interdisciplinary Perspectives*. London: Routledge. Also, see E. Soja (19890, *Postmodern Geographies: The Reassertion of Space in Critical Social Theory*. New York: Verso; and G. Benko and U. Srohmayer (1997), *Space and Social Theory*. Oxford: Blackwell.

[3] For an excellent systematic account of space and place in the history of Western philosophy, including the significance of place in recent thought, see E. Casey (1997), *The Fate of Place: A Philosophical History*. Berkeley: University of California Press. For an accessible introduction to the history and production of space and

spatial practice and performance, see D. Gregory (2008), *Spaces*. London: Routledge.

⁴ For a variety of perspectives on the spatial turn in recent education, see K. Gulson and C. Symes (2007), *Spatial Theories of Education*. London: Routledge.

⁵ All of these terms, along with 'experiential education,' 'problem-based learning,' and 'collaborative learning,' are often understood to intersect with one another as forms of 'engaged' or 'student-centered' pedagogy.

⁶ See, for example, A. Colby, T. Ehrlich, E. Beaumont and J. Stephens (2003), *Educating Citizens: Preparing America's Undergraduates for Lives of Moral Responsibility*. San Francisco: Jossey-Bass; P. Theobald (1997), *Teaching the Commons: Place, Pride, and the Renewal of Community*. Boulder: Westview Press; G. Smith (2002), 'Going Local'. *Educational Leadership* 60 (1), 30–33; D. Hutchison (2004), *A Natural History of Place in Education*. New York: Teachers College Press; D. Sobel (2004), *Place-Based Education: Connecting Classrooms and Communities*. Great Barrington: The Orion Society; and the special issue of *Ethics, Place and Environment* devoted to place-based and environmental education, 8 (3), October 2005.

⁷ Sobel, *Place-Based Education*, p. 7.

⁸ See K. A. Appiah (2005), *The Ethics of Identity*. Princeton: Princeton University Press, especially pp. 213–272.

⁹ See G. Smith (2002), 'Place-Based Education: Learning To Be Where We Are'. *Phi Delta Kappan*, 83, 584–594.

¹⁰ J. Dewey (1959), *The School and Society* in M. Dworkin (ed.), *Dewey on Education*. New York: Teachers College Press, p. 76.

¹¹ W. Berry (2001), *In the Presence of Fear*. Great Barrington: The Orion Society, pp. 37–38.

¹² D. Orr (1992), 'Place and Pedagogy', in *Ecological Literacy: Education and the Transition to a Postmodern World*. Albany: State University of New York Press, p. 126.

¹³ In addition to the essays on education in *Ecological Literacy*, see also D. Orr (1994), *Earth in Mind: On Education, Environment, and the Human Prospect*. Albany: State University of New York Press.

¹⁴ See, for example, C. Ruitenberg (2005), 'Deconstructing the Experience of the Local: Toward a Radical Pedagogy of Place', in K. Howe (ed.), *Philosophy of Education*. Urbana: Philosophy of Education Society, pp. 212–220; and D. Gruenewald (2003), 'The Best of Both Worlds: A Critical Pedagogy of Place', *Educational Researcher*, 32 (4), 3–12.

¹⁵ S. Haymes (1995), *Race, Culture, and the City: A Pedagogy for Black Urban Struggle*. Albany: State University of New York Press.

¹⁶ Ruitenberg, 'Deconstructing the Experience of the Local', p. 215.

¹⁷ See Colby, et al., *Educating Citizens*.

¹⁸ For a discussion of the theory of engaged pedagogies and how they are being applied in higher education, see Colby, et al., *Educating Citizens*.

¹⁹ See K. Strand, S. Marullo, N. Cutforth, R. Stoecker and P. Donohue (2003), *Community-Based Research and Higher Education: Principles and Practices*. San Francisco: Jossey-Bass.

²⁰ T. Nagel (1986), *The View From Nowhere*. New York: Oxford University Press.

²¹ L. Code (2006), *Ecological Thinking: The Politics of Epistemic Location*. New York: Oxford University Press.

22 E. Thompson (2007), Mind in Life: Biology, Phenomenology, and the Sciences of Mind. Cambridge: Harvard University Press. See also F. Varela, E. Thompson and E. Rosch (1991), *The Embodied Mind: Cognitive Science and Human Experience.* Cambridge: MIT Press.

23 M. Johnson (1987), *The Body and the Mind.* Chicago: University of Chicago Press.

24 A. Clark (1997), *Being There: Putting Brain, Body, and World Together Again.* Cambridge: MIT Press.

25 C. Preston (2003), *Grounding Knowledge: Environmental Philosophy, Epistemology, and Place.* Athens : University of Georgia Press.

26 D. Haraway (1988), 'Situated Knowledges: The Science Question in Feminism and the Privilege of Partial Perspectives', *Feminist Studies,* 14 (3), 575–599.

27 S. Harding (1998), *Is Science Multi-Cultural? Postmodernisms, Feminisms, and Epistemologies.* Bloomington: Indiana University Press.

28 See, for example, the special issue devoted to 'Epistemology and Environmental Philosophy: The Epistemic Significance of Place', *Ethics and the Environment,* 10 (1).

29 Preston, *Grounding Knowledge,* p. 2.

30 J. Malpas (2006), *Heidegger's Topology: Being, Place, World.* Cambridge: MIT Press, p. 305.

31 M. Heidegger (1994), 'Creative Landscape: Why Do We Stay in the Provinces?' in A. Kaes, M. Jay and E. Dimendberg (eds.), *The Weimar Republic Sourcebook.* Berkeley: University of California Press, 426–428.

32 E. Levinas (1990), 'Heidegger, Gagarin and Us', in S. Hand (trans.) *Difficult Freedom: Essays on Judaism.* Baltimore: Johns Hopkins University Press, pp. 231–234.

33 For an account of service learning in philosophy see Drew Leder's chapter in this volume.

34 C. Linsman and I. Harvey (2000), *Beyond the Tower: Concepts and Models for Service-Learning in Philosophy.* Washington, DC: American Association for Higher Education.

35 For syllabi of service learning courses in philosophy, see *http://www.compact.org/syllabi/list.php?discipline=Philosophy* [accessed, 28 May 2008].

36 D. Lloyd, 'Sojourning in the Art World: Service-Learning in Philosophy of Art', in *Beyond the Tower,* p. 202.

37 See R. Frodeman (2006), 'The Policy Turn in Environmental Philosophy', *Environmental Ethics,* 28 (1), 3-20.

38 Casey, *The Fate of Place.*

39 See Colby, et al. *Educating Citizens,* 136–138.

40 For an account of the significance of emotions in teaching philosophy, see Brendan Larvor's essay in this volume.

41 D. Havlick and M. Hourdequin, 'Practical Wisdom in Environmental Education', *Ethics, Place and Environment,* 8 (3), 385–392.

42 G. Snyder (1980), *The Real Work: Interviews and Talks (1964–1979).* New York: New Directions Books.

43 W. Jackson (1996), *Becoming Native to This Place.* Washington, DC: Counterpoint.

Chapter 6

Escaping the Cave: Experiential Learning in the Classroom, Community and Correctional Institutions

Drew Leder

Philosophy is often thought of as a discipline preoccupied with abstruse and abstract ideals, and therefore disconnected from the 'real world'. The first practitioner of Western philosophy and natural science, Thales of Miletus, was said to have fallen into a well one night while gazing up at the stars. A passing maidservant from Thrace scoffed at him for being so absorbed in the skies he couldn't see what plainly lay at his feet (Plato's *Theaetetus, 174a*). I must admit I sometimes fit the caricature of the absent-minded professor. Absorbed in thought, I can be a danger to myself or others.

But to thus understand philosophy, and philosophical teaching, is to do a grave disservice to its practitioners. Socrates' questions were not, for the most part, prompted by abstract philosophical speculation but by very real and human dilemmas. For example, Plato's *Euthyphro* commences when Socrates meets Euthyphro on the courtroom steps; a discussion of the true nature of 'piety' is crucial because one is accused of impiety, and the other an accuser, in two trials about to commence. Plato's long series of arguments in the *Phaedo* concerning the soul's immortality is a very real response to the existential moment; Socrates is preparing to drink the hemlock.

The existential rootedness of philosophical inquiry is as, or even more, evident in the Eastern philosophical traditions which I teach as often as I do the Western. The *Tao te Ching* begins with the famous 'buyers beware' warning, 'The tao that can be spoken is not the everlasting Tao./ The name that can be named is not the everlasting Name'. The Tao must be intuited, embodied, *fully lived* to have any meaning, not simply talked about in a classroom.

Krishna's learned discourse on yoga which constitutes the lengthy *Bhagavad Gita* unfolds in an anguished moment frozen in time: on the battlefield of Kurukshetra, two armies poised for slaughter, Arjuna stops, unable to decide whether to throw down his arms or to proceed with the killing of his own family members and teachers. Knowledge must illuminate action, and do so immediately.

Buddha goes even farther to say that disconnecting knowledge from action can be dangerous. He compares this to a man shot with a poisoned arrow refusing to have it removed until he clarifies who shot the arrow, their caste, colour, home city and height, as all the while he sickens and dies from the wound. Such happens when we idly speculate about the eternality of the world or soul, leaving the poisoned arrow of our present suffering to fester.

Since ancient times true philosophy has thus been tied to experience and action. In Socrates' allegory of the cave from Plato's *Republic*, the prisoner doesn't just discuss matters; he is released from chains, turns around, walks out of the cave, is dazzled, blinded and illuminated by a new world, and then re-enters the cave to assist others perhaps at the peril of his life. How can we make the classroom in some way resemble this challenging and transformative experience? How to be more than puppet-masters ourselves, drawing blackboard images for our student prisoners chained to their seats by distribution requirements and grade-threats? How to help students think in a way that *moves* them out of the cave of unreflective preconceptions and social training – moves them intellectually, emotively, politically, behaviourally? Otherwise, it's all just words.

One method I've chosen, or really a series of methods, is the use of experience-based learning. Surely we all hope our students will connect the concepts we are teaching to their own lives. To facilitate this we use experiential examples in class. We guide discussions that provoke students to reflect on their experience. But we can also go one step farther – we can *design* experiences for our students that provoke and further philosophical reflection.

Such experiences may involve engagement with the *polis*, the broader community outside of the prison/cave walls of the confined classroom. Service-learning is a primary example of this pedagogy. But experiences can also involve not simply moving outward but penetrating inward through contemplative exercises. Meditation can be incorporated into the classroom.

In a variety of ways, instead of thinking, with the hope it may sometimes affect our doing, we can ask our students to do something that provokes them to think anew. We might call this Dewey-doing, in honour of the pragmatist philosopher John Dewey, whose writings portray the educational process as deeply experiential.[1] In life, he suggests, we learn by confronting problematic situations which provoke data gathering and reflection. This process leads us to formulate hypothetical solutions that are then tested in real-world action, and subsequently refined as we discover what works and what does not. We learn in the midst of doing, and the thinking it calls forth.

Off the beaten track: service-learning

The place I have most incorporated experience-based learning is within a course I teach each year on Asian Philosophy. Focusing on Hinduism and Buddhism, I give each student a choice between three different experiential 'tracks' that supplement traditional readings and assignments. The first track I'll address involves service-learning.

Because it makes extra demands upon the students – at least ten two-hour site visits, and additional writing – compared to the other tracks, I reward these students with extra-credit contingent on completion of the project and the quality of their written work. I give my students a choice between two service sites that have been prearranged with the assistance of my college's excellent Center for Community Service and Justice. For example, one might be a home for residents with AIDS, the other a shelter offering multifaceted assistance to the homeless and indigent. I choose sites whose mission and clients relate closely to many of the topics of the course, including questions of personal identity, self-body relationship, karma, death and reincarnation, suffering and techniques for mastering and transcending it, compassion, interdependency, the caste system, social justice and social activism. I also allow students to choose or continue to work with an alternate site, if it fits well with course themes.

Pedagogically, I long ago learned not to simply say, 'keep a journal in which you connect your experiences to course content'. The students need much more explicit assistance on how to link the often disorienting, emotional, inchoate and unpredictable raw material of their service experiences to the formal concepts of the course. I now provide very specific questions for the students to respond to, along with the option of formulating their own.

For example, when studying the life of Buddha we read a famous account of how he, as a spoiled young prince, artificially protected by his father from any glimpse of human suffering, first encounters 'four passing sights' – an old man, a sick man, a corpse and a renunciate – whereby he learns of the inevitability of bodily decay, and the need for and possibility of escape from the accompanying misery. I ask the students to submit electronically a 1–2 page essay on the following questions:

> Have you (or your clients) witnessed something analogous to the sick person, old person, or corpse, that shock Siddhartha out of his 'artificial kingdom'? Has this served as a force of positive awakening for you or them?
>
> In the Four Noble Truths, Buddha said that life is filled with *dukkha* (suffering) and the root of this suffering is *tanha,* our self-centered cravings. Do any of your service experiences bear on this thesis? What kinds of suffering do you see in your clients, and/or yourself? What seems to be the root of these sufferings, and how might the pain be relieved?

To give a concrete example of this pedagogy in action, I supply a student response submitted by Monica Bauer, who served in a 'Project Health' needle exchange program. I will quote her response at length, if not in its entirety:

> At my service site I talked to this lady suffering from HIV, cancer, a drug addiction, poverty and an abusive husband. For some reason she really took to me, and we talked for over an hour. I had trouble understanding her half of the time, but I tried my hardest to listen to her story. She told me everything I could ever want to know about her life. On the needle exchange van, I'm supposed to connect those who are interested in the resources they need, but this day, my role on the van was to be a friend. When I first laid eyes on this woman, of course I thought that what happened to her could never happen to me. But what was really surprising was that the more this lady talked about her life, the more I began to see that she was just like me. She and I both have a very religious, over-the-top, Catholic mother, we both like it better where the weather's warmer and the people are nicer, we both love movies, and we both have nieces/nephews who we love a lot but rarely get to see. What was really touching was when she started to cry as she told me the story of her father's death. She spoke about how her father and she were never close, but that she respected and loved him because he had done so much for her in her life. Something I can also relate to. In class, we talked about how we always view sick people, old people and those who've died as 'them.' We find it hard to comprehend that 'them' could ever be 'us.' This was one of the first times I actually remember sitting on the van and thinking, this woman comes from a family just like mine and has a background just like mine – this could be me.

The more service I do, the farther I seem to separate myself from the artificial kingdom. Growing up, I was never refused anything. Every need and every want was fulfilled. Yet I was still never that happy. My goal in high school was to be a star athlete. I made the varsity lacrosse team and the varsity soccer team at a young age and I worked really hard. But I just remember being so unhappy . . . I agree with Buddha's theory that life is filled with *dukkha* (suffering) and that the root of this suffering is *tanha,* our self-centered cravings. These egotistical cravings are what keep others down. If Americans weren't so self-interested, maybe we would care more about the homeless and the poverty stricken. We are all responsible for letting the terrible wrongs in this society happen, and continue to happen. When someone falls into bad times, the community should be there to pick them up and help them get back on their feet. But instead, in our society, we ignore and marginalize them. So much suffering could be relieved if people stopped focusing on themselves, and started putting others first. (Monica Bauer)

Over the years I have discovered that a student's first response often provokes or leaves unanswered questions that need follow-up to maximize learning. The electronic submission format allows me to fire off a brief response, and to ask other students to do the same for one another (diminishing my workload), followed by a brief 'part two' submission from the originating student. For example, I asked Ms. Bauer whether she thought her experience of commonality with her client was unusual, or something that we would sooner or later arrive at with every human being we encountered. Another student asked whether the homeless, sick and poverty-stricken are suffering as the result of *their own* desires, or more from the egotistical desires that render *others* indifferent. I think this is an important issue in understanding Buddhism – is personal suffering caused by individual karma and craving, and/or that of the collectivity? Such questions, which could be quite abstract, take on an existential meaning and urgency when tied to vital experience – in this case, that conversation with a woman struggling with adversity, so different from, yet similar to, Ms. Bauer. I suspect lessons learned in this way are thought through, understood and retained in greater depth than those generated by a teacher at the blackboard. For example, while I won't quote from it, Ms. Bauer's follow-up response reflected upon and integrated her own family history, her personal encounter with illness, the crises of Baltimore and the ways in which we are trained to 'ignore' or 'expel' those around us who are suffering rather than work to alleviate their pain.

Service-learning is not for everyone, student and faculty alike, or for every course and occasion. I am blessed by having the support of an institution whose Jesuit values are congruent with such work, which has an excellent service-learning office and infrastructure, a supportive Philosophy Department, and even faculty incentives for those who utilize this pedagogy. There also exist many helpful materials available for anyone interested in service-learning pedagogy, including some specific to the discipline of philosophy.[2] Even so, with 56 students in my two sections of Asian Philosophy, it would be overwhelming to try to arrange and oversee service-learning work for them all. Nor do I feel it pedagogically necessary. In studying Hinduism, we learn that there are many 'yogic' paths to enlightenment. Service-learning most corresponds to *karma yoga* wherein one's work in the world, now viewed as selfless service, becomes a method of liberation from ego-self. Yet there are also paths of devotion, knowledge and meditation which may be more appropriate for individuals of different temperament. In harmony with this I like to let my students select their own experiential track from a menu of options, the others of which I will now address.

Off the beaten track: meditation, and philosophical games

Another way in which I am blessed within my department is to have a colleague, Bret Davis, who has lived for over a decade in Japan, and is an advanced practitioner and teacher of Zen meditation. Even without his presence, however, I have not hesitated in my own imperfect way to teach meditative practices inside and outside the classroom. Meditation is viewed in most Eastern traditions as an essential aid to the process of self-exploration, the dissolving of delusions and painful cravings and aversions, and the realization of the fundamental Source from which we come. Fortunately, the fundamental elements of many forms of meditation – posture, focus on the breath, non-resistance and non-clinging to passing thoughts, are not 'rocket science' to understand and teach. Even when transmitted imperfectly, a taste of meditation can be valuable. We cease talking about Hindu or Buddhist views of mind, and actually witness our own mind in action, experience its flaws and recalcitrant chatter, and perhaps its capacity to arrive at moments of stillness.

For such reasons I not only often begin class with a brief meditation – which frequently elevates the energy and attention-level of the students and myself – but also include meditation practice as one of my three experiential tracks. Participating students read an excellent primer, *Meditation for*

Dummies,[3] do some prescribed meditation on their own (at least they're supposed to), and engage in a weekly Zen sitting (where attendance is taken) with the colleague mentioned above. Written reflection takes place through electronic submissions. I'll again share a brief and illustrative excerpt:

> Now that we have begun to weed out most of our annoying feelings and emotions during meditation we can begin to really concentrate on those thoughts that simply will not go away. The book tells us to stop viewing these emotions as distractions and to begin including them in our meditation with mindful awareness . . . and just continue to welcome everything that happens to us. It is important that we find a happy medium between allowing our emotions to run our lives and simply shutting them out altogether.

> I have began to treat every incoming feeling with deep consideration and if the specific thoughts happen to be more involved than I may have first realized I calmly try and examine them with an open mind. It is important to remember that 'feeling your feelings does not make them bigger or worse, it actually allows them to move through and release!' As I continue with my meditation I am going to try and use these skills next time I meditate and an overwhelming emotion comes my way. Instead of allowing myself to get sucked in to the feeling, I will embrace it and let it pass through me. (Teresa Pollet)

Whether the student is successful or not in achieving this goal, she is learning something about the Buddhist ideal of right mindfulness, the methods and rigors involved in attaining it, as well as the pattern of her own emotions. Again, we have the process John Dewey describes: Problematic situations provoke reflection and hypothetical solutions, which then are tested and refined in action. This particular mode of experiential learning – the integration of contemplative practices with higher education – has become something of a 'cutting-edge' national phenomenon, with supportive professors, institutions, even fellowships, available to help interested teachers.[4]

Not all my students happily commit to a weekly service-learning placement or Zen sitting. Experience can be packaged in other, user-friendly but still effective, forms. Many students choose a third 'experiential game' track I have designed utilizing exercises from my book *Games for the Soul*.[5] The concept behind it is simple, easily adapted or extended. I presume that the techniques used in most spiritual traditions – meditation, prayer, ritual and techniques for generating gratitude, compassion, service, focused attention and self-awareness – while often thought of as 'spiritual disciplines,' and hence hard work, are really 'games' in disguise. The practitioner learns to count breaths, or count blessings; imagine and speak with God in a certain way; play a part in a costumed ritual; assume a posture that induces a corresponding experience; etc. Imagination, dress-up, pretend – these are things children naturally understand and enjoy, and along with rules, prescribed roles and challenges that develop skills, are the ways in which games are structured. In spiritual games, winning is less about competitive triumph than advancement toward a life-transforming goal – be it that of inner peace, God-awareness, enhanced joy or an open heart. That's what it might mean to 'win' at such a game.

During the semester, students who choose this track play seven simple games I have devised that reflect Hindu or Buddhist principles. For example, they are asked to go through a day experiencing whatever happens as a 'karmic' educational opportunity; or seeking constantly to be of service, like the *karma yogi*; or 'practicing the witness', a Buddhist *vipassana* technique, wherein they watch their thoughts arise in a dis-identified fashion, as if a spectator in the movie theatre of their mind. Again, I'll provide a brief sample of student writing, in this case on playing a game involving mantra recitation, for which the student has chosen a translation of the famous Tibetan and Mahayana *Om mani padme hum*:

> I decided to pick the religious mantra 'the jewel in the lotus of the heart'. I liked this one because it is basically trying to see the beauty in everyone. It started around 3:00 pm when I was at [the café] patiently waiting to check out. The cashier was moving at a abnormally slow pace and my rumbling stomach was getting annoyed. I repeated the mantra in my head and took a second to think about it. I then thought of if I was in her position I would probably be moving slower. She probably was there working before I even woke up and has probably had a long, exhausting day catering to bratty Loyola kids. A second time I found my mantra coming into play was when I was studying for this test. I was sitting at a table and I looked up and spotted this boy. He was overweight and eating 3 slices of pizza with a chocolate milk to drink. He had acne covering his face with greasy brown hair. I repeated the mantra in my head and thought I bet this guy is one of the nicest people, but I'm sure many people wouldn't even give him a chance . . . Throughout the day I kept repeating the mantra and found [myself] to be wondering what people were like on the inside, rather than immediately judging them from

the outside. This relates to the course because we are all from the same source . . . Hindus would say our divine atmans are who we are, not these temporary bodies. (Erin Meyer)

Simply talking about the use of mantra is here supplanted by the experience of actually working with one and the discovery of vital, perhaps unanticipated, results.

This would also describe my experience with the pedagogical methods I've been enumerating. It's one thing to consider them in abstraction, another to actually try them out and see the results that, for good or ill, accrue. A reader sympathetic to such techniques may yet have questions such as: Will this actually work given *my* students, subject matter and teaching style? Can such methods be easily incorporated into my existing courses? I'm already way too busy – how much extra work would they generate? And while these techniques may be suited to Asian Philosophy are they adaptable to topics in Western thought? I'll try to provide a few quick and honest responses.

As with any pedagogical method, results are uneven, depending on the commitment and skill of teachers and students alike. For every student who wows me with an experiential realization, there may be another whose submissions are disappointing. Nonetheless, I find on my course evaluations that the notion of having 'experiential tracks,' and a choice among them, is highly valued by students. The individual tracks generally receive strong ratings, with service-learning often at the top. At semester's end I consistently feel that the experiential components have made the course more vital, personal and/or understandable for the majority of my students.

While there is a time-cost to any alteration in an existing syllabus, I find these methods do not add inordinately to my workload. Except in the case of service-learning write-ups, which I feel the need to respond to personally and provocatively, I often skim or check in electronic submissions without providing comments, simply giving full credit for the proper completion of the assignment. This may be less than optimal pedagogy but it stops me from being swamped.

Occasionally I have students read and respond to one another's work electronically either within their own experiential track or across tracks. I can also use this material to foster classroom discussion that enables all students to benefit from hearing about a range of experiences (meditative, service-learning, etc.) that they may not be directly participating in. I am conscious that I can do much better in exploiting such options, yet consoled by the thought that next semester I surely will – or at least hope to, given the rich possibilities of this pedagogy.

Regarding its adaptability to Western philosophy, I think there too the possibilities are rich. To give but a few examples, imagine service-learning, meditative exercises and/or experiential games in relation to: the Socratic inquiry into values and virtues; the Aristotelian doctrine of the virtuous mean; the Stoic prescription for how to handle suffering and adversity; the Augustinian quest for relationship with God; Cartesian meditations on the *Cogito*; Hume's questioning of personal identity; Nietzsche's reflections on herd-morality, the will to power and the free spirit; Marx's critique of class-driven and alienated capitalism; Foucault on disciplinary institutions; de Beauvoir's analysis of women as 'the second sex'; and on and on. These topics in ethics, epistemology, metaphysics, philosophical psychology and social philosophy all have experiential correlates for students to fruitfully explore.

Going into the cave: teaching philosophy in prison

The use of experiential methods helps to also suggest ways of teaching philosophy in a variety of non-traditional settings to older or unconventional students who need more to sink their teeth into than abstract tomes. One of my most powerful learning experiences – really a transformative service-learning experience for me – began when I first stepped out of the 'Loyola bubble' to teach a course in 1992 at the Maryland Penitentiary. The oldest continuously operating penitentiary in the Western world, it is situated in downtown Baltimore. At the time it served as Maryland's maximum-security facility. I volunteered to teach a college-level seminar in philosophy that attracted some of the most motivated and educated inmates. We began by studying the theme of imprisonment and freedom, reading about Socrates' trial, the Stoicism of Epictetus, and Martin Luther King, Jr's call for justice in his letter from Birmingham Jail. Most of the inmates were serving life-sentences. They weren't going anywhere and soon I found that neither was I – the class, originally designed as a six-week summer seminar, continued over two years until the prison was re-classified, and most of my students shipped out.

To sustain a two-year classroom conversation is a luxury one rarely has in a college setting, along with that of teaching students as passionate and committed as these. Paradoxically, for my Loyola students taking philosophy as part of their required core curriculum, it can all seem like a prison sentence to be served until release, in the form of a diploma, is finally granted. How very different was the attitude of the inmates for whom the life of the mind *was their release*. Even while suffering bodily confinement, the spirit can take flight. The great thinkers of every historical period, culture and faith lay open through the pages of the books we studied under the watchful gaze of the prison guards.

Dwelling in a world of ideas, the inmates were better able to disconnect from the harshness around them – the bars and barbed wire of maximum security. Yet our work was not primarily about disconnecting, but the men reconnecting with crucial questions and insights that life in the inner city and prison had obscured. Who am I, beyond my identity as a drug dealer, criminal and tough guy? What is life all about now that I'm serving a life sentence? What went wrong in my past? How can my future be different? How do I cope with the present, waking up each morning to a life in hell, or if I'm lucky, purgatory? How can I be useful? How can I be happy? How can I control my demons, and contact my inner angels?

Such questions were not merely intellectual, though intellectual they were. The very lives of the men seemed to ride on the answers adopted – their emotional, social and spiritual lives, and on the streets, and in prison, sometimes their physical lives. Perhaps that is true for all of us to a degree as we struggle to define our identity and goals of our lives, but for the prisoners this was uncommonly clear.

Our class conversations proved so powerful that I began to tape, transcribe and edit them, and they formed the basis for a book, *The Soul Knows No Bars: Inmates Reflect on Life, Death, and Hope*. Trained as a phenomenologist, I was particularly interested in exploring what happens to lived-time and space, embodiment, personal identity and sociality, when one is confined for long years in a prison environment. We did not hesitate to read challenging texts – Heidegger, Foucault, Nietzsche – albeit with explanation and discussion. A brief excerpt from the *The Soul Knows No Bars*[6] will give an example of the class in action, here discussing an article on 'Lived-Space' by the German phenomenologist O. F. Bollnow[7]:

Drew Leder: Bollnow suggests that to have a house, or we might say a *home*, to build a home, to feel a sense of *being-at-home*, is essential to being human. But can a prison constitute a home in this sense?

Selvyn Tillett: I'd say yes and no. I don't want it to be a home because I don't want to be here. I consider home what I left on the street. But since I have to be here for a long time, the cell is somewhere I can go and keep unto myself. So I might fix it up a bit, paint the wall just to get a different color.

Charles Baxter: And the cell's where you actually get your schoolwork done, or work for organizations you're in, or work to get out of prison. Man is created from one cell, right, and as man grows he adapts into another cell, and that cell's also a place for growth and development. When you read the Koran and the Bible you'll see that different prophets went to the *cave* for comfort and isolation. And the cell's like that cave.

Tray Jones (Arlando Jones, III): . . . But you can never really have a home in here. Because the officers could come with the key anytime they want and uproot you. Like right now, everything that I own I brought out with me (my toothbrush and all) because *I'm the cell*, my own body, rather than some hole cut out of space.

John Woodland: We always had a concept around here about keeping yourself distant from prison activities and the prison mentality. Don't participate in a whole bunch of prison groups, don't get caught up in playing football, basketball, don't think about fixing no cell up to make it comfortable. Let it stay raggedy. You want to keep a mindset that this is not some place for me to get comfortable.

Charles Baxter: [*laughing*] I call my cell my *palace*. As a matter of fact I just got it painted last week and paid the dude four packs to do it. He painted the floors, my ceiling, the whole thing. I got my Oriental rugs laid down. I don't care where I'm at, I'm going to make it heaven while I'm there. Even in this hellhole, I'm going to find some heaven.

Wayne Brown: It's different being in a double cell. I could feel at home laying on my bunk. But when I got up and took one step to the wall, I felt like I'm in a danger zone 'cause I had somebody else on the top bunk. I was under their scrutiny. There's somebody watching . . .

Tray Jones: Yeah, when I used to sleep in a double cell, if I was in there with a person I didn't like, I felt like Wayne. But when I was in the cell with T – the only cell buddy that I really got along with – a bond developed, and in our closeness we were so brotherly . . . It seemed like I had *more* room in the cell with him than I do now when I'm alone. We'd play cards and talk, and it felt like there was a lot of room!

For this conversation to unfold I had no need to prescribe experiential exercises of the sort used at Loyola. For the inmates, prison *was* their extended experiential exercise. My job was to help them analyze it, survive it and, as much as possible, make productive use of it. Again, the Deweyan dialectic of reflection and action was crucial to these men. In one man's words, he sought to figure out not only how to 'serve time' but have 'time serve me'. The conversation above addresses a correlative task: how to expand, hallow or escape a space that threatens to crush both body and spirit. We see even in this brief excerpt strategic disagreements – for example, concerning whether to embrace or resist viewing the *prison-as-a-home* – and experiential realizations – that the presence of another can both contract or expand space. I hoped to present texts and facilitate discussions that might assist these 'lifers' in their quest to positively re-form their lives.

In pursuing this goal, inmates act in accord with the original meaning of the 'penitentiary' which institutionally began in the late eighteenth century as a religious and humanistic penal reform. The penitentiary cell was modelled on the monastic cell, a place meant for spiritual reflection, repentance and transformation.

We see this ideal realized in Charles Baxter's reference to his cell as a place for 'growth and development,' something akin to the cave to which prophets repaired. Teaching philosophy in such a setting – or writing, meditation or yoga – can provide a crucial aid to this process. I and others have compiled a list of contemplative resources around the country that inmates can access.[8] Then, too, there are many teachers doing exciting work linking colleges and prisons, students and inmates, on a journey of mutual education.[9]

Of course, the contemporary 'penitentiary' does much to undermine its putative mission. Conditions are harsh and overcrowded – the United States incarcerates people at 6–10 times the rate of other comparable countries, holding fully one-quarter of the world's prison population. Treatment by authorities is often dehumanizing and disempowering. Opportunities for educational, therapeutic and occupational advancement are deficient. The men to whom I taught Heidegger were prepared in many cases by having previously received college degrees through prison extension programs. These were largely shut down by the 1993 Omnibus Crime Bill which made inmates ineligible for the Pell Grants which finance higher-education for low-income Americans.

Whereas Charles Baxter re-imagines the cell as a prophet's cave, too often it more resembles Plato's cave. In this allegory, all that is visible to the chained prisoners are shadows cast on a wall which they take to be real, having no object of comparison. This is an apt description of many a prison. Those who might bring light from the outside world are often sadly absent, with the inmates left to contemplate shadows on a wall – the contempt of authorities, the society of other criminals and the memories of a failed life. Not surprisingly, upon release inmates are often poorly equipped psychologically, educationally and occupationally to make it in the outside world. Recidivism rates are high, though significantly reduced for the fortunate few who secure college education.

I earlier said that when we utilize experiential learning in traditional academic settings we, to some degree, release our students from the classroom 'cave' wherein they are forced to study chalk-images drawn on blackboards by their teacher/jailers. (I apologize for the metaphor, but am trying to adopt a student perspective.) Escaping into the sunlight of immediate experience, whether through service-learning, meditation, experiential games or other methods, can refresh and illuminate the academic experience. My own work in and with prisons, which has continued off and on to this day, has similarly provided illumination for me. I have found that one of the most powerful ways to escape the classroom cave is to enter the many other caves our society constructs (ideally bringing our students with us) – the penitentiaries, homeless shelters, youth programs, hospices, senior centres, halfway houses – to humbly learn from the rich experience of those who therein dwell, and assist them, with whatever tools we have, in their own struggle for freedom.

Notes

[1] Dewey, J. (1938), *Experience and Education*. New York: Collier Books; Giles, D. E. Jr and Eyler, J. (1994), 'The Theoretical Roots of Service-Learning in John Dewey: Toward a Theory of Service-Learning'. Michigan Journal of Community Service Learning, 1 (1), 77–85.

[2] Eyler, J., Giles, D. E. Jr and Schmiede, A. (1996), *A Practitioner's Guide To Reflection in Service-Learning: Student Voices & Reflections*. Nashville: Vanderbilt University;
Howard, J. (ed.) (2001), *Michigan Journal of Community Service Learning, Service-Learning Course Design Workbook*. Ann Arbor: University of Michigan;
Jacoby, B. and Associates (1996), *Service-Learning in Higher Education: Concepts and Practices*. San Francisco: Jossey-Bass;
Crews, R. J. (2002), *Higher Education Service-Learning Sourcebook*. Westport: Oryx Press;
Lisman, C. D. and Harvey, I. E. (eds) (2000), *Beyond the Tower: Concepts and Models for Service-Learning in Philosophy*. Washington, DC: AAHE (American Association for Higher Education Series on Service-Learning in the Disciplines).

[3] Bodian, S. (2006), *Meditation for Dummies*. New York: Wiley Publishing.

[4] See, for example, academic programs supported by 'The Center for Contemplative Mind in Society', *http://www.contemplativemind.org/programs/academic/* last viewed on 05/12/2007.

5 Leder, D. (1998) *Games for the Soul: 40 Playful Ways to Find Fun and Fulfillment in a Stressful World.* New York: Hyperion.

6 Leder, D. (2000), *The Soul Knows No Bars.* Lanham: Rowman and Littlefield, pp. 55–58.

7 Bollnow, O. F. (1961), 'Lived-Space'. *Philosophy Today*, 5, 31–39.

8 *Freedom Within: Sharing on the Power of Meditation.* (2007) Baltimore: Bridge Project, Center for Community Service and Justice, Loyola College in Maryland. *www.loyola.edu/bridgeproject*, last viewed on 09/27/08.

9 Pompa, L. Inside-Out Prison Exchange Program. Philadelphia: Temple University Dept. of Criminal Justice. *http://www.temple.edu/inside-out/*, last viewed on 05/12/2007.

Student Interlude II

Once I remember we had a simulation of a debate: Plato against Karl Popper about the ideal city. The teacher divided the class into two groups. Half of the class supported Plato's ideas and the other half supported Popper's thought and he (the teacher) was the judge. The precise outcome of the debate was not important, but the process of the argumentation that we (students) engaged in was interesting and challenging.

Corinna Casi,
University of Helsinki, Finland
(talking about her philosophy classes in Italy)

Sometimes philosophy seems too abstract and the practical applications of philosophy, with real world applications, would be helpful (almost to the point to keep a student sane!). Psychologically speaking, stories are how people best communicate. Through stories, people can relate. The most fun courses are those with stories to back up the lecture.

Joe Kim,
Colby College, USA

Use more diagrams! If not in teaching, in the notes provided. A picture speaks a thousand words. I know philosophy typically does not use graphics, but to have that visual aid, if only so to then identify the argument with an image would anchor the argument deeper in memory.

Phillip Brightmore,
University of Liverpool, UK

A philosophy teacher should always engage the students, pull questions and answers out of them even if it will entail intense moments of silence. Basically avoid as much as possible the straightforward lecture style, lecture when necessary for background info and the like. The best philosophy classes I have had have been the ones where students were engaged, and enticed into answering and questioning; I think one must force discussion as hard as it may be at first.

Christopher Fischer,
Marshall University, USA

Chapter 7

Philosophy is/as the Power of Words

Matt Lavery and Rupert Read

What is the use of studying philosophy if all that it does for you is enable you to talk
with some plausibility about some abstruse questions of logic, etc. & if it does not
improve your thinking about the important questions of everyday life . . .
                    Wittgenstein, in a letter to Norman Malcolm, 22 June 1940[1]

This essay is about how teaching philosophy can be a very different
thing than it is often thought of as being. It is not entirely unusual for
philosophers – especially Wittgensteinians – to insist that teaching philosophy is nothing like teaching a body of knowledge, or a science. Going
beyond this, *we* think, though, that Wittgenstein's idea of philosophy as a
method to be applied in dealing with a certain substantial and important
genre of problems rather than as a series of instructional theses[2] renders it
not only a quite common-sense affair but also more relevant to the current
state of the world than it ever has been in the past – *and*, more relevant to
teaching (in and of) that world. A Wittgensteinian inspiration can offer
tools for teaching philosophy that make it intensely relevant to life far from
any ivory tower.

What is perhaps unusual, and what is (we hope) of some importance, is
our thought that a broadly-Wittgensteinian conception of philosophy and
method of teaching philosophy[3] can be put to work in helping to teach
students about living well, and thinking clearly, in direct connection with
matters ethical and political. (Though, as Wittgenstein himself suggests
in the above epigram, we believe that this idea is not taken nearly as seriously as it should be, not even by most avowed Wittgensteinians.) Our essay
concerns the power of words, how to not be over-awed by that power, and
how to learn to use that power to unleash wisdom and goodness. To love
wisdom, and thus love the world.

This doesn't sound neutral. Doesn't our approach violate the canons of
a liberal education? Yes. But this is, we submit, simply a direct result of

taking seriously the idea of philo-sophia. We reject the *core* idea in and of
a 'liberal education' of *the neutral hand-over of a body of knowledge or at least of
'the state of the debate' from professor to pupil.*[4] We reject the notion of neutrality
in education itself because it is *a fiction*. Liberalism is a dangerous delusion
that plays at objectivity and neutrality while smuggling along with it deeply
embedded perspectives and prejudices that lead to self-contradictory and
highly-undesirable consequences (when applied to education and, as we
will show below, not coincidentally to politics/political philosophy).[5]

All (or at least, most) of mainstream 'liberally taught' philosophy is, by
our lights, already politicized; only: in the wrong way. Take, for example,
the most famous device of teaching logic that there has ever been: namely,
the following syllogism:[6]

> All men are mortal.
> Socrates is a man.
> *Therefore* Socrates is mortal.

This syllogism, the first *paradigm* of sound logical reasoning that many students learn, is questionable. For presumably 'All men are mortal' is not
meant to refer only to males, as opposed to to women (leaving open, as
it were, that maybe women aren't mortal . . .). And yet, if one replaces
'Socrates' with 'Hypatia,' one gets this:

> All men are mortal.
> Hypatia is a man.
> *Therefore* Hypatia is mortal.

. . . And this seems unsound; for 'Hypatia is a man' surely induces a
bizarreness-reaction, and indeed would probably always have done so.

The conclusion is uncomfortable indeed: the first paradigm of logical
thinking typically taught to students arguably *equivocates*(!)[7] because of a
failure to think beyond the gendered assumptions subtly present in much
traditional language-use. A liberally-trained logician with a care for truly
educating her students needs to provide – to engage in, to make perspicuous to those students – some thinking about her teaching when using this
model, as what one says in teaching logic is profoundly political in the
sense that it tends to implicitly argue *for a particular kind of thinking,* and for
certain things and certain ways of thinking being allegedly less important
or less valid or less 'hard'. (As a further example, our gradually-becoming-
standard (?) use of the female pronoun here is of course intentional, itself a

'calling-out' of 'smuggled in' patriarchal thinking, and one that is regularly *dismissed* as 'mere' 'political correctness' – as though it were better *not* to be correct in the all-important sphere of politics?!)[8]

Now compare/contrast with the above the following fragment of our own classroom process:

If we are teaching Wittgenstein, say, we don't pretend that Norman Malcolm might be as good a reader and as good a philosopher as (say) Peter Winch. To extend the point: It would be ludicrous – a parodic postmodernist pose – to suggest that maybe anyone's view on a philosophical question is as good as anyone else's. But at the same time, for reasons already implicit in our outline above of our rejection of all scientistic visions of philosophy (appealing though they are, as a prop, to the teacher in search of legitimation), we reject any self-deluded elitist idea of philosophical knowledge as the possession of a few who can simply impart it to the many. When we say for instance that Wittgenstein wrote in the strange way that he did not randomly nor for reasons of personality defect or pathology but because doing so was/is internal to his philosophy, we have no authority for so saying other than our integrity, the trust we can justly generate in our students, and (of course) *the reasons that we offer* for so saying. In effect, we stand before our students intellectually naked: our ideas, our wisdom, our reasoning, and yes, no doubt, our prejudices, exposed clearly to their view. That is our aim in teaching: to let our students see us and why we think what we do clearly, so that they can learn what *they* think, too. We are, as it were, an 'object of comparison' for our students (Cf. *PI (Philosophical Investigations)* 130). We aim to be a mirror in which their own thinking in its excellences, its inadequacies, and its deformities can be seen clearly, and thus changed.

Thus, there is no privileged non-neutral 'Archimedean point' from which philosophy can be taught without an assortment of what some would call 'baggage': political, intellectual, etc. We speak to our students in a vital respect as equals. We aim to be true inheritors of Socrates' mantle, taking seriously (as he did not) the claim to 'ignorance'. To take seriously that there is no philosophic knowledge is, ironically, to give up the claim to teach a body of knowledge neutrally. For no such body exists.

Our suggestion is that philosophy needs to drop the paradigm of knowledge, and recover the paradigm of wisdom. Of valuing what is valuable. Without bad faith on this score, there is no avoiding hereabouts of ethical (and political) commitment.

Now: Having said that, we nevertheless don't think it proper or really necessary (read on to see why) for philosophers per se to simply proselytize or otherwise 'stump' for a moral/ethical stance. But, philosophical clarity has (more so now than ever) become an essential antidote to a moral skewing resulting from a manipulation of language by various embedded, monied power interests deliberately working to confuse the real underpinnings of their actions in a manner that is as studious and purposeful as the sexism of the paradigmatic syllogism's is claimed to be inadvertent by the overwhelming majority of those who have used it in logic instruction.[9] The corporate media are ever shortening the length of sound-bites; 24-hour rolling news is replacing serious current affairs analysis.[10] These realities, not coincidentally, impinge especially hard on many students brought up in a highly consumeristic, materialistic and 'relativistic' world.[11] Utilitarian economistically minded under-resourced education is churning out students with short attention spans and little sense of underlying systems and holistic effects. In this respect, the media serve ill not only *philosophy* and *the teaching of philosophy* but they also indirectly pose more immediate and important challenges to our political system.[12]

Given these challenges, a key task of (particularly Wittgensteinian) philosophers is to find *effective* ways of enabling people to see things clearly *in political life*. As we suggested above, in the current political/economic climate, where language is used to obscure clear (perhaps we ought to say 'philosophical') vision, the philosopher seeks out and values clarity; and always bears in mind that *clarity begins at home.*

So we need to think about what is closest to home. And what could be closer than what one believes about what is most important: about all things political.[13] Again: we reject the liberal conceit of neutrality in political theory/philosophy – and likewise in education. Good philosophy teaching is honest philosophy teaching. Honest philosophy teaching is teaching that simply offers our students the world as we find it. Vividly re-seen, provocatively described across or against the grain of the dominant culture. Honest philosophy teaching makes no pretence to neutrality. It facilitates Critical Thinking in a number of ways: not least, through forcing students to think for themselves, *not* by setting before them a mythical row of quasi consumer goods between which they can freely choose, but by forcing them to choose in the crucible of presenting them always with live options that are actually supported/held by those proposing them. Our paradigm in teaching ought not to be the pretend-neutrality of packaging, but the real non-neutrality of honest disclosures of how we take the world to be.

So we don't hesitate to (among other things) deck out our lectures with accounts and examples of a political bent, described as we would and do honestly describe them. We don't pretend to offer a (fantasized) neutral or impartial description of the intellectual options facing our students: we describe the landscape as we honestly see it, and leave it to them to find their own way among it or re-make it or re-vision it. (And we don't hesitate to tell them that we don't admire the mere pretence of following us in seeing the landscape as we do: that attempts to ape our way of seeing the world may well pass, but will never earn high marks.) We submit that the worst – and most common – way that philosophy teachers implicitly 'spin' is to offer an account of the world or the mind etc. as if the last thing they would ever do is spin that account to help out their own actual perspective upon it . . .

Now, 'spin' is a word that is bandied about a lot in our media-saturated times and it is one that most people would claim to understand without there being a single, universally recognized definition; it means some-thing like dissembling that one cannot call all-out lying due to the thin-nest connection to reality of the words making up the lie.[14] It has become almost commonplace for the electorate to expect that issues are being spun, and to thus distrust politicians. If fatigue towards political double-speak resulting from over-saturation of spin makes such blatant obfusca-tion a bit *less* dangerous than it has been in the past, it has become no less difficult for individuals to see through it to discover the real (or 'cash') value of political speech. Demystifying spin, thus, becomes not the apogee of philosophical insight but rather a valuable 'warm-up' for the more tax-ing, 'bloody-hard way'[15] of deconstructing the verbal structures that place a veil over the political and practical agendas of special interests[16] – and reconstructing them in a better way. This more challenging philosophical clarity requires looking into oneself carefully to see the more subtle ways that language can play upon us to (mis)understand such agendas, in part *by* establishing new (or recapturing buried or forgotten) alternative con-ceptual '*frames*' that are not simply new verbal poses, not simply pictures that can be used and discarded in the way that spin *can* be (and needs to be) un-spun. Frames disclose value(s) (the values upon which one's 'pos-ition' is based) in the same way that spin tries to conceal it. Frames cannot be deconstructed in the same way that spin can: spin is superficial, framing is more substantial. A frame concerns the entire way an issue is formulated, the way it is conceived of.[17]

To be truly effective in aligning actions with values, then, frames must be completely reworked, issues must be reframed[18] in the same way a pic-ture must be if we are to appreciate, say, the subtleties of one of its colours or textures. Then, *once* one has reframed, one can add additional consid-erations, counter-objections and factual evidentiary support. But making the initial 'paradigm-shift' is critically important. Fail to do so, and you are simply batting on your opponent's wicket, playing away rather than at home. You might get quite a good score, but your chances of *winning* are minimal. So, for example: if one speaks of how we ought to conserve our natural resources rather than just turning them all into disposable consumer goods and throwing them away, one is already half-way to losing the argument. To have a decent chance of winning, one has to reject the very conceptulization of the world as a collection (a 'standing reserve', as Heidegger puts it) of mere 'natural resources'; one has to reject the idea that there is any 'away' where things can truly be thrown; and so on. (See below, for a little more detail on how positively to reframe an issue such as this one.)

Key to this project, as we have hinted at above, is that framing, deframing and reframing are *very difficult,* and this is rational: otherwise, one is constantly floundering around without an over-arching paradigm, flitting from one set of grounding principles to another like a 'fashionista'. To effect a scientific revolution is rightly rare; otherwise there would be no science.[19] Reframing requires *re-seeing.* And unlearning old hard-dying habits.

For a more concrete understanding of the difficulties and importance or reframing, we turn to an example: images of freedom conjured up in adverts to persuade people to buy flashy new cars; but just imagine what our roads would look like if people acted absolutely freely upon them. What would happen if, for instance:

there were no impediments like traffic lights or stop signs (or if these were routinely, universally ignored)
If people invariably parked wherever they wanted (e.g. in the middle of the street; or making it impossible for other parked vehicles to move).
If people drove on both sides of the road, willy-nilly . . .[20]

What makes 'the freedom of the roads' work, in practice, is, first, that we have rules of the road (such as driving on the left) which are very widely observed, and, secondly, that at least some drivers do show genuine consideration to other road-users (for instance, letting people out of side-roads). Without these two things, our roads would be scenes of total chaos, and of far worse carnage than they actually are. What's more, developments in technology continually factor out the 'freedom' of the person behind the wheel:[21] GPS is already giving way to concept cars with piloting systems that will remove most elements of choice in route from a driver; cars will have automatic speed-management to maximize fuel economy and to keep the car below the speed limit . . . we may end up, within a generation, with cars that are in effect entirely driven by electronic chauffeurs. This will free up 'car drivers' to read the newspaper etc. while going from A to B . . . just as riders on public transport are free to do already! The reality is that the only means of transport that almost deliver complete freedom to go where one will, under one's own direction, ironically, are the oldest and most low-tech of all: cycling (whereby you can quickly bypass road congestion, congestion that stops buses and cars alike), and walking. Walking is the most reliable mode of transport of all. Nothing (save something going wrong with your legs) can stop you. You have almost total flexibility to change position and direction at any time, when you walk . . .[22]

The reality is that drivers do not have much freedom, on the roads, within the Highway Code.[23] The much-vaunted absolute freedom of the motorist, which can seem so much more attractive than depending on other people all the time (as one obviously does if one takes public transport), is a grand illusion. Car-driving needs to be tightly constrained by the law to work well, and, as a car driver, one always depends just as deeply on other people as one does when one is a public transport passenger. One person driving down the wrong side of a busy street can demonstrate that, in an instant. By contrast, real freedom is arguably the preserve of the pedestrian, not really of the motorist at all;[24] and yet the frame of freedom surrounding owning a car and driving is not easily undone by the many lobbyists and grass-rooters – like the New York City based bicycle activists 'Critical Mass' – at work to bring about the much-needed paradigm shift: *freedom of the pedestrian, freedom of the non-motorist* (It's hard to reframe: Even having looked closely at the example it still seems paradoxical to enunciate these new slogans!).

It is difficult to shake off the wrong-headed idea of driving as 'pure freedom' in part because to do so works against the interests of the car-economy – the manufacturers, the salespeople, big oil, *advertisers.* These interests have powerfully structured the entire debate, our very frameworks for making sense of freedom. If one's *paradigm* of freedom is 'the open road', then it just seems like madness to think that cars might be making us unfree. (Much as, if one's paradigm of the unmoving is the Earth, then it just seems like madness to think that perhaps the Earth itself moves through space, spins on its axis . . .)

Now cross-apply this frame on a much larger scale: Those, such as the British 'journalist' and motor enthusiast Jeremy Clarkson, who advocate the 'freedom of the motorist' sound very similar to those economists and politicians who advocate 'the free market'. We often hear these days that there is no alternative to capitalism, no alternative to globalization, no alternative to 'free' markets – this is what Thatcher and Reagan famously said in the 1980s; New Labour and the American neo-cons say almost the same now. We are told that the little pleasures of our lives, from the ability to buy just about anything at a supermarket to discount airfare allowing inexpensive travel around the world (but surely not, as anyone who has ever flown economy-class could attest, 'freedom') are all built upon this globalized 'free' market economy, but the utter failure and impossibility and undesirability of a truly 'free market' on the roads should give us a clue to why unfettered freedom and selfishness do not work in the economy and society in general. Yet see how much play such arguments get in primetime speeches on trade pacts like NAFTA: policy-makers are frustratingly slow to take concrete action to curb such free selfishness for fear of alienating corporate constituents with the suggestion of policies that will impact their profit margins and voters with talk of the need to, for example, 'give up,' 'sacrifice,' and 'go without'. Anything which sounds like a constraint on a crudely-marketed personal (corporate?) freedom is 'hard to sell'. Thus the way the issue of genuinely sustainable – green – economics ('Sustainable development' often in practice means simply development that can go on and on – i.e. endless economic growth – i.e. something by definition unsustainable!) is framed for the mass audience has been the primary barrier to adopting social and political policies that can counteract the devastating effects of global 'free' markets.[25]

In this most important and practical sense, the project of philosophy and of teaching philosophy in the Wittgensteinian sense described at the outset of this essay can be rightly seen *as* the disposition to uncover *the power (of) words*: it is the disposition to see how words take power over us . . . or can empower us. What's more, this disposition, as the basis for any possibility of reframing, *is the power of words* to effect change that can benefit all those currently disenfranchised or threatened by entrenched power structures. Our intelligence has been bewitched by a certain language; but it is by means of language too that we can overcome the bewitchment . . .

Wittgenstein strives for philosophical freedom. For liberty. He strives to find what are, for a given occasion and person, the liberating word(s). But one cannot have this freedom, unless one frees oneself from the grip of the thought-constraints of the dominant culture: for instance, the ideal of freedom itself as a pure thing, an absolute – a fantasy held out by driving, for instance, as we have just deconstructed. The fantasy of 'the American dream' – the idea that anyone, everyone, can attain freedom by having lots of money – fails to recognize that money only works as a device to ensure that one has access to certain freedoms only if one is able to buy others' labour-time with it, i.e. if others are *unfree* to do as they please in inverse proportion to one's own financial freedom . . .

As we have been arguing above, the primarily philosophical task of *deframing* and *reframing* increases in importance accordingly as the political weight of the issues at hand impact life on the planet. Presently, how to realize/seize the power of words in regard to 'green issues' – for instance, the knotty and literally-all-important need to reduce the carbon emissions for which we are responsible – has been taken up and developed to a certain extent[26] by the major American linguist George Lakoff. His seminal work, *Moral Politics,*[27] argues that much of American politics can be understood as the clash between the 'Strict Father' morality of conservatism and the 'Nurturant Parent' morality of what he calls 'liberalism' (or, more recently, 'progressivism' – we think it wise of him to have left behind the label of liberalism, in part because of its being a hate-word for the Right, but (much more importantly) for the reason sketched above: that liberalism is *inherently undesirable,* is already an enormous compromise toward consumerism, a failure to seriously value the Earth, a huge drag on any seriously radical reframing project),[28] and that environmental care naturally falls under the purview of the latter; just as self-interested exploitation of one's 'property', and *not* conservation, is the logical consequence of ('conservative') 'Strict Father' morality. This is right, as far as it goes, but Lakoff seems to miss the need for deeper reframes in this account. One extremely obvious one is the reframe that *we* would urge: of thinking of the Earth as first and foremost our mother ('Gaia'), or our parent, rather than the other way around.[29] We *are* the nurtured, all of us, deeper than deep. Another such deep reframe, related though not exactly the same, is that promoted by Ecological Economics, the 'deep-Green' version of which is what Green Economics must ultimately replace mainstream 'neoclassical' economics with: of the economic system as a finite *sub*-system of our (also finite) *life-support system,* the Earth (as opposed to: of the ecological system as a mere 'externality' appended to the economic system, which is, in neoclassicism – the economic ideology of contemporary capitalism – taken to be in principle limitless). This revolution that is perhaps taking place right now in economics is something the basis of which and need for it takes philosophical thought to see (which is one reason why the greatest advocate of ecological economics, Herman Daly, appeals explicitly to philosophy throughout his *oeuvre*[30]).

As important as it is for the philosopher to see the need for these reframes, it is also, if we are right in our conception of philosophy, her task to help see them through, to get them applied/working in the lived world – and here that philosophical vision, that teaching of philosophy, is of the utmost importance because it bridges the gap between an over-intellectualized solution and the actual experience of the people for whom the solution is intended.

The first of these conceptions – the Earth as our mother – is as yet too esoteric, too 'spiritual,' for widespread usage. The second – that of ecological economics – is as it stands too technical, but it can easily be simplified: the Earth can be conceptualized as our *home* (and one doesn't plunder one's own home), as our *nest* (and one doesn't soil one's own nest), even (to make clear as crystal the stakes here) as our *life-support system*. The traditional Left (as in much of what remains of the 'Labour' movement, and as in many of the left-wing splinter groups, such as the multiple 'Respect' Parties that have emerged from George Galloway's failed experiment in Britain) uses the 'nurturant parent' metaframe (unconsciously) to foreground 'the deprivation model', under which poor people and working class people have been deprived of what is rightfully theirs, and thus deserve more money, more things. But here the nurturant parent frame is in the end inadequate for greens, because it commits the error of insufficient holism hinted at the beginning of this essay: it despoils the Earth, depletes 'resources', promotes consumerism, dishes out pollution – to try (hopelessly) to make up for the bad time that the poor and the working class have had at the hands of the rich; to deliver them their 'rights' to what they have been 'deprived' of (as if it is a *deprivation* to not be decadent). Thus, within the 'nurturant' frame, we all talk about 'deprived areas', even though the absolute standard of living in those areas is frequently higher than the *average* standard of living in the 1960s, a time when most Americans and Britons *were happier than they are now.* Quality of life – not 'deprivation,' not improvements in 'standard of living' – is above all what matters. Additionally, what makes people unhappy is relative poverty, not absolute levels of standard of living (above a certain threshold minimum, above 'rich subsistence' levels). But relative poverty *cannot* be tackled by relieving 'deprivation' (because that still leaves the poor relatively far worse off than the rich, than celebrities whose culture they are continually forced to bear witness to, etc.); it can only be tackled by actively pursuing *equality.*

And so then the biggest thing that needs to be altered in Lakoff's approach, the first additional radical metaframe that he requires, which to some extent eclipses entirely (or at least radically . . . reframes . . .) 'nurturance', is the *centrality* of the Earth,[31] the ungainsayable value of the ecosphere. The very first central issue must be not the (vital) issue of basing our lifestyle, our education system, and our politics around care (rather than strictness, toughness, etc.), nor the (vital) issue of reorganizing our economy to work for people: It's not (first) education, education, education, nor the economy (stupid): *it's our life-support system.* Human politics simply does not exist, without human survival. This – Earth – is our home. Here we stand; *we can do no other.*

Nurturance is only a half-way house. True love, whether it be of parents and children, of siblings, of friends, of those struggling for a better world – a better and long-term habitable home – together, *begins at home*, in the true sense of 'home'. And therefore such true love is wide, and mutual; for our home is thoroughly shared. What is also then missing from Lakoff – what again ultimately makes his 'nurturant moral politics' perhaps suitable for progressive 'liberals', but not for green-minded forward-thinking philosophers, as a key meta-frame – is *mutuality*. The ethos of team-work, of us accomplishing great things together, is an ethos that can animate the broad socio-political forces necessary to affect *real* change. As an ethical task, mutuality appeals to 'pioneers' and progressives. It can appeal to 'fashionistas', who won't want to be left out of smart, attractive, creative teams. And it can appeal even to the hold-outs, the security conscious, older people: as in for instance 'the spirit of the Blitz' (Just as people pulled together under threat from bombing, so they may pull together under threat of the long climate emergency); and similarly, as, for instance, in the way in which even many radicals who were in New York on September 11 found the experience empowering and not (in the violence of the event, and of the vicious patriotism it set off) demotivating: for they felt that they were living in a *community*, where people – friends and strangers alike – *spoke to each other*, and *helped each other*, for the first time . . .

Ours may seem a strange, politicized, vision of philosophy, of teaching philosophy with a moral politics at its core, or even: as its end. But by our lights, mainstream philosophy is intensely politicized: with the politics of a more or less Rawlsian liberalism/conservatism (Rawlsian liberalism being a highly-conservative doctrine,[32] the doctrine of the liberal who, as Stokeley Carmichael rightly had it, is enormously keen to change the world for the better – so long as his own power and financial position is not in the slightest threatened by the potential change . . .). Rawlsian liberalism, the dominant ideology of our times in the world of political theory and of the intellectual, pretends that it is not an ideology at all: it pretends to a kind of neutrality between conceptions of the good. This offensive pretence is in fact merely a veil for liberalism's relentless promotion of a vision of the good according to which we are isolated individual desiring-machines. Rawlsianism is a proxy for the crudest consumeristic materialism. It is this veiled politics that we want to flush out into the light of day. To enable our students to see it as figure, rather than just as ground. Philosophical reflection, the power of words made spirit-and-flesh through the array of reframing devices that we have outlined above, enables one to see the human being as more than just an atom that exists only to satisfy its wants.

There is no possibility of philosophy and of teaching what is of value without challenging that picture of the human being that seems not to be a picture at all, and that structures so much of our politics *and so much more.*

So: the kinds of reframes that we have outlined above, in the body of this paper, are only a very small sample of the kind of thinking that is needed *across the entirety of philosophy teaching;* and of life. The reframes that we have outlined above, the making figural (so that they can become the new *ground*) of an inherent mutuality, and of the Earth being what makes life possible and not some mere source of 'raw materials' that we are free to turn into trinkets and throw away (Because again: There *is* no 'away' . . .), do not deprive students of freedom. They enable.[33] They enable a way of thinking, of seeing and speaking and acting, that is no longer under the thumb of a hidden set of unchallengeable assumptions concerning what is valuable: roughly, assumptions as to the absolute value of *things* and the insatiability of human desire for those things.

We believe that the reframes outlined above should be made available to students. Taught. But students are not of course *compelled* to accept them. (Indeed, they have the option of arguing consciously and clearly against them, which they probably never had before.) Rather, they are given the realistic *possibility* of seeing beyond the grammar that tends to dominate our lives. The grammar of objects (that are called, euphemistically and prejudicially, 'goods'); the grammar of greed.

Liberty from such grammar is a philosophical task of the utmost importance that offers yet another reason for not teaching in a neutral way. It would seem to us abominable, for instance, to present things as if maybe producing a 'good' that will lead to vast suffering of beings who cannot even complain is just as good a way to lead one's life as acting so as to satisfy real human needs, or acting so as to produce an understanding of our interconnectedness, our utter dependence upon this beautiful blue-green rock; and so on.

So ours is, we hope to have demonstrated in this essay, at the very least no stranger a vision of philosophy than the ones that too-often dominate in academics: philosophy as a veiled apologia for the status quo, or philosophy as a kind of intellectual game of chess, or abstract theorizing, or philosophy as mere historical analysis. By contrast, this (our) vision of philosophy as a kind of social critique, and a communicative tool for enhanced reflection and better vision – a view reasonably well represented even within the traditional academic philosophical 'canon' from the Ancient Sceptics through Nietzsche and up to and beyond Richard Rorty today – is, we think, more appealing and appropriate.

We are philosophers. We are the world, grown conscious of its plight, but also aware that another, better world really is possible. It is literally insane to think that we (we philosophers, we humans) ought to be indifferent between the suffering of the world and the flourishing of the world, between the extinction of humanity or the flourishing of humanity. The fantasy of teaching philosophy neutrally between life and death, between eco-philia and eco-cide, is a fantasy that only someone dead to their feelings – to their broader self (other beings, the ecosystem that they are always already part of), to anything but abstractions – would cling to. Cling to, rather than allowing themselves to take the world as it is and as it ought to be – in short, to see it aright.[34]

That is what we think. We have made no effort to dress it up or to hide its assumptions or consequences. Now it is up to you: to agree, to disagree, to struggle with us, or against us. Just as the choice of how to think and how to live is set before students plainly, when one teaches them honestly. When one aims to teach with all of oneself; not just with one's mind, but with (one's) humanity.[35]

Notes

[1] For context and commentary, see Ray Monk's (1990) excellent *The Duty of Genius* New York: Macmillan, p. 425.
[2] Think here, for instance, of the Preface to the *Tractatus Logico-Philosophicus* (hereafter *TLP*) with its insistence that Wittgenstein's book is 'not a textbook'.
[3] A conception and method influenced also, we hope, by Kuhn and by others mentioned and discussed below.
[4] In this rejection, obviously, we are influenced by some educational philosophers and pedagogues, such as Paulo Freire.
[5] There is a lot to say here, to expand upon this, that we cannot do in the present place. Two good places to start are Michael J. Sandel's (1982) *Liberalism: The Limits of Justice* Cambridge: Cambridge University Press and Chapter 3 – 'Religion without Belief' (pp. 44–56) in Read's (2007) *Philosophy for Life* London: Continuum (ed. Lavery).
[6] One of us (Read) was once taught about this example in a class on Feminism and philosophy.

[7] Of course Wittgenstein's work is full of (usually less politically-charged) examples of similar language traps, notably the long and detailed exposes of how first-person reference carries with it certain 'philosophical' baggage about minds, identity, etc. (See, e.g. Hans Sluga's (1996) 'Whose House is that?': Wittgenstein on the self' in his and David Stern's (eds) *The Cambridge Companion to Wittgenstein* Cambridge: Cambridge University Press, pp. 320–353 for one treatment of this discussion). Often these exposes did not resolve themselves in overt political commentary, as ours has done here, but it has been argued (see, e.g., Alice Crary's (2000) 'Wittgenstein's philosophy in relation to political thought' in hers and Read's (eds) *The New Wittgenstein* London: Routledge, pp. 118–146; see also Naomi Scheman's piece in Sluga and Stern's volume) that Wittgenstein's methodology is one that fundamentally calls us towards being always mindful of the 'rational responsibility' of our words: 'Wittgenstein's writings in this respect teach us something about the kind of challenge we confront when we turn to investigate established modes of thought and speech (such as those that bear directly on political life), sorting out their injustices and developing more rigourously just and consistent ways of thinking and speaking.' (Crary, p. 141).

[8] Compare also the discussion of certain canonical philosophical inequities in Lavery's (2004) 'Vox populi?: Morality, politics, and *The New York Times*' Ethicist' *The International Journal of Applied Philosophy*, 18 (1), 53–68.

[9] See for instance Newt Gingrich's famous memo on language as a tool of control: *http://www.fair.org/index.php?page=1276*, last viewed on 15/05/2008; or Frank Luntz's cynical material very-usefully archived at *http://www.politicalstrategy.org/archives/001118.php*, last viewed on 15/05/2008.

[10] See Nick Davies's (2008) *Flat Earth News* London: Chatto and Windus, for a strong analysis of *why*.

[11] See the paper by Hutchinson and Loughlin in this volume.

[12] For one strikingly relevant discussion of this – for it concerns precisely the failure of the media to reflect the moral concerns that almost invariably *frame* political issues – see Lakoff's (2002) *Moral Politics: How Liberals and Conservatives Think* Chicago: University of Chicago Press, pp. 384–388.

[13] To some, this claim will seem odd. We aim to make it crystal clear – natural – as this essay proceeds. We have to re-see what our home *is* . . .

[14] See Steven Poole's (2006) useful book *Unspeak: How Words Become Weapons, Weapons Become a Message, and How That Message Becomes Reality* New York: Grove Press, for useful dissection of the spin (i.e. the 99% lie) involved in the very concept of 'spin' . . . For a book in the same field that contrariwise simply embraces spin in the basest possible way, one need look no further than Frank Luntz's (2007) *Words That Work* New York: Hyperion. See e.g. Luntz's wikipedia entry, for illuminating for-instances of his especially-influential (form of) spin.

[15] For an interesting discussion of the intersection between philosophy and ethical responsibility (and teaching!) of this phrase of Wittgenstein's, see James Conant's (2002) 'On going "the bloody hard way" in philosophy' in J. Whittaker's (ed.) *The Possibilities of Sense* New York: Palgrave, pp. 85–130.

[16] By which of course we mean things like the interests of the rich, of big corporations, etc.; we are not using the term as it has been spun into contemporary American parlance, where, outrageously, it tends actually to refer to the interests of

substantial numbers of ordinary people! For detailing of this point, see Chomsky's work, e.g. at *http://www.thirdworldtraveler.com/Corporate_Media/Terrorism_Chomsky_ STP.html,* last viewed on 15/05/2008.

[17] To understand fully the difference between reframing and spin, go to *http://www. rockridgeinstitute.org/research/lakoff/luntz/view,* last viewed on 15/01/2008. The truth about the success of the conservative movement in the U.S. is that it is founded in significant part on successful, cynical and destructive use of spin . . . but often more profoundly on the use of frames that reflect what conservatives actually think. Conservatives are willing to speak their minds, to activate conservative values among the populace. Those with different values – e.g. progressives, greens – must do the same. The liberal delusion of prevailing through a purported absence of any value-commitment *is* a delusion, and moreover a hopeless and failed (and covertly conservative) political programme.

[18] Reframing is an idea discovered perhaps in many places/minds (most recently, in Lakoff), but certainly (among others) in Wittgenstein, and elaborated by the Wittgensteinian philosopher of science Thomas Kuhn's idea of a 'paradigm shift.' Consider the need for reframing, and not just for radical critique, that is central to Wittgenstein's philosophy. A picture often holds us captive. One displaces such a picture . . . with another picture. (Ideally, in philosophy, one is now freer than one was before – i.e. the second picture doesn't *capture* one, because one is aware now of one's tendency to overly attach to pictures. In science, things are different – 'normal science' under a new paradigm *depends* upon being captured by the new picture.) That second picture may be a genuinely more attractive alternative. Becoming aware of seeing-as – of reframing – the central topic of Part II of Wittgenstein's *Philosophical Investigations* – often introduces new possibilities for seeing-as, e.g. by means of pointing up or creating internal relations. *Seeing things under new aspects the possibility of which one has been alerted to is having those things reframed for one.* In situations of 'seeing-as', there is no 'just seeing the facts'; one sees-as one thing, or as another. Kuhn was concerned above all to perform exactly this kind of therapy upon his readers – to enable them to see why they were attracted to out-of-date 'Whiggish' interpretations of the history of science, and to enable them to replace those histories of science with histories giving proper attention to the way in which paradigm instances of science (e.g. Newton's laws) prepare the ground for a puzzle-solving tradition that follows them, through structuring fundamentally the way the world is seen: through changing what looks natural. In short, Kuhn enabled his readers to see the world in a new way, roughly as one does after a successful course of therapy. This is exactly what Kuhn says happens in the lived world of scientists during a scientific revolution. For more, see Read's and Sharrock's (2002) *Kuhn: Philosopher of Scientific Revolution* London: Polity

[19] (For explication of this point, see Read's *Kuhn*). Thus we are *not* pushing a voluntaristic, liberal fantasy of (re-)framing: reframing is always non-neutral, values-based, challenging – it is of a completely different order from quasi-consumeristic 'Coke vs. Pepsi' choices which *can* be more or less voluntaristically understood.

[20] The example we are developing here is much the same as that famously employed by Charles Taylor in his 'What's Wrong With Negative Liberty' in arguing against

Isiah Berlin and for a notion of positive liberty. Those wishing to see a deft carrying out at length of a philosophical reframe could do little better than to study the whole article of Taylor's. His deconstruction of Berlin's very famous but disastrously crude and covertly right-wing conceit of (negative) liberty is the kind of ambition we aspire to, and aim to engage in with our students.

[21] And consider for instance guided busways.

[22] One might object that our polemical re-visioning here doesn't work: Am I free to walk to Manchester from London tomorrow? I am free to get the train there and I'm free to drive there (if I can afford the ticket or the hire car and I have a licence) but I could not walk the 150 miles there tomorrow. Of course we don't mean to deny that: but it is useful and interesting to reflect that those freedoms depend upon being extremely unfree as one makes the journey. And it remains true that walking, for all its limitations, involves (for the able-bodied) a *kind* of *über*-freedom: an ability to change direction at any moment; a lack of dependence upon any machine etc.

[23] At least, in the 'standard', crudely over-simplified sense of freedom that is generally in play within 'the American dream', within Berlin's 'negative' liberty conception, etc. *Within* the Highway Code drivers do have freedom. That is to say, once the facticity of the code is accepted. If the facticity of the code is not accepted then we see it as a restriction on freedom. But only in the negative sense of freedom – again this is the point made at length by Taylor against Berlin.

[24] For amplification of this theme, see the radical 'metaphorical' reframing effected in Read's newspaper op-ed pieces, at *http://oneworldcolumn.org/2.html*, last viewed on 15/05/2008 and *http://oneworldcolumn.org/4.html*, last viewed on 15/05/2008.

[25] This essay was written before the "global financial crisis" of 2008 which not only provides a lived-world example of 'the devastating effects of global "free" markets' but that also suggests the tendentiousness of that term: as (particularly green) critiques have pointed out, the 'rescue plans' promoted by the developed world reveal that the 'free' market is anything but.

[26] Though much more is needed, on this front. Read is at present working on a handbook on green reframing, to fulfil this need.

[27] Lakoff (2002). See also the still available (and vital) work of the Rockridge Institute at *http://www.rockridgeinstitute.org/*, last viewed on 15/05/2008.

[28] It is easy to see how these labels apply to some areas of policy in UK much the same as in the US, or at least how they used to apply. Take 'crime', for instance. It used to be the case that the Conservative Party was a 'Strict Father' Party while Labour and the Liberals were 'Nurturant Parent' Parties. But all that has been swept away – all three major British Parties are advocates of 'Strict Father' attitudes. Of course the same has happened in the States, and not for no reason. New Labour and the New Democrats in America gave it up because they thought it a millstone around their necks; they decided to paint themselves as tough on crime, unforgiving to criminals. This policy-orientation tends to be popular because of how much 'common sense' and media discourse assumes the same, and thus grounds a 'moral politics' of blame and punishment.

[29] Of course, these can be brought together, as in this profound Native American chant, 'The Earth is our mother, we must take care of her; The Earth is our mother, we must take care . . . of . . . her.'

[30] Most strikingly, in his *magnum opus*, (1994) *For the Common Good* Boston: Beacon.

[31] In a certain very limited (and ultimately-superficial) way, one can say that, ironically, the ecological economics (the 'Dalyan') revolution *reverses* the Copernican revolution, in that it places the Earth at the centre of things again . . . But this disguises the deeper way in which the Dalyan revolution *continues* the displacement work of Copernicus: for conventional neo-classical etc. economics places *us* centrally, just as Ptolemaic astronomy did, whereas Copernicus instead had us think about us as comparatively peripheral, as Daly does: we are peripheral to the Earth, which is the fundamental unit. Economics is a *subset* of ecology.

[32] Rawlsian liberalism, born out of despair at the non-action-guidingness of a Utilitarianism that is not morally repellent in its results, is itself just as non-action-guiding: virtually any inequality, however extreme, can be 'justified' by an apologist for it who claims that its trickle-down consequences are still the best possible for the worst off in society. (A notion which we, by the way, find morally repellent . . .)

[33] As does the Highway Code.

[34] Cf. *TLP* 6.54.

[35] Our thanks to Phil Hutchinson and to the editor for very useful critical comments on previous drafts of this paper.

Chapter 8

Teaching Philosophy through Metaphor

Panayiota Vassilopoulou

We usually associate the term 'metaphor' with poetry or rhetoric, and understand it as a trope, a figure of speech (alongside allegory, simile, paradox and many others), which expresses or establishes a new connection between words, things or actions that appear otherwise, or initially, unrelated. In these cases, the reader is invited to explore and interpret metaphors, since their ambiguity is considered as an essential ingredient of the poetic experience or the rhetorical force of the text. In contrast to both poetry and rhetoric, philosophy is often seen as an intellectual endeavour where conceptual precision is both a prerequisite and an objective, where truths are to be expressed in as literal statements as possible and where the laws of logic are omnipresent. Do 'philosophy' and 'metaphor', then, point to two incompatible activities? If one adopts such narrow definitions of both metaphor and philosophy, then this may indeed be so. However, the understanding of the term metaphor adopted here is broader; and so is, I hope, the understanding of philosophy.

In order to expand these commonly held views about metaphor and philosophy, I start with an exploration of some less familiar, yet very significant, aspects of metaphor, and then draw attention to certain elements of philosophical activity and education that seem to be closely related to metaphor. The first two parts of this paper serve thus as a background for a pedagogical practice – illustrated in the third part through an example drawing on my teaching experience – which I believe that could be further developed and systematized as to form a valuable component of contemporary philosophical education. My main contention is that an educational practice of guided awareness and interpretation of metaphors found in philosophical texts, informed by an understanding of metaphor as an active, on-going and open-ended intellectual process, will help students and teachers of philosophy to engage more actively with philosophical texts and ideas, to gain deeper understanding of philosophical problems and the responses to these, and to develop their thought in more creative directions, mostly by establishing connections with other philosophical or cultural contexts with which students may have been already familiar.

Metaphor

To begin with, a broader conception of metaphor appeals, *firstly*, to its prominent status over other figures of speech. Aristotle, the first philosopher to provide a systematic account of metaphor, exemplifies metaphor not only as one figure of speech but as the 'genus' to which other figurative devices (including, most notably, simile, proverb and hyperbole) belong as species[1] – a view shared by many theorists of metaphor, including Paul Ricoeur, who comments that, '. . . for Aristotle the word *metaphor* applies to every transposition of terms. Indeed its analysis paves the way for a global reflection concerning *the figure as such.*'[2] The generic status attributed to metaphor, and thus its prominence over other figures of speech, indicates that metaphor, whether directly or indirectly, informs all other ways of verbal expression (including, in a certain sense at least, non-figurative speech). At its best, a metaphor *creates a similarity,*[3] while other devices either rely on an already identified, more obvious, or partial, analogy or similarity (as, for example, in the case of metonymy: 'the daily *press*'), or are more elaborate and perhaps less striking than the metaphor or sets of metaphors (as, for example, in the cases of similes and myths), which they seem to unravel. However, from this point of view, and for the purposes of the present discussion, whether simple or complex, brief or extended, similes, myths, metonymies, synecdoche, etc., will all be treated as kinds of metaphors, as instances of the metaphoric process in this broad sense.

Secondly, as already implied above, another important aspect attached to a broader conception of metaphor is the connection between metaphor and creativity. Although creativity is not confined to metaphor, and all metaphors are not equally or evidently creative, the two seem to be intimately connected. By creativity, I mean here the exercise of our ability, rooted at the very nature of human beings, to respond to what is already existing or known (as, say, a puzzle, a lack, an opportunity) in a way that cannot be captured with the help of a set of determinate descriptive or normative rules (and thus issues to something initially unknown), but which, however, transforms eventually our understanding and experience, giving rise to new descriptions and norms, contents and forms. This is not intended as a rigorous definition of creativity, of course, but as a point of orientation in the exploration of the relationship between metaphor and creativity. It seems then that this relationship is quite complex: at one level, a new metaphor may itself be considered as something new, created without the help of rules and requiring a process of reception in order to be understood; at another level, the use of metaphors is crucial in almost any instance of creativity, since a successful metaphor establishes connections that enable us to move between the known or familiar and the unknown or strange (whether in creation or reception), in ways that often extend further and beyond rationality, rely on intuition, and presuppose the exercise of imagination.

In Aristotle's words, to create (presumably good) metaphors is 'by far the greatest thing' the 'token of a genius', and strictly speaking it cannot be taught to one by another.[4] It may be precisely the work of genius to deliver a novel and sustainable insight into reality, but even if one is not a genius, there is still the task and opportunity for critical reception: in the attempt to understand a metaphor one may produce an interpretation or series of interpretations that will shed new light into the aspect of reality that the initial metaphor attempts to articulate. And it is often the case that when a new, additional, interpretation of a given metaphor is attempted, one ends up 're-creating' this metaphor by seeing in it and through it a new meaning. Following this process through, one may add something genuinely new to world, especially if one thinks that the world does not consist (merely) of factual truths to be discovered, but of a network of relations and interpretations which, although established through history and culture, are nevertheless available to be re-constructed and transformed.

In the light of this last remark, it becomes gradually apparent that what is of particular interest, at least for the present paper, is that a broader conception of metaphor involves, *thirdly*, treating metaphor not only as the static result of a process but, dynamically, as *the process* of transferral itself. To illustrate this with an example deriving from a philosophical context, we are not just interested in a metaphor such as 'metaphysics is the battlefield of endless controversies', found in the *Critique of Pure Reason*,[5] but also, or primarily, in the process which makes this transferral possible and meaningful. That is, the process through which a concept like 'battlefield' may be applied to 'metaphysics' in a way that something which when taken literally may be meaningless, becomes metaphorically meaningful in a variety of new ways – obviously not only in the way in which Kant, for instance, intended it. Needless to say, there are also ways in which this metaphorical connection would make no sense at all.[6]

The metaphoric process involves transferring one term from the semantic field where it ordinarily belongs to another as yet 'alien' field; a new pair of previously unrelated terms is thus constructed. The emerging pair relies on the identification of similarities between the two terms, which, in relation to the focal point established by the metaphor are brought in the foreground, while their differences (some of which may already be implicitly also identified) retreat in the background. This new pairing, this new connection, affects our cognition of either or both of the terms involved, and if powerful enough, it may transform our previously established conceptual structures. To engage in the metaphoric process involves being sensitive to the unconventional aspects to which the metaphor draws attention, while attempting to identify the basis on which a metaphor may be justified, the reasons for its being productive or misleading.[7] In the course of this process we may gain a deeper understanding of the questions that prompted any given metaphor in the first place, we may evoke other metaphors in order to further elaborate or correct the initial one, and we may address the limitations of relevant literal expressions.

It is at any rate true that metaphorical expressions are not only used in order to illustrate a thought which is otherwise 'fully available to the thinker in purely literal terms', but 'on the contrary, the metaphorical description itself serves as an invitation, to its originator and to others, to develop its ramifications'.[8] As a process, 'to metaphor' (to verb yet another noun), is integral part of both the construction and expression of our own ideas, revealing a peculiar dialectic of reason and the imagination, implicated in the various types of discourse available to us. It is this process then, through which we make connections between words, concepts or images that properly or ordinarily belong to different spheres, rather than just the specific metaphors at which the process peaks and becomes visible, that plays such an important role in our creative understanding, or misunderstanding, of the world and of the cognitive tools and patterns informing the various types of discourse around us. By accepting the invitation extended by a metaphor, we become actively involved in the attempt 'to find or invent new and fruitful descriptions of nature'.[9]

But in discussing metaphor as a continuous and to a certain extent open-ended process, I have shifted from words to concepts, and this move, already anticipated by Aristotle, is systematically articulated by such contemporary theorists as Lakoff and Johnson, who in their seminal work on metaphor have shown that, 'metaphor is pervasive in everyday life, not just in language but in thought and action. Our ordinary conceptual system, in terms of which we both think and act, is fundamentally metaphorical in nature'.[10]

That, *fourthly*, metaphors do not solely concern words but concepts, allows us to understand metaphor as the very transference of meaning from one domain or medium to another, 'a borrowing between and intercourse of thoughts, a transaction between contexts',[11] albeit verbal or non-verbal, in ordinary or sophisticated contexts. So conceived, metaphors pertain to various types of discourses or practices that we encounter; paintings, maps, pieces of music, games, even actions may be thus considered as metaphors with cognitive, volitional or emotive relevance.

One needs to be cautious here, however, because such view, especially if coupled with Nietzsche's famous exhortation that truth is, '[a] movable host of metaphors, metonymies, and anthropomorphisms: in short, a sum of human relations which have been poetically and rhetorically intensified, transferred, and embellished, and which, after long usage, seem to a people to be fixed, canonical, and binding',[12] may result in there being ultimately no essential distinction between literal and non-literal discourse. Regardless of one's position on this claim, a 'rehabilitation' of metaphor, as is often called, that is, an appreciation of metaphor not simply as an unavoidable and necessary evil but as an important and indispensable component of our thinking, expression and life, need not appeal to such extreme a view.

For our present concerns, it suffices to note that the dichotomy between literal and metaphorical meaning, even if indispensable, is often blurred: whether an expression is thought to be (still) metaphorical and what its content may be depends on the situation in which it is used and the point of view from which it is interpreted. On the one hand, it may be true that many metaphors are no longer recognized as such: we immediately, to use two examples from everyday life, understand what the *World Wide Web* is, and when someone tells us that they *see* what we mean we are not puzzled. In these cases, the specific historical or conceptual context in which these expressions are used allows for their almost instant and straightforward 'translation' into a literal expression, whether consciously or unconsciously. On the other hand, however, these very same expressions when placed in a different context, or when employed for different purposes, may be better understood and appreciated if we become aware of their metaphorical nature. For instance, and to take the *World Wide Web* example again, the fact that a system of communication and information exchange was conceptualized and then organized in terms of a 'web', consisting of 'pages' 'uploaded' or 'downloaded' by its users, was not inevitable, since these were only some of the possible *metaphorical* ways in which such a system could be conceived.[13] Explicit reflection on the conditions, advantages and limitations of such a cluster of metaphors could lead to their revision, or the conception of new metaphors to replace them; the gain of such an engagement with the metaphoric process would not only be a better understanding of the nature of the *World Wide Web*, but also the emergence of innovative conceptions that could guide future developments in this field.

Philosophy and metaphor

The relationship between metaphor and philosophy is not exhausted, of course, by the fact that metaphor has been throughout the history of philosophy an object of theoretical preoccupation for many philosophers. As in other types of discourse, here too metaphors are woven into the very fabric of philosophical thought and word, and even a cursory glance at the philosophical corpus would be enough to provide us with an inexhaustible wealth of examples of various metaphorical devices. Metaphors do not only appear in the more literary philosophical texts of writers such as Plato or Nietzsche (writers who do share an interest in metaphorical language and display in their work a corresponding sensitivity to the metaphors they employ), but they are often used in less prominent or sustained ways even in texts that are, for the most part, devoid of any 'poetic' elements, as shown by the famous example from Kant cited earlier. Confronted with the presence of a metaphor in a philosophical text, one may be tempted to overlook or bypass it, either as a harmless or harmful disruption of the flow of rational argumentation, or as source of gratuitous or intolerable ambiguity, or as a sign of philosophical frivolity perhaps motivated by stylistic considerations, or finally as a 'neutral' or 'transparent' device that does not introduce any complications in the text. However, one may equally well accept the fascinating challenge of understanding a metaphor and its motivation, and thus find oneself caught up in the metaphoric process. But let us take a closer look here.

Obviously, any sustainable attempt to read a substantial philosophical work in a way that takes into account its metaphorical dimension cannot deal evenly with every metaphor present in the text. Implicitly or explicitly, the context created by the limitations, exigencies or objectives of a given reading will decide which of the metaphors found in the text perform an important function (whether positive or negative) in the process of rendering intelligible the thought of the philosopher, or, in other words, which metaphors merit further reflection and philosophical speculation. Some of the metaphors present in the text will be thus unavoidably considered as 'just' figures of speech, contributing to the aesthetic qualities or style of a philosopher's prose, or as 'transparent' devices that do not deserve further consideration, even if the lines drawn do not reflect any objective fact about the text and can be re-drawn differently in the context of another reading. If, however, the attempted reading is alert to the metaphorical dimension of the text, there will be invariably cases in which the presence of a metaphor cannot be dismissed easily; in the present context, I may distinguish, briefly and schematically, two such cases, on the basis of the source of this metaphorical material.

First, there are metaphors that reflect habitual uses of language, echoing wider cultural and historical traditions. These metaphors could appear in a variety of forms: simple terms (e.g., 'a *theory* that *delivers* truth'), idiomatic or proverbial expressions, even fully articulated myths. These metaphorical formulations may be considered as crystallizations of ideological, religious and social influences (or, even, as results of 'forgotten' philosophical articulations) and their sheer familiarity often prevents us from putting into question their validity or explanatory force. Being conscious of the merits and dangers of the role these metaphors play in the historical and epistemological construction of reality, philosophers often concentrate their attention on these and devote considerable time and effort to their revision.[14] The revision of such metaphors is at times judged imperative in order to shake off resilient historically established beliefs that dominate our conceptual framework and hinder us from identifying or taking seriously novel or alternative solutions to a given problem. Retrieving the original source of a metaphor, following the metaphoric logic guiding its inception, making visible the points of view from which it fails or fulfils its purpose, are some of the ways in which a critical examination of such metaphors can be conducted. This process of revision, however, does not necessarily culminate with the mere critical analysis of a metaphor into literal statements. Rather, it may lead to the construction of alternative metaphorical formulations, claiming to satisfy the same need for pervasiveness, persuasive strength and succinct articulation that motivated the introduction of the metaphors to be replaced.[15]

The second kind of metaphors deserving philosophical investigation are thus those that are the products of philosophers' own creative thinking and mark their personal contribution to the development of philosophical ideas. These are, indeed, the clearest cases in which the metaphors employed are not easily translatable into a series of literal statements without considerable loss in the understanding of their meaning; in fact, it may be the case that in view of the shape of certain philosophical questions a metaphorical response is the most concise and appropriate one available. The very identification of a 'new' solution to an 'old' problem, let alone the conception of a 'new' problem itself, establishes a set of new connections, a nexus of previously unidentified similarities, and introduces a new way of looking at what may have appeared as known or self-evident. The metaphoric process, especially as instantiating the ability to recognize similarities in things that would otherwise appear dissimilar, is in this way organically linked with the process of philosophical thinking. It is actually for this reason that Aristotle, in his discussion of metaphor in the *Rhetoric*, draws a parallel between the two processes and notes: 'metaphors should be drawn from objects which are proper to the object, but not too obvious; just as, for instance, in philosophy it needs sagacity to grasp the things that are apart,' while in the *Topics* he makes this connection more explicit by stating that:

> The examination of likeness is useful with a view both to inductive arguments and to hypothetical deductions, and also with a view to the rendering of definitions. It is useful for inductive arguments, because it is by means of an induction of particulars in cases that are alike that we claim to induce the universal; for it is not easy to do this if we do not know the points of likeness. It is useful for hypothetical deductions because it is a reputable opinion that among similars what is true of one is true also of the rest.[16]

That is not to say, of course, that the ability to discern similarities is itself identical with the ability to create metaphors. There are, after all, ordinary similarities that may group things, words, or concepts together, or similarities that can be identified through determinate rules and systems of classification, in which case no metaphoric process needs to be in operation.[17] The point is, however, that the metaphoric process, rather than competing with the discursive modes of philosophical reasoning (that is, the arguments, syllogisms and definitions, that structure philosophical thinking and writing), constantly informs and is informed by these, and thus it forms an integral part of philosophical creativity. By transferring what is regarded as known to an unexpected sphere – a yet unexplored ground – metaphors enrich our understanding, expand our philosophical vocabulary and widen our conceptual horizon.

But if metaphors are indeed such essential components of philosophical thinking, their importance should be addressed by, and reflected in, the way we practice and understand the nature and priorities of philosophical education. If our aim is not just to teach students the history of philosophy, but also to expose them to philosophical activity itself, or even teach them how to be philosophers themselves (in other words, to help them develop both critical and creative thinking), a guided awareness and interpretation of metaphor may have a lot to contribute in this respect. The pedagogical strength of metaphor has been long recognized by many educationalists in various fields.[18] I will at present mention just a few of its possible merits.

To begin with, to an all-increasing pressure for clarity and immediate outcomes promoted by contemporary academia, which inevitably often leads to superficiality and an illusion of understanding, the ambiguity inherent in metaphor comes in as a refreshing cognitive challenge, able to stimulate the mind of both teachers and students of philosophy. We should discourage our students from believing that 'conclusions are imma-nent in the text rather than emerging from the active thinking process of thinkers' and that 'ambiguity is attributed to faulty thinking rather than to rationally justifiable qualitative differences between different readers of the text'.[19]

Metaphors that, as identified above, invite and deserve special attention from a philosophical point of view, offer multiple insights into the situation or problem examined and display both intelligence and acute perception or imagination. With this kind of metaphors there is rarely, if ever, a single correct way of interpreting them, of straightforwardly 'explaining' what a metaphor means. It has been argued, for example, that, 'when we try to say what a metaphor "means", we soon realize that there is no end to what we want to mention'.[20] In our attempt to unravel a metaphor we end up saying too much and yet too little, as there always seems to be room for an 'and so on'; our interpretations thus seem to only asymptotically capture the meaning of the metaphor. This wealth of interpretations should not be attributed solely to the polysemy intrinsic in metaphor; rather it is also, or primarily, associated with the fact that interpretations are undertaken from a multiplicity of points of view that inevitably shape them. A shift in the perspective from which we approach a metaphor results in alternative interpretations; some of which may contradict each other, while some may be better or more informative than others. Exposing students to this array of possibilities encourages them to engage more actively with philosoph-ical texts and ideas, to appreciate the value of the otherwise often highly frustrating proverbial saying that in philosophy there are 'no conclusive answers'.

Most importantly however, this practice guides students to adopt a well-defined perspective, drawing largely on their own available resources, beliefs and inclinations, which may then become visible and subsequently be put into question.[21] Even in cases where a more sensitive and critical appreciation of the metaphors employed in a philosophical context will not lead us to a 'clearer' understanding of the problem at hand, it may still lead us to a better understanding of ourselves, our preconceptions and limitations. In other words, it may lead students a step closer to self-knowledge, a priority goal for any philosopher still aspiring to the Delphic commandment which, starting from Socrates, has been guiding many philosophers in their thought and practice over the centuries.

Finally, metaphors enthuse and surprise us, intrigue not only our curiosity with riddles that we cannot easily unravel, but also capture our imagination and stimulate our perception. In this respect, metaphor is a very effective way to learn something new and may also serve as a mnemotechnic device. Appealing to Aristotle once more,

> We all find it agreeable to get hold of new ideas easily: words express ideas, and therefore those words are the most agreeable that enable us to get hold of new ideas. Now strange words simply puzzle us; ordinary words convey only what we know already; it is from metaphor that we can best get hold of something fresh.[22]

Viewed in this light, metaphor seems to play a cardinal role in philosophical education precisely because it engages us – students and teachers alike – with something more than reason alone, placing the emphasis of philosophical activity on personal understanding rather than on the acquisition of an impersonal and 'objective' body of knowledge. And we would all agree, I suppose, that we would prefer it, were we to be taught in a way that would make learning both challenging and pleasurable, stimulating and memorable.

An example

It is against this background that I would like to illustrate how metaphors can be employed in the teaching of philosophy, by outlining briefly a way of structuring a two-hour teaching session. The session is delivered as a workshop during which students are divided into three groups; each group has to introduce material provided by the teacher, sometimes in advance, in the form of handouts, which is subsequently discussed by the whole class. Except for preparing the material to be used, the teacher facilitates the discussion and intervenes when this is deemed necessary. The philosophical theme of the workshop is the soul (or mind) and body problem, which addresses questions such as: 'What is the nature of soul and body?', 'What is the relationship between them?', 'Is the soul immortal?' This is one of the first philosophical problems with which students of philosophy are introduced to the discipline, and a problem that they have the chance to revisit many times during their course of study. What follows derives largely from my personal experience and practice in teaching Ancient, Hellenistic and Late-antique philosophy to second and third-level students, and thus it has not benefited from a more comprehensive implementation. However, I hope that it will contribute to the development of a more systematic model to be developed in this direction, which could be employed in other modules taught, primarily but not exclusively, to University philosophy students.[23]

My approach unfolds in three distinct, yet not altogether independent, directions, presented here as stages in a unifying process. The first stage is to concentrate on the metaphors found in a particular set of philosophical texts and encourage students to discuss and explore them, in order to assess how these contribute to the understanding of the philosophical ideas that these texts introduce. The second step is to help students to make connections with similar metaphors that they may have encountered previously in philosophical contexts other than those examined during this session. The third step is to encourage students to use metaphors as a bridge of communication between the philosophical texts under discussion and other cultural creations, such as literary texts or works of art in other media, with a special emphasis on popular culture or on particular backgrounds that may figure prominently in their personal experience.

From the point of view of Ancient Greek philosophy, a rather familiar starting point in order to examine the soul-body problem is Plato's *Phaedo*, a dialogue that students are likely to remember from their A-Levels, GCSEs or their first year at University, as the text where one can find three unsuccessful attempts to argue for the immortality of soul (occasionally students do not actually remember what these arguments really are, but they still remember that they fail to prove the point). The first group of students are asked to consider the metaphor 'the body is a prison for the soul' and, together with the immediate contexts in which it appears, they are also given a selection of additional passages from this dialogue to help them construct their interpretations.[24] The second group is given a very different philosophical articulation of the soul-body relationship on which to reflect, coming from Hellenistic philosophy, and in particular the Stoics, who presented their views with the help of the metaphor 'the soul is an octopus with its tentacles stretching out into the body'. Students in this group have on their handouts a selection of texts sufficient to create the necessary philosophical background to which they may appeal in order to understand the content of this metaphor.[25] Students in the third group are asked to follow Plotinus' critique of metaphors used by his predecessors, including 'the soul is in the body as the steersman is in the ship' and 'the soul is present in the body as fire is present to air', and to evaluate his own metaphorical formulation, according to which 'the body is a net immersed in the soul-sea'.[26]

The spokesperson of each group undertakes then to introduce the metaphor they had to study, make the necessary connections with the philosophical ideas that it conveys, and formulate a first assessment of the respects in which it may be adequate or inadequate. In their attempts to explore and interpret the selected metaphors, students are confronted with questions such as, 'How are we to understand the nature of body and soul and their interaction through this metaphor?' or 'Are body and soul two different entities, and if so, how do they communicate with each other?' Students may further be encouraged to play along with the metaphor and follow its logic, through a series of additional questions. Consider for example questions like, 'If the body is a prison for the soul, as Plato claims, is the embodied life thought to be a sentence, a punishment, an accident?'; or, 'If the body is a prison for the soul, and it is through death that the soul can be freed, why is not suicide an option for Plato'?; or, 'If both soul and body are of the same bodily nature, as the metaphor suggested by the Stoics indicates, how is it possible for two bodies to occupy the same space at the same time?' As the discussion progresses and the groups interact with each other, students may be prompted to make more explicit comparisons between the metaphors examined so far. For example, 'What are the philosophical implications of substituting the vocabulary of imprisonment with that of symbiosis?' or 'Why is it misleading, as Plotinus claims, to adopt metaphorical expressions for the relationship between soul and body that rely so sharply on a distinction between inside and outside?'

This sketch is probably enough to give us an idea of the kind of questions that the teacher should introduce, entertain and encourage at the first stage of the session. As the discussion unfolds, more connections are attempted that allow students to move into further layers of philosophical thinking. The vividness and compactness of metaphors allow students to easily remember their content and the association with the implicated philosophical ideas; they are thus the perfect building blocks for the establishment of a context, which in its turn illuminates the metaphors and leads invariably to a revision of the initial understanding of the metaphors themselves. As a result, students become more actively engaged in learning, develop their interpretative skills and realize that philosophical activity is not exhausted by the discussion of the validity of given arguments; in sum, they may get a taste of philosophers' efforts to conceive of something new and of the way in which this effort mobilizes both discursive and non-discursive elements of thought.

The second stage in this process involves making connections with other philosophical contexts. Within a similar framework of structured questioning and dialogue, the students are asked to examine texts that they have already explored in their first-year syllabus; this time, however, the texts are approached in the light of the preceding discussion and with an extra sensitivity toward the metaphors they contain.[27] This material is selected and introduced in class by the teacher and may include metaphors such as: 'the soul relates to the body in the way a king relates to his kingdom' (Aquinas),[28] 'the soul is like a wind permeating the body' (Descartes),[29] or 'the body is a manifestation of the will' (Schopenhauer).[30]

During this stage, students are presented with an opportunity to incorporate what they learnt during the first stage, what is 'new' to them, to what they already know, that is, to built actively on their prior knowledge in order to assimilate the new material. At the same time, by re-examining philosophical works already familiar to them with reference to the metaphors found in these, they become aware of aspects of philosophical thinking that they may have failed to notice, especially if their attention had previously concentrated solely on the relevant arguments. As a result, students do not only learn something new; they are guided to look afresh at something they already 'know' in a way that may issue in a new understanding of texts and ideas. In other words, they are exposed to a learning practice that is itself a constructive and transformative process – a creative philosophical process – rather than a process of accumulating data or storing arguments. Moreover, through the establishment of a network of thematic connections between the various metaphors (a process facilitated by the vividness of the metaphors), the students may appreciate both the persistence of certain philosophical problems throughout the history of philosophy and the broad variety (the imaginative and conceptual wealth) of the different responses to these problems.

In the final stage, the teacher may assist students to make connections with metaphors embedded in other contexts or media. Obviously, from this point onwards the backgrounds, interests and aspirations of any particular group of students, as well as the resources that are readily available in a given occasion, may vary significantly and could lead the discussion in directions that cannot be easily anticipated. However, the main objective of the teacher would be to motivate students by, say, evoking examples from literature, or by providing visual examples of art works, or by appealing to familiar examples from popular culture. I shall limit myself to a few examples immediately relevant to the problem of the relation between body and soul.

An appropriate classical literary work that could be used in this context is John Donne's poem *The Extasie*. Donne, within a poetic depiction of the experience of love, discusses, in the last part of the poem, the relation between body and soul with the help of a set of metaphors that derive from the classical tradition (and thus are similar to some of the philosophical metaphors that the students have already examined, including a reference to the Platonic metaphor of the prison), but at the same time revises these (rather dualistic) metaphors towards a more positive re-evaluation of the function and the importance of the body, expressed with the help of new metaphors. The poem establishes thus a very helpful framework for the discussion of the evaluative or hierarchical aspect of the dichotomies that inform a large part of the traditional philosophical discussion of the soul-body problem. From the world of contemporary art, the striking and enigmatic *Lighted Performance Box*, Bruce Nauman's installation of an aluminium rectangular containing a 1000-watt halogen lamp, can be another useful example. Some elements of this work (such as its position and dimensions), as well as Nauman's well-documented preoccupation with the issue of selfhood, suggest that it may be viewed as a representation of a human being, a minimalist statue, and as such can be read as a visual metaphor for the soul-body relationship. An exploration of the work in this context can thus thematize other aspects of the metaphorical conception of this relationship, such as the 'spatial' relations between a container and the contained, or the problematic juxtaposition of the solidity of the body with the 'elusiveness' of the soul. Finally, an example from the world of popular culture, to which the students may be able to relate more easily, could be the current 're-imagined' version of the science fiction series 'Battlestar Galactica'. In this series, we encounter the Cylons, human-made machines, who have evolved in a way that makes them virtually indistinguishable from humans from 'the outside', that is, in terms of their bodily appearance, but differ from humans in two respects that, from a Platonic perspective, appear rather startling: on the one hand, they have no souls (at least, this is how they understand themselves), while, on the other hand, they enjoy a certain type of immortality, in that they can be resurrected by 'downloading' their memories and experiences into a different body. Once more, a discussion of the nature of Cylons can lead to a further exploration of the classical nexus between body, soul, mortality and immortality, of which the Cylons are a particular metaphorical expression.

The objective of this last step is to alert students to the pervasiveness of metaphors in contexts other than the philosophical ones that they have been so far examining, contexts that determine not only what they know, but also how they live and act. And it is not uncommon, for example, for students to realize that their tacit dependence on certain metaphors is a barrier to new ways of understanding; or to notice some disparity between their explicit beliefs and the metaphors that they use in their descriptions of their personal views, even on what matters to them most. Had they known the implications and presuppositions of these metaphors, they probably would have avoided them, or opted for ones that they may have been more comfortable with.[31] Consequently, the expanded metaphorical vocabulary to which they have been exposed does not only allow them to clarify their expressions but most importantly to clarify their thinking and being, by becoming more consistent and committed to that which they profess.

The pedagogical practice that I have been suggesting is not meant to replace traditional teaching methods, nor is it meant as a panacea for the problems confronted by many educationalists and students in their attempts to teach and learn philosophy. There may be other ways, and better ways, of achieving what I intend; but if students' responses do provide some indication of the weaknesses and strengths of our teaching methods, then indeed my hypothesis is strongly confirmed:[32] teaching philosophy through metaphor resulted almost invariably in a deeper, more enduring and internalized understanding of philosophy and its methods.[33]

Notes

[1] Aristotle, *Rhetoric*, trans. R. Roberts, in Barnes (1984) (ed.), *The Complete Works of Aristotle: The Revised Oxford Translation* Vol. 1, Princeton: Princeton University Press, 1406b20ff; 1413a15ff.

[2] P. Ricoeur (1978), *The Rule of Metaphor*, London: Routledge, p. 17; for a similar conception of metaphor as a unified concept, see also N. Goodman (1968), *Languages of Art: An Approach to a Theory of Symbols*, New York: Boobs-Merill Company, and J. Searle (1979) 'Metaphor', in A. Ortony (ed.), *Metaphor and Thought*, Cambridge: Cambridge University Press, pp. 92–123.

[3] A claim advanced primarily, but not exclusively, by Max Black (1962), see 'Metaphor' in *Models and Metaphors*, Ithaca: Cornell University Press, pp. 25–47 and 'More About Metaphor', in A. Ortony (ed.), ibid, pp. 19–43.

[4] Aristotle (1991), *Poetics*, 1459a5–7, W. Hamilton Fyfe (trans.), Cambridge and London: Loeb Classical Library.

⁵ E. Kant (1998), *Critique of Pure Reason*, P. Guyer and A. W. Wood (eds. and trans.), Cambridge: Cambridge University Press, A viii.

⁶ More often than not, a metaphor makes sense only if read in one direction from *tenor* to *vehicle*, that is, in our case, from 'metaphysics' to 'battlefield', and not the other way around. However, by taking into account the extended context in which a metaphor is found, it may prove that some metaphors are also reversible or bidirectional. On this issue, see, for example, C. Forceville (1995), '(A)symmetry in Metaphor: The Importance of Extended Context', *Poetics Today*, 16 (4), 677–708.

⁷ As H. J. N. Horsburgh (1958) notes in his article 'Philosophers against Metaphor' (*The Philosophical Quarterly*, 8 (32), 231–245), that the sense and degree in which a metaphor may be 'misleading' in terms of the 'logical confusion' it may cause or reinforce vary significantly. Although it is the 'logical confusion' resulting from metaphors on which the attack of philosophers against metaphors often concentrates, I use the term 'misleading' here in a more general sense: a metaphor may be misleading at least in some respects when it does not advance or encourage further philosophical engagement.

⁸ I. Scheffler (1988), 'Ten Myths of Metaphor', *Journal of Aesthetic Education*, 22 (1), 45–50, p. 47.

⁹ Ibid.

¹⁰ G. Lakoff and M. Johnson (2003), *Metaphors We Live By*, Chicago: University of Chicago Press, (first edn 1980), p. 3.

¹¹ I. A. Richards (1996), *The Philosophy of Rhetoric*, New York: Oxford University Press, p. 94.

¹² F. Nietzsche (1873), 'On Truth and Lies in a Nonmoral Sense', in D. Breazeale (1979) (ed. and trans.) *Philosophy and Truth*, New Jersey and London: Humanities Press International, p. 84.

¹³ The fact that metaphorical language is indispensable in order to understand and communicate revolutionary technological innovations, such as the recent 'digital revolution', is evidenced by the extensive use of metaphorical expressions in the relevant contexts. See, for example, P. C. Adams (1997) 'Cyberspace and Virtual Places', *Geographical Review*, 87, (2), 155–171. For a more general discussion on the role of metaphor in the development of science, see M. Hess (1988), 'The Cognitive Claims of Metaphor', *The Journal of Speculative Philosophy*, 2 (1), 1–16.

¹⁴ Certainly, on many occasions these metaphorical elements may function as 'blind spots' in the thought of a philosopher, and then it falls to the reader to engage critically with them in the way described above.

¹⁵ A typical example would be Kant's 'Copernican Revolution', in which a conception of knowledge articulated metaphorically around the paradigm of vision is replaced by a conception of knowledge articulated around the paradigm of making; Kant, *Critique of Pure Reason*, vxvi–vxviii.

¹⁶ Pickard-Cambridge (trans.), in J. Barnes (1984) (ed.), *The Complete Works of Aristotle: The Revised Oxford Translation*, Vol. 1, Princeton: Princeton University Press. On this point and for a comprehensive discussion of Aristotle's position on metaphor, see J. T. Kirby (1997), 'Aristotle on Metaphor', *The American Journal of Philology*, 118 (4), 517–554.

¹⁷ In this connection, see D. Davidson (1978), 'What Metaphors Mean', *Critical Inquiry*, 5 (1), Special Issue on Metaphor, 31–47.

[18] See, for instance, in connection with religious studies, E. Ashton (1993), 'Interpreting Images: An Investigation of the Problem of Literalism in Language Use and Religious Thinking', *British Journal of Educational Studies*, 41 (4), 381–392; with science, J. Bump (1985), 'Metaphor, Creativity, and Technical Writing', *College Composition and Communication*, 36 (4), 444–453; with art, H. Feinstein (1985), 'Art as Visual Metaphor', *Art Education*, 38 (4), 26–29.

[19] See G. Labouvie-Vief (1990), 'Wisdom as Integrated Thought: Historical and Developmental Perspectives', in R. J. Stenberg (ed.), *Wisdom: Its Nature, Origins and Development*, Cambridge: Cambridge University Press, p. 70 and G. Corradi Fiumara (1995), *The Metaphoric Process*, London and New York: Routledge, p. 55.

[20] The quote comes from Davidson, 'What Metaphors Mean' (p. 46), who follows S. Cavel. Unlike Cavel, however, Davidson does not see the endless character of attempts to spell out a metaphor (marked with qualifiers such as 'and so on') as distinguishing metaphorical from literal discourse. Rather, he would 'say the same for any use of language' (ftn. 16). Even so, the fact remains that what may hold also for other or all uses of language can be illustrated and experienced more clearly and convincingly when dealing with metaphor. This is enough to justify the particular importance of metaphor as a component of philosophical teaching that I have been advocating here.

[21] On this, see also my (2003) 'From a Feminist Point of View: Plotinus on Teaching and Learning Philosophy', *Women. A Cultural Review*, 14 (2), 130–143.

[22] Aristotle, *Rhetoric*, 1410b10–13, R. Roberts (trans.), in Barnes (ed), *The Complete Works of Aristotle*, Vol. 2.

[23] A possible direction to pursue has been suggested to me by Andrea Kenkmann, the editor of the present volume. Her idea is to create a kind of virtual 'museum' by bringing various resources and media together, which students will explore philosophically in a manner similar to what I propose here. I would like to thank her for sharing her views with me and for her input in the development of the present paper.

[24] E.g., '[the soul] . . . is imprisoned in and clinging to the body', 'it is forced to examine other things through [the body] as through a cage and not by itself', *Phaedo*, 82d5ff. G.M.A. Crube (1981) (trans.), *Plato. Five Dialogues*, Indianapolis: Hackett.

[25] As reported by Aetius 4.21.1–4; the selection of passages included in the handout comes from Long and Sedley (1987), *The Hellenistic Philosophers*, 2 vols., Cambridge: Cambridge University Press, sections 45, 'Body' (pp. 272–274) and 53, 'Soul' (Vol. 1, pp. 313–323).

[26] 'The universe lies in the soul which bears it up, and nothing is without a share of soul. It is as if a net immersed in the waters was alive, but unable to make its own that in which it is. The sea is already spread out and the net spreads with it, as far as it can; for no one of its parts can be anywhere else than where it lies' (*On Difficulties about the Soul I*, IV.3.9.37–44, A. H. Armstrong (1966–1988) (trans.), *Plotinus*, 7 vols Cambridge: Loeb Classical Library. Plotinus develops his critique of other metaphors in other passages, such as IV.3.21–22. These texts are part of the selection of passages appearing on the handout.

[27] All our first-year students attend the introductory modules '*Analysing Philosophical Texts* I & II' (in the first and second semester respectively). These are text-based

two-hour weekly seminars, during which students are acquainted with extracts from various philosophical works, following roughly the thematic order and selection of J. Cottingham (1996) (ed.), *Western Philosophy*, Oxford: Blackwell Publishers.

[28] Evoked by T. Aquinas in *Summa Theologiae* in response to the question 'Is the soul man?' The text reads: 'a thing seems to be chiefly what is principal in it; thus what a king does, the kingdom is said to do', ibid, p. 143.

[29] 'But as to the nature of this soul, either I did not think about this or else I imagined it to be something tenuous, like a wind or fire or ether, which permeated my more solid parts'. R. Descartes, *Meditations*, ibid, p. 146.

[30] 'If every action of my body is the manifestation of an act of will . . .', notes Schopenhauer in the *World as Will and Idea*, 'the whole body then must be simply my will become visible', ibid, p. 163. The way in which Schopenhauer conceives of the relation between *my* body and *my* will (which replaces here terms like 'soul' or 'mind') is not strongly metaphorical (except that, as usual, visibility is metaphorically associated with reality). However, his analogical elaboration of this claim toward the generalization that all matter is a manifestation of will, is an almost classic example of metaphoric reasoning and students can appreciate it much better if they think of it this way.

[31] A characteristic example comes from a similar workshop that I run on the philosophy of love. Students are usually surprised by the philosophical implications of an expression such as 'my other half' brought to the surface through a discussion of Aristophanes' speech in the *Symposium*, and are subsequently hesitant to use it when referring to their beloved.

[32] I am referring, first, to students' immediate response during the sessions: in the course of the workshop they feel increasingly more confident to voice their views, to co-operate with each other and to work effectively as members of a group; second, to positive feedback communicated through student questionnaires: students often refer to these sessions as 'unique opportunities to learn' and even as 'life-changing experiences'; finally, to the way students perform in their assessment: they achieve significantly higher marks for modules that included such workshops.

[33] I am grateful to the Academy of Finland for funding part of my research on metaphor.

Chapter 9

Feeling the Force of Argument

Brendan Larvor

Higher education requires students to make judgments about the evidence and arguments placed before them, and all judgment has an aesthetic aspect. A mathematics student must be *struck* by the validity and elegance of a proof; a science student must *feel* the weight of evidence (or the lack of it). In the humanities, a lot of bad writing is the result of students trying to articulate and defend judgments that they have copied from secondary sources but have not felt in their viscera. This is not to say that judgment is all unreasoned, inarticulate conviction. Nor is it to suggest that logical relations between premises and conclusions are somehow subjective. On the contrary, the point is that students should perceive logical relations as objective realities. A student who knows that the argument on Page 84 is a good one simply because it satisfies the rules set out on pages 64–73, but who does not *feel* the force of its logic, will lack all motivation to internalize the rules or use them on other occasions. The difference that validity makes to an argument must be vividly real to a student if that student is to see why it matters. Nor is this merely a matter of motivation. A student with no feeling for the logical structure of the subject-matter will struggle to apply techniques in new contexts. One of the proper goals of higher education is to equip students to do their own research. A student who does not feel the badness of a bad argument is unlikely to produce many good ones. After all, good arguments usually start out as not-so-good arguments that don't *feel* quite right.

In this paper, I will contrast the case of philosophy with that of mathematics, using the work of George Polya. I will then claim that mainstream English-speaking philosophy is ill-equipped to think about the aesthetic and emotive aspects of the experience of doing and learning philosophy. I shall blame the Enlightenment for this state of affairs. More specifically, I shall find fault with the view that humans are naturally rational, where we understand 'rational' to mean something like the dispassionate, formal rationality on display in the end-products of the mathematical sciences. I shall then offer the work of R. G. Collingwood as a route out of this bind, and conclude with some practical consequences for teaching.

Mathematics

In mathematics, there is a standard distinction between seeing the validity of the individual steps in a proof, and understanding the proof as a whole. For example, here is George Polya, 'The intelligent reader of a mathematical book desires two things: First, to see that the present step of the argument is correct. Second, to see the purpose of the present step.'[1] Since the purpose of the present step is to advance the overall proof-strategy, the intelligent reader needs a sense of that strategic overview. Without it, even the most intelligent reader becomes 'dismayed and bored, and loses the thread of the argument'. Elsewhere,[2] Polya explains that in a formal derivation of a mathematical theorem, the purpose of a step may not become clear until later in the proof, and even then, it may remain mysterious how the theorem and proof came to be. A proof that pulls just the right rabbit out of just the right hat at just the right moment may compel assent, but (at least on first reading) it does not supply the intelligent reader's second requirement. Moreover, it offers no heuristic lessons to students. For this reason, Polya recommends telling the story of how the theorem and proof emerged (or rather, a streamlined version thereof). If students see how theorems are arrived at and proofs discovered, they may become intelligent readers of mathematical books. They may even eventually become intelligent writers of mathematical books.

Notice that Polya runs together boredom, dismay and losing the thread of the argument. This attention to the motivational and affective state of the student is a regular motif in Polya's work on mathematical pedagogy. The first move in solving a problem, he says, is to adopt it as one's own:

> You need not tell me that you have set that problem to yourself, you need not tell it to yourself; your whole behavior will show that you did. Your mind becomes selective; it becomes more accessible to anything that appears to be connected with the problem, and less accessible to anything that seems unconnected . . . You keenly feel the pace of your progress; you are elated when it is rapid, you are depressed when it is slow.[3]

Here, in the mind of the mathematician or mathematics student committed to a problem and striving to solve it, we find an intense form of intellectual sensibility. The objective structure of the subject-matter and the logical relations constituting arguments about it are not merely vivid; they are salient to the exclusion of all else. For Polya, mathematical problem-solving requires an appropriate motivational and affective condition. You cannot practice the discipline without a feel for the subject-matter, where 'feel' has two senses: an intuitive grasp and a caring concern.

Like mathematics, philosophy demands commitment, a ready familiarity with the subject-matter and a vivid sense of the logical relations among its elements. One of philosophy's differences with mathematics is the role of intuition. In mathematics, intuition is unwelcome in final, published proofs, despite the heuristic importance of mathematical sensibility. Appeals to intuition are more difficult to avoid in philosophical argument than in mathematical proof. Even the final, ready-for-publication version of a philosophical argument may appeal to intuitions of one sort or another. For example, 'ordinary language' philosophy took the intuitions of sophisticated native speakers as its data. Arguments in ethics have to reckon with moral intuitions, even if these are not part of the theory at hand (utilitarianism, for example, must respond to the complaint that it gives counterintuitive results). In many philosophical enquiries, pre-theoretic intuition serves as a test-bed or evidential field.

The role of intuitions in philosophical argument requires a difference in practice from mathematics: in addition to *using* their intuitions heuristically, philosophy students must also *examine* their more spontaneous judgments about philosophical questions. To do this, they must first *have* spontaneous reactions to philosophical questions. Philosophy seminars often fail simply because students do not have spontaneous responses to the more technical philosophical questions. For example, what are the 'truth-makers' for statements about the past? It is possible, and I believe common, for students to understand a question like this, understand why it matters, and yet have no intuitions tugging them towards one solution or away from another. Tutors are sometimes baffled when seminars fail for this reason. The question is not complicated (past events are, by definition, non-existent, so how can terms refer to them?) and was explained slowly and carefully. The students understood the motivating examples (the truth about war-crimes and genocides matters, so there had better be true statements about the past). So what is the problem? Most likely, it is that the students, while they have feelings about genocides, do not have intuitions about metaphysics or semantics to guide their next moves. Lacking a sense of direction on the technical question, they sit still and wait for guidance. To the frustrated tutor, this inertia can look like laziness or indifference.

The students look as if they are waiting to be spoon-fed. In fact, the students are often simply waiting for an instruction that they can follow. Many of them cannot express their intuitions about the metaphysics of time for the same reason that they cannot follow an instruction to 'Open the lid of your harpsichord'. 'Sorry, Sir, I don't have one of those.' When students do have spontaneous intuitions about technical philosophical questions, they may not recognize them as such, but rather as unhappy confusion. Philosophy gets going when we have conflicting intuitions, but students may feel those conflicts as personal inadequacy.

Of course, students in any discipline may lack feeling for their subject, but in many disciplines, they can press on with some practical activity and hope that light will dawn. You can follow the recipe for an experiment even if you have little sense of what it is about. Most disciplines have motions that students can go through with or without understanding – students who lack understanding come unstuck later, when they have to cope with new cases or unfamiliar material. In philosophy, the articulation and examination of one's spontaneous intuitive responses is a central activity and occupies much classroom time. Philosophy students who lack spontaneous responses to the matter in hand cannot participate. It is as if healthy medical students had to learn about diseases by examining their own bodies.

This point applies with special force to logical relations. As I said at the outset, students of any subject must develop a sense for the characteristic arguments of their discipline. They should feel the 'hardness of the logical *must*' (or the statistical or evidential *must* as the case may be). This is doubly true in philosophy because logic is part of our subject-matter. To engage with the philosophy of logic, a student must have an intuitive grasp of logical structure that is sufficiently robust for the student to test logical theory against it. For example, a logic student should feel *both* the oddness of material implication considered on its own *and* the neatness of the system(s) of which it is a part.

The practical problem for teachers, then, is how to cultivate this sensibility in students. What exercises can we devise to make philosophical concepts and logical relations vivid to them? Polya has something to say about the corresponding question in mathematics. Teachers should offer students problems at the correct level of difficulty that arise naturally (as an example, Polya suggests finding the diagonal of a rectangular parallelepiped, using the classroom as a model[4]). The teacher should check that the student understands the problem by asking: *What is the unknown? What are the data? What are the conditions?* Further support should take the form of general heuristic questions, such as 'do you know a related problem?'

(not 'can you apply the theorem of Pythagoras?').[5] With enough practice of this sort, the student may internalize the heuristic questions and develop the confidence, commitment and intellectual stamina to tackle more demanding problems. Ultimately, says Polya, 'Teaching to solve problems is education of the will'.[6]

Polya could say all this and meet no opposition because he did not threaten anything in the self-description of mathematics and mathematicians. On the contrary, he articulated something of the experience of mathematical problem-solving and teaching in a way that resonated with mathematicians and mathematics teachers. His path was clear because in mathematics, feelings and intuitions play little or no part in the end-products (the proofs, theorems, structures and calculations). Polya was free to explore the subjective experience of mathematics researchers, teachers and students precisely because the objectivity of mathematics is not in doubt. This is not the case in philosophy. The apparently ineradicable presence of intuitions in philosophical argument and the lack of an agreed technique for resolving philosophical questions make it difficult for philosophers to claim objectivity for their arguments. This may explain why some philosophers insist on the rigour of philosophy, at the risk of protesting too much.

The knight of reason

Western philosophy traditionally sees itself opposed to mystery-mongering and intellectual chicanery. Its principal weapon against these two foes is clarity in thought and speech. This self-image is especially prevalent among English-speaking heirs to the analytic tradition, who sometimes signal this self-understanding by practicing a wilful pedantry. ('You don't really mean that you're *in two minds*. It doesn't even make sense to say that you're *in* one mind. Minds are just not the sort of things one can be *in*.' *Etc.*) In some versions of this tradition, philosophy is nothing but the activity of clarification; where other disciplines have a definitive subject-matter, philosophy has a mission. The picture of the philosopher as a knight-errant of clarity and rigour turns up in accounts of the value of academic philosophy to the taxpaying public. These accounts typically depict a world plagued with mystifying hocus-pocus and sophistical spin, in desperate need of disambiguation.

Challenges to this self-image sometimes elicit a comically shrill response. For example, the most zealous clarifiers regard Jacques Derrida as a mystery-monger of the worst sort, who peddled precisely the kind of mumbo-jumbo that philosophy is supposed to expose and eradicate. That the public should associate such a person with philosophy is intolerable. From this point of view, for Cambridge University to award Derrida an honorary degree was like appointing Mystic Meg[7] to the post of Astronomer Royal. 'Continental'[8] philosophers such as Derrida do not merely fail to write in the constipated, legalistic prose favoured by the analytic school.[9] They seem to suggest that clear speech is impossible, or at the very least, indicative of shallowness. Derrida did not merely fall short of the prevailing standards of clarity and rigour; he insinuated that the knights-errant of clarity and rigour are in fact so many Quixotes. Whether Derrida deserved either the honorary degree or the opprobrium is a question for another day. The episode is instructive for the touchiness that it exposed in his detractors. A more confident response would have been to observe with a shrug that universities often award honorary degrees to persons of uncertain academic merit.[10]

We owe the image of the scientific philosopher ministering clarity and rigour to an intellectually fallen world to the Enlightenment.[11] The lingering influence of the Enlightenment manifested in the treatment of those writers, such as Feyerabend, Duhem and Polanyi, who insist on the importance of feeling and passion in science. Feyerabend claimed that scientific progress sometimes depends on a scientist's willingness to stick with an idea in the face of all the available evidence. A new idea needs time to develop a theoretical framework that can articulate its own evidential base and respond to counter-arguments without falling into ad hoc defensive moves. For that, a new idea needs obdurate partisans who are willing to use propaganda as well as logic.[12] In other words, science will not progress if scientists always approach their hypotheses with perfectly disinterested rationality. The truth or falsehood of Feyerabend's claim is a subtle question for specialists. For our purpose, what matters is the scandalous reputation that Feyerabend enjoyed among philosophers (and he did enjoy it). Philosophers routinely disagree with each other, so the fact that they all disagreed with Feyerabend is not remarkable. The point is that they did not merely reject his view – they despised it. In the consensus of philosophers of science, Feyerabend was not merely mistaken, but dangerously and scandalously so.

Long before Feyerabend,[13] Pierre Duhem introduced feeling into the very logic of science. Rather than focussing on the scientist's passionate commitment to an idea, Duhem emphasized the scientist's feeling for the phenomena, which he called 'good sense'. Experiments often give unexpected results. In most cases, this is due to a failure in the execution or the equipment. There is fog on the lens; the chemicals are not pure; the computer software has a bug; the shielding-devices allowed some extraneous influence; *etc.* Sometimes, very occasionally, an unexpected result heralds the discovery of a new phenomenon. But, argues Duhem, logic alone will not identify these special cases.[14] Therefore, a scientist must use 'good sense' to direct the search for an explanation of the anomaly. 'Good sense' is not common sense. It is the scientist's acquired knack of judgement, like a mechanic's ear for changes in the tone of an engine or a doctor's ability to diagnose a chest complaint from the pattern of wheezes and rasps. In other words, an expert requires trained eyes and ears as well as a disciplined brain. Thomas Kuhn argued that the prevailing scientific theories of the time influence the training of the scientist's senses and intellect.[15] The scientist's convictions affect the way he or she perceives the evidence. Consequently (argued Kuhn), the defeat of one scientific theory by another is not entirely a logical process; it requires a kind of conversion experience in the scientific community.

These philosophers all gained outlaw status, except for Duhem, who was pardoned on account of his association with Quine. Philosophers of science regarded them as purveyors of dangerous doctrines, which responsible philosophers should take care to refute. Philosophers rejected as heresy the suggestion that feeling plays an essential role in scientific practice because it seemed to undermine the rationality of science. This conviction gained intensity during the 'science wars' of the 1990s. On one side were various sociologists, anthropologists and literary intellectuals who seemed to want to deny that natural science gives us a uniquely reliable kind of knowledge. A resentment of science seemed to animate them. They presented natural science as a hegemonic discourse that left no room for non-western medicine, traditional agriculture, any kind of religion or anything else that looked strange or silly from the western scientific point of view (such as art, love, altruism, consciousness and narrative explanations).[16] Ranged against these critics of science were philosophers (and some scientists) who insisted that natural science is our best source of knowledge, including medical and nutritional knowledge, and that to suggest otherwise is dangerously irresponsible. Moreover, the defenders of science argued, this is not an accident; natural science is a reliable source of knowledge on account of its rational method. Thus, the rationality of scientific method became politically important. Both sides of the 'science wars' thought that if feeling plays an important role in scientific practice then science is not wholly rational. For one side, the suggestion that science is not altogether rational gives undeserved comfort to opponents of progress.[17] The other side found the same suggestion liberating. Notice the shared assumption that rationality and feeling are mutually exclusive.

We do not have to make our minds up about philosophy of science now. The point is that this was not a debate within philosophy. It was a debate in which philosophy (or at least, English-speaking philosophy) took one side against the other, and this reveals something about that philosophy. As one unusually candid insider put it, 'To be a card-carrying philosopher of science it is almost obligatory to reject Kuhn's point of view'.[18] Specifically, one had to reject those views (attributed to Kuhn, Feyerabend and others) that seemed to contradict the conviction that science is essentially dispassionate. This a priori separation of passion from logic runs beyond the philosophy of science and back to the Enlightenment. For example, the standard starting-point[19] in philosophical psychology is the 'Humean'[20] model of the mind consisting of a 'belief box', a 'desire box' and a formal system that works out how best to satisfy the contents of the desire box given the contents of the belief box. The beliefs and desires have an experiential, aesthetic aspect – the agent feels them. But most versions of this model present the operation of the formal system (in other words, thinking) as imperceptible to the agent. Whatever its merits for the specific aims of cognitive science, this model offers little insight into the felt experience of thinking, and still less into the experience of learning to think. Polya's elation at rapid progress and depression when stymied are not present in this model (though one might tack them on as epiphenomena). Duhem's good sense and Feyerabend's scientific passion can appear in the belief and desire boxes respectively. However, the separation of felt beliefs and desires from dispassionate formal reasoning fails to do justice to the intimacy of thought and feeling that we found in Polya, Feyerabend and Duhem, and which is part of the common experience of teachers and students of philosophy.

Similarly, almost all systematic philosophy of language (written in English) sets aside the emotive or expressive aspect of language in order to explore semantics and syntax. The standard topics in philosophy of language are reference, truth-conditions, analyticity, rule-following and the like. The principal problem is (still) to explain how speakers can assert propositions, and the starting-point is still formal logic. Of course, many philosophers of language move beyond the dream of a logically perfect language. In his *Tractatus*, Wittgenstein gave an exquisite version of the view that language is a logical system, and then in later works devoted himself to explaining why it is untenable. Wittgenstein pointed out that we use language to express emotion and sensation as well as to make statements.

Indeed, he suggested that our ability to talk about our feelings originates in our natural expression of them.[21] In spite of Wittgenstein's efforts, however, the picture of human language as a system that might run just as well in a robot that did not share our feelings (if it had any feelings at all) is alive and well. It is still, in many contexts, the default position, against which dissenters must endlessly protest. We can easily locate the perennial rhetorical advantage belonging to the picture of language as a logical system to which feeling is inessential. The enduring appeal of this picture in English-speaking philosophy (and cognate disciplines) is part of our inheritance from the Enlightenment.[22] It is the philosophy-of-language correlate of the 'Humean' model in philosophical psychology. It is of a piece with the responsibility (felt by philosophers of science) to insist that science is essentially dispassionate. It is part of the theology of the Knight of Reason.

What is wrong with the Enlightenment?

Our enquiry is about teaching, and one might ask how the Enlightenment could pose a problem for teachers of philosophy. Surely, the Enlightenment ideals of dispassionate enquiry sustained by clear thought and language are precisely what philosophy should teach. Well, yes, so long as we remember that these qualities are ideals, that is, distant beacons that we should not expect to reach. An ideal is like the Pole Star. It is always available as a navigational aid precisely because we never arrive at it. The trouble with the Enlightenment is that it makes formal rationality seem like something we already have, which we only need use more carefully. On the 'Humean' model of mind, formal rationality is at work within each of us, quietly examining our beliefs in order to devise actions that will lead to the satisfaction of our desires. If we are not always rational, it is because something has distorted or hampered our natural reason. Similarly, according to 'tractarian' models of language, we have logic already built in to our grammar. If we sometimes speak illogically, it is only because we allow ourselves to be muddled. For the 'card-carrying' philosopher of science, natural science is rational (not 'tries to be' but 'is'). According to the nineteen philosophers who protested against Derrida's honorary degree, clarity and rigour are not distant ideals; they are the minimal requirement for professional philosophical status.

This idea, that humans are essentially rational, did not originate in the eighteenth century. However, it is the central thought of the movement we now recall as 'the Enlightenment'. It is the motif of Kant's major works, and finds political expression in his essay *What is Enlightenment?* The first paragraph reads:

> Enlightenment is man's release from his self-incurred tutelage. Tutelage is man's inability to make use of his understanding without direction from another. Self-incurred is this tutelage when its cause lies not in lack of reason but in lack of resolution and courage to use it without direction from another. *Sapere aude!* 'Have courage to use your own reason!' – that is the motto of enlightenment.[23]

This idea is attractive because it is egalitarian – all humans are rational, not merely a lucky few. All that enlightenment in Kant's sense requires is 'resolution and courage'. In other words, becoming rational largely consists in removing self-imposed impediments to the use of one's reason.[24] This, though, is a poor model for thinking about teaching philosophy, because it assumes that formal rationality is already present in students and lecturers alike, and needs only to be drawn out and exercised. Experimental psychology has shown this to be false.[25]

We humans (including students) live first in a world of connotations and associations, which are only later resolved into thoughts, facts, hypotheses and suchlike.[26] What is more, our world of images, feelings and meanings comes painted in ethical colours. Words and deeds, people and things strike us as admirable, mean, unfair, compassionate, and so on. Dispassionate formal rationality is not natural to us, even when we are engaged in rational activities (recall Duhem's scientific 'good sense', the passionate propaganda of Feyerabend's Galileo and the intense emotional commitment of Polya's mathematician). Scientists and mathematicians write up their theories and explanations, their theorems and proofs in dispassionate language, but the scientists and mathematicians must be passionate, or they would not subject themselves to the hard rigour of scientific rationality.

Collingwood to the rescue

So far, I have argued that English-speaking philosophy (particularly philosophy of science, logic, mind and language) struggles to recognize the emotive aspect of intellectual life, and the expressive character of language, because Enlightenment conceptions of human nature still shape it and direct it.[27] As philosophers, we would like to think about the business of teaching philosophy in philosophical terms. That is, we would like to think about teaching philosophy using resources drawn from philosophy itself, rather than having to borrow from psychology or educational theory. At the same time, we would like our philosophical pedagogy to avoid the shortcomings we found in mainstream English-speaking philosophy, hampered as it is with its Enlightenment residue. Happily, such resources do exist. As we saw already, Wittgenstein emphasized the expressive origins and function of sentences that look like reports of inner states (e.g. 'I have toothache'). However, Wittgenstein's discussion did not extend far beyond raw sensations such as pain and grief. We need a discussion of the *intellectual* passions (ironically, it is clear from his writing that Wittgenstein felt the intellectual passions unusually strongly). Also, Wittgenstein's conception of philosophical puzzlement as a kind of bewitchment that requires therapy is not the obvious basis for a philosophical pedagogy.[28] A better source for our purpose is the view of language that R. G. Collingwood set out in his *Principles of Art*.

Collingwood's chapter on language is the hinge between his philosophical psychology and his account of the nature of art. From the beginning of his discussion of philosophical psychology onwards, he sustains an electrostatic metaphor: experiences and activities (including intellectual experiences and linguistic activities) have an 'emotive charge'. Sensations typically come with an inseparable emotional aspect ('When an infant is terrified at the sight of a scarlet curtain blazing in the sunlight, there are not two distinct experiences in its mind, one a sensation of red and the other an emotion of fear: there is only one experience, a terrifying red.'[29]). He goes on to claim that modern education encourages us to attend to the sensation at the expense of the emotion, so that highly educated adults hardly notice the emotional charge of most of their sensory experience. In contrast (says Collingwood), artists and children tend to feel the emotional charge of their experiences keenly.[30] Unfortunately for our pedagogical interest, Collingwood does not identify what it is about 'modern education' that suppresses this sensitivity. His chief aim in his philosophical psychology is to develop a theory of imagination, because for Collingwood, imagination is the capacity that allows creatures who feel to become creatures who think, write books and create art.

With his philosophical psychology in place, Collingwood proceeds to elaborate his account of language. Like Wittgenstein, he claims that language begins as emotional expression, and only later becomes a vehicle for the articulation of thoughts.[31] It is a great mistake, he argues, to suppose that 'intellectualized' language or 'symbolism' (that is, language used to articulate thoughts) makes sense in isolation from its expressive function. The temptation to make this mistake arises from writing, because bad writing, and especially bad technical writing, often lacks tone.[32] Lying on the page, the formula 'H$_2$O' has no obvious emotive charge. When spoken by a teacher, it will express an emotion – perhaps boredom or excitement – and the pupils will respond accordingly. As soon as we take up 'symbolism' for some purpose, we give it an emotional charge. Collingwood makes the point by mocking one Dr. Richards, who earned his disdain by treating language as an object (rather than an activity) and then separating the scientific and emotive uses thereof. I quote at length, as the scene has a bearing on our topic:

> When Dr. Richards wants to say that a certain view of Tolstoy's about art is mistaken, he says 'This is plainly untrue.' Scientific use of language, certainly. But how delicately emotive! One hears the lecturing voice, and sees the shape of the lecturer's fastidious Cambridge mouth as he speaks the words. One is reminded of a cat, shaking from its paw a drop of water into which it has been unfortunately obliged to step. Tolstoy's theory does not smell quite nice. A person of refinement will not remain in its company longer than he can help. Hence the abruptness: those four brief words say to the audience: 'Do not think I am going to disgust you by dragging to light all the follies into which unreflective haste led this great man. Take courage; I dislike this chapter as much as you do; but it is going to be very short.'[33]

We lecturers naturally worry about the content of our lectures rather than the emotions we express in giving them. As human beings, students respond immediately to the emotive charge, even if they do not understand the content. The lecturer may have tried to give a balanced account of the debate between X and Y, but his preference for Y shines through. When the students come to write the essay on the relative merits of X and Y, they know where to put their money. The lecturer might try to balance the lecture by suppressing his enthusiasm for Y, but this 'objective' presentation will make a mystery of the whole exercise. The students will wonder why they have to sit through all this stuff about X and Y when even the lecturer does not seem to care much for either of them. The better strategy is for the lecturer to plunge into the works of X, reconstruct X's mental world and re-enact X's thoughts until he shares some of X's intellectual passions. We can be sure that X had intellectual passions, else we would not now have the works of X.

Collingwood's emphasis on the expressive character of even the most technical speech has a bearing on e-learning. At present, most electronic communication is in writing. In order to express the emotive charge on one's words (without which they will not speak to the students), one has to write well. One has to write so that the student-reader 'cannot make nonsense of [the lecturer's words] by reading them, aloud or to himself, with the wrong intonation or tempo'.[34] This strenuous literary requirement has not received much attention in discussions of e-learning. Audio recordings of lectures preserve the lecturer's tone of voice, and video captures more of the expressive performance (on the other hand, repetition can work strange transformations on these recorded performances, and in any case, well-written text has the advantage that both writer and reader go slowly).

Collingwood's chapter on language ends as this paper begins, with the emotional aspect of mathematical work. Here, he insists that 'the emotions which mathematicians find expressed in their symbols are not emotions in general, they are the peculiar emotions belonging to mathematical thinking'.[35] Earlier in the chapter, and in other works, Collingwood is rather hostile to formal grammar and logic.[36] Here, he makes peace with them (on his own terms, of course):

> The progressive intellectualisation of language, its progressive conversion by the work of grammar and logic into a scientific symbolism, thus represents not a progressive drying-up of emotion, but its progressive specialisation. We are not getting away from an emotional atmosphere into a dry, rational atmosphere; we are acquiring new emotions and new means of expressing them.[37]

Collingwood is not the whole story, of course. He does not pretend to offer a comprehensive philosophy of language (he leaves the questions about reference and assertion unanswered) and the details of his philosophical psychology may not convince. His hostility to experimental psychology deprived his view of empirical nourishment. Nevertheless, he offers a way for philosophers to think about the human process of learning and teaching from within our discipline. He suggests approaches to problems that more mainstream philosophies of mind and language struggle even to articulate.

Classroom Tips

What practical consequences, if any, follow from all this? I count five:

1. Take time to respect and develop the intuitions that students already have:
When learning formal logic, for example, students have to master conventions that do not always sit well with their understanding of natural speech. It is unnatural to read 'Some S are P' as 'Some, possibly all, S are P'. For

obvious Gricean reasons, we read 'Some S are P' as 'Some S are P and some are not'. If the lecturer brushes this intuition aside (perhaps for lack of time), the students will learn that logic is weird, that their intuitions are irrelevant and that questions are not welcome. Better to tell the students that at least one serious logician agrees with them,[38] and to explore the consequences of working this intuition into the formal system. If you have to reduce the content of the course to make time for these excursions, do it. If you turn the students on to logic, they can read about ω-completeness and paraconsistency for themselves.

2. Tell the students what is going on:
Explain that examining naïve intuitions is a standard part of what philosophers do. Explain that, when asked for their intuitions about this or that question, they are not being fobbed off with trendy teaching that promotes self-expression ahead of 'proper' learning. They are in fact doing philosophy. Explain also that philosophy gets going when our intuitions conflict. Students who feel confused because they sense the force of both ends of the conflict are actually doing well, and someone should congratulate them. (Of course, confusion is not always a sign of philosophical sensitivity.)

3. Design exercises to induce suitable intellectual experiences:
I like to teach philosophy of science using historical scientific examples. But the history of science detail often obscures the philosophy. So I introduced parlour games to allow students to get a feel for the underlying logical point. For example, I set small teams the task of defending rich-but-dubious theses of their own choice before a hostile press (played by the rest of the class). This exercise gives them a feeling for the logical complexity of refutation. Thus, they have relevant experiences and logical intuitions of their own to bring to a discussion of the Duhem-Quine hypothesis.

4. Ensure that all your material is alive:
Remember Dr. Richards on Tolstoy? If Tolstoy's view really is 'plainly untrue' then there is no point mentioning it. If Tolstoy's view is worth mentioning, then it is worth inhabiting Tolstoy's position, reconstructing his thought and thus feeling the force of his motives. Nothing less will bring Tolstoy's thought to life, which you have to do if the students are to see any point in learning about it. Victory over a corpse is no less pyrrhic than victory over a straw man.

5. Retrace the route to here:
Polya pointed out that advanced mathematical concepts can seem either arbitrary or magical until one learns how they emerged through trail

and error. There is little educational value in proofs that merely compel assent. Similarly, the philosophy curriculum will seem arbitrary without some effort to contextualize its content. Philosophical questions do not spring from nowhere and philosophical texts do not make sense in isolation. Moreover, the students' reflections on their intuitions will be rudderless unless the students appreciate enough of the history of the problem in hand to see why some putative solutions are regarded as serious while others have been discarded.

These few tips do not amount to a pedagogy. But they may indicate the typical consequences of including 'acquiring new emotions and new means of expressing them' among our educational aims.

Notes

1. Polya (2004), p. 207.
2. Polya (1954), volume II (*Patterns of Plausible Inference*) p. 147.
3. Polya (1954), volume II (*Patterns of Plausible Inference*) pp. 144–145.
4. Polya (2004), p. 7.
5. Polya (2004), p. 22.
6. Polya (2004), p. 94.
7. The in-house astrologer at *The Sun*, a British daily newspaper. In 1992, the University of Cambridge awarded Derrida an honorary DLitt. Nineteen philosophers signed a letter of protest, citing Derrida's failure to meet accepted standards of clarity and rigour.
8. The analytic/continental distinction makes little sense as it contrasts a methodological bent with a geographical area. It is, as Bernard Williams put it, 'like classifying cars as Japanese and front-wheel drive' (Williams (2006), p. 201). As he points out, the geography is misleading, since some of the principal sources of analytic philosophy arose in the German-speaking world.
9. To take an arbitrary example of the style:

   > For the only objection brought above against this account was that it failed to establish that Wittgenstein was committed to denying that it is possible for the majority of speakers of a given language to go wrong because it seems to them that they mean something quite definite by their words though in fact they do not (Holzman and Leich (1981), pp. 9–10).

   Someone careful with language wrote this sentence. No-one who cares for language could have.
10. For a list of honorary doctorates awarded by the University of Cambridge, see *http://www.admin.cam.ac.uk/univ/degrees/honorary/* last viewed on 27/03/08.
11. 'Other men are carried away by their passions; their actions are not preceded by reflection: they are men who walk in darkness. A philosopher, on the other hand, even in moments of passion, acts only after reflection; he walks through the night, but is preceded by a torch.' (Diderot (1965), pp. 284–285). The metaphor

of the light of (scientific) reason as an all-too-easily-extinguished candle recurs frequently. See for example Sagan (1995). In the eighteenth century, natural science was still called 'natural philosophy'.

[12] See *Against Method* (1975), in which Feyerabend considers Galileo's defence of Copernican astronomy against the tower argument (if the Earth is moving, why does a stone dropped from a tower fall in a straight vertical line?). The observational evidence was all against him until he could persuade people to look at matters his way. That is to say, Galileo needed propaganda to introduce a novel observational framework. Even then, Copernicans had to explain why no-one observed stellar parallax until Bessel in 1838.

[13] See Oberheim for Feyerabend's debt to Duhem.

[14] Duhem (1954), pp. 216–218. Duhem carefully restricted his discussion to those disciplines whose experimental instruments embody theories drawn from physics (pp. 182–183), but when he wrote this book (1905) there were few exceptions to this criterion and there are fewer still now.

[15] Kuhn (1970). Kuhn seems to have acquired this view from the French historian of science Alexander Koyré, who in turn got it from Husserl. See Larvor (2003).

[16] Feyerabend makes a version of this argument, but he makes it clear that he is not against science or reason; rather he is against people bullying other people and using words like 'science' and 'reason' to do it. Crucially, *scientists* are sometimes bullied in this way, to the detriment of science and humanity.

[17] See, for example, Bricmont and Sokal (1998); Gross and Levitt (1994); Stove (1982).

[18] Forster (2000), p. 231.

[19] Of course, many philosophers and psychologists have moved beyond this starting-point – this is not the place to do justice to individuals. *The discipline as a whole* shows its prejudices in choosing the 'Humean' position as the point of departure.

[20] Inverted commas represent doubts about the extent to which Hume was committed to the 'Humean' model of mind.

[21] 'Here is one possibility: words are connected with the primitive, the natural expressions of the sensation and used in their place. A child has hurt himself and he cries; and then adults talk to him and teach him exclamations and, later, sentences. They teach the child pain-behaviour'. 'So you are saying that the word "pain" really means crying? – On the contrary: the verbal expression of pain replaces the crying and does not describe it.' Wittgenstein (1953), §244.

[22] Of course, 'the Enlightenment' is the name of a historical complex; the Scottish Enlightenment was different in temper from the French Enlightenment, and both from the German Enlightenment. Moreover, the major philosophers of the period were much more subtle than broad-brush treatments of 'the Enlightenment' suggest (see footnotes 20 and 24). However, we are here concerned with the discipline of philosophy as a whole. At this level of magnification, broad-brush treatment is appropriate.

[23] Kant (1963), p. 3 (first published in 1784).

[24] In fairness, 1784 also saw the publication of Kant's *Idea for a Universal History*. Here, Kant argued that 'those natural capacities which are directed to the use of [man's] reason are to be fully developed only in the race, not in the individual' (1963 p. 13).

[25] See Plous (1993) for a summary of the research.

[26] The Capgras delusion (believing that your family have been replaced by replicas) and Cotard delusion (believing that you are dead) arise when subjects experience empirical sensations without feeling the corresponding emotions. For example, a subject might see his or her spouse without feeling anything beyond what one would feel in the presence of a stranger. See Capgras, J. and Reboul-Lachaux, J. (1923); Cotard, J. (1882).

[27] Of course, the Enlightenment left traces in other philosophical cultures too. The discussion here is restricted to English-speaking philosophy in order to limit the (already generous) scope of its generalizations.

[28] See Wittgenstein (1953), §121ff, §309. One might argue on Wittgenstein's behalf that the fly who has escaped from the fly-bottle is richer in wisdom than the fly who never went in, but there is little in Wittgenstein to licence this extension of his view and some reason to doubt that he would approve of it.

[29] Collingwood (1938), p. 161.

[30] Collingwood (1938), pp. 162–163.

[31] 'In its original or native state, language is . . . an imaginative activity whose function is to express emotion.' Collingwood 1938 p. 225.

[32] Collingwood (1938), pp. 264–265.

[33] Collingwood (1938), p. 264.

[34] Collingwood (1938), p. 265.

[35] Collingwood (1938), p. 268.

[36] In a footnote to his *Autobiography*, he mentions that 'frightful offspring of propositional logic out of illiteracy, the various attempts at a "logical language", beginning with the pedantry of the text-books about reducing a proposition to logical form', and ending, for the present, in the typographical jargon of *Principia Mathematica*. Collingwood (1978), pp. 35–36.

[37] Collingwood (1938), p. 269.

[38] Blanché (1953). See Larvor (2004). In a similar spirit, Luciano Floridi thinks that students who fail simple tests on material implication are in fact competent Bayesians.

References

Blanché, R. (1953) 'Sur l'opposition des concepts' *Theoria* vol. 19 pp. 89–130.

Bricmont, J. and Sokal, A. D. (1998) *Fashionable Nonsense: Postmodern Intellectuals' Abuse of Science.* New York: Picador USA.

Capgras, J. and Reboul-Lachaux, J. (1923) 'L'illusion des "sosies" dans un délire systématisé chronique' *Bull. Soc. Clinique de Médicine Mentale* 11, pp. 6–16.

Collingwood, R. G. (1938) *The Principles of Art.* Oxford: Clarendon Press.

—(1978) *Autobiography.* Oxford: Oxford University Press. First published in 1938.

Cotard, J. (1882) 'Du délire des négations' *Arch Neurol* 4:152–170, pp. 282–296.

Diderot, D. (1965) *Encyclopedia: Selections by Diderot, D'Alembert, and a Society of Men of Letters.* (Tr. by Nelly S. Hoyt and Thomas Cassirer) Indianapolis, New York and Kansas City: Bobbs-Merrill.

Duhem, P. (1954) *The Aim and Structure of Physical Theory.* (Tr. Philip Wiener) Princeton: Princeton University Press.

Feyerabend, P. (1975) *Against Method*. London: New Left Books. (Third edition containing additional material: Verso 1993).

Forster, M. R. (2000) 'Hard problems in the philosophy of science: idealisation and commensurability' in Nola and Sankey (eds) *After Popper, Kuhn and Feyerabend: Recent Issues in Theories of Scientific Method* pp. 231–250. Dordrecht: Kluwer Academic Publishers.

Gross, P. R. and Levitt, N. (1994) *Higher Superstition: The Academic Left and Its Quarrels with Science*. Baltimore: The Johns Hopkins University Press.

Holzman, S. and Leich, C. (eds), (1981) *Wittgenstein: To Follow a Rule*. London: Routledge and Kegan Paul.

Kant, I. (1963) *On History*. New Jersey: Macmillan. White Beck (ed.).

Kuhn, T. S. (1970). *The Structure of Scientific Revolutions* (second edition). Chicago: University of Chicago Press. (first edition 1962).

Larvor, B. (2003) 'Why did Kuhn's *Structure* cause a fuss?' in *Studies in History and Philosophy of Science*, vol. 34/2 pp. 369–390.

—(2004) 'The case for teaching syllogistic logic to philosophy students' *Discourse* Vol. 4 No. 1 pp. 130–136. Reprinted in Gil, Lancho and Manzano (eds) (2006) *Proceedings of the Second International Congress on Tools for Teaching Logic*.) pp. 81–86.

—(2006) 'Students are human beings (discuss)' *Discourse* Vol. 6 No. 1 pp. 225–236.

Oberheim, E. (2005) 'On the historical origins of the contemporary notion of incommensurability: Paul Feyerabend's assault on conceptual conservativism' *Studies in the History and Philosophy of Science* 36 pp. 363–390.

Plous, S. (1993) *The Psychology of Judgment and Decision Making*. New York: McGraw-Hill.

Polya, G. (1954) *Mathematics and Plausible Reasoning*. Princeton: Princeton University Press.

—(2004) *How to Solve It: A New Aspect of Mathematical Method*. Princeton Science Library Edition with a new foreword by John Conway. (Original publication 1945.)

Sagan, C. (1995) *The Demon-Haunted World: Science as a Candle in the Dark*. New York: Random House.

Stove, D. (1982) *Popper and After: Four Modern Irrationalists*. Oxford: Pergamon Press.

Williams, B. (2006) *Philosophy as a Humanistic Discipline*. A. W. Moore (ed.). Princeton: Princeton University Press.

Wittgenstein, L. (1953) *Philosophical Investigations*. Oxford: Blackwell. (Tr. Anscombe).

—(1961) *Tractatus Logico-Philosophicus*. New York: Humanities Press. (Tr. D. F. Pears and B. F. McGuinness).

Student Interlude III

I have witnessed and experienced numerous methods of teaching philosophy in the classroom. To my surprise, the most applicable and sublime insights often arrived via a round of beers and hot wings at the local pub or outside the classroom in some unexpectedly creative and kind way. The compassion and insight philosophers are capable of is profound, but rarely put into action. This is an incredibly ironic and disappointing situation to find oneself in when all their life they have only wanted to seek continuous understanding in an open, non-hierarchical, fun, and inspiring manner.

In traditional philosophy classrooms we are taught to sit quietly and listen. Those who follow this implicit rule are recognized and rewarded. We are groomed within what Paulo Freire called the 'banking system of education' where the teacher knows more than the student and is there to instruct only, fill the student's empty, ignorant head with *how* to think, *how* to speak, *what* to know, and *how* to live 'well'. I have often been made to feel intellectually inadequate unless I was studying my Greek, Latin, or formal logic, for example. Analytic philosophy is necessary and useful, but it is only half the story (if even that) of the history of philosophy, and of profound philosophical insights that have and can change humanity in an affirmative manner.

Instead, I wanted to dialogue, wanted to express and discuss the truths as I have lived and understood them, and listen to how others have experienced their truths. I wanted to enact what the philosopher George Yancy now advocates in his classrooms: a *pedagogy of Parrhesia* or fearless speech. Instead, I have typically, but not always, been at a disadvantage in some way for not fitting into the white, male-dominated mold of what it means to be a 'philosopher'. This seems to be the case only with Western philosophy. It is my hope (and duty) that we begin to transcend borders, boundaries, horizons, gates and, most of all, limits, leaving the door unlocked in case our neighbors need a friend, instead of remaining in the realm of symbols, traditional texts, logic exams, and the confinement of your 'average' or traditional philosophy classroom.

Christina Rawls,
Duquesne University, USA

Chapter 10

Philosophy and Education for Wisdom

Maughn Gregory and Megan Laverty

Since philosophy is the art which teaches us how to live, and since children need to learn it as much as we do at other ages, why do we not instruct them in it? . . . They teach us to live when our life is over.

Michel de Montaigne[1]

Wisdom and education

Though rarely mentioned in the documentation of curriculum objectives or educational standards, wisdom is an educational aim that most educators, parents and students acknowledge. In spite of the tremendous resources we spend to help our children and students acquire sufficient knowledge and skills to make their way in the world, to contribute to society, to make the most of their talents, and even to make their mark on the world, hardly anyone believes that these aims constitute the full value of education. Additionally and perhaps most importantly, we hope that education contributes to making our children and students wise, in the sense that they will learn to make good judgments, to cope with life's vicissitudes, to find their 'moral compass,' and in other ways to live well. In both professional and amateur educational discourse, wisdom has the status of an ultimate aim or a meta-objective of education: an objective to which other objectives contribute. Though it often goes unnamed, this meta-objective is made evident by such trans-disciplinary and non-academic educational objectives as the development of good character, responsible citizenship, critical-thinking acumen, socio-political tolerance and appreciation of ethnic and religious diversity – each of which has spawned countless grant initiatives and curricular programs.

Since antiquity educational philosophers have both called for education to focus on wisdom and have criticized educators and educational programs that focused on more materialistic and mundane objectives at the expense of teaching students to cultivate their own wellbeing. For instance, Pierre Hadot notes that in ancient Athens,

> Sophists had claimed to train young people for political life, but Plato wanted to accomplish this by providing them with a knowledge . . . inseparable from the love of the good and from the inner transformation of the person. Plato wanted to train not only skillful statesmen, but also human beings.[2]

Contemporary scholars like Jerome Bruner, Wifred Carr, Nicholas Maxwell, Nel Noddings, Parker Palmer and Robert J. Sternberg[3] have also called for schools to prepare young people, not only to *perform* well academically, athletically, artistically and technologically, but to *live* well, with meaning and purpose.[4] Noddings, for example, has argued that the primary purpose of schooling is to help individuals become capable of caring for themselves, their ideas and their environment, as well as for their families, friends and larger communities.[5]

There are numerous obstacles to bringing education to aim at wisdom, including: regulative restrictions typified by the No Child Left Behind Act; increased standardization of educational interventions and outcomes; economic demands for greater educational efficiency; the constant threat to colleges of education presented by alternate route certification and detractors from the disciplines; the diminishing role of teachers as curricular and pedagogical experts; and the demands of students and parents for more idiosyncratic choice in educational content and format. Many of these obstacles both arise from and give rise to a largely unarticulated view that the primary purpose of education is to prepare students to be successful at pursuing relatively unexamined desires in a free-market economy. In Sternberg's words:

> Education is seen more as an access route . . . not so much toward the enhancement of . . . learning and thinking as toward obtaining through education the best possible credentials for individual socioeconomic advancement. Education is seen not so much as a means of helping society but of helping one obtain the best that society has to offer socially, economically, and culturally.[6]

What is needed to counteract this view and these obstacles is a shared understanding of the kinds of wisdom-oriented objectives that education ought to aim for, as well as strategies that teachers can use toward those aims. We contend that philosophy is an important resource for both.

Philosophy as a wisdom practice

Philosophy first evolved, in Asia and in the West, as a wisdom tradition – as the study and practice of *living well* – a deceptively simple phrase that, nevertheless, differentiates wisdom-oriented philosophy from most other modes of philosophical practice, e.g. theory and epistemology, that have comprised the greater part of academic philosophy since medieval times.[7] Whereas most philosophical practices aim at some kind of knowing or understanding, wisdom-oriented philosophy aims at a far-reaching transformation of the self. Thus, Richard Shusterman recommends 'the idea of philosophy as a deliberative life-practice that brings lives of beauty and happiness to its practitioners,'[8] and observes that 'philosophy's solutions to life's riddles are not propositional knowledge but transformational practice'.[9]

The Stoics distinguished three inter-related components of living wisely,[10] which make a useful heuristic for organizing the theories and practices of other wisdom-oriented philosophers: a moral component: living ethically, virtuously and with integrity; a psychological component: enjoying peace of mind in the midst of chaos and tribulation; and an intellectual component: disciplined thinking and the construction of a value-oriented vision of the world and one's place in it. The Stoics correlated these three aspects of wellbeing with the disciplines of ethics (behaviour), physics (perspective) and logic (thinking), each of which involved both a theoretical and an applied or lived component.[11] This tripartite distinction corresponds roughly to earlier distinctions found in Plato and Aristotle: *phronesis, sophia* and *episteme*, and to contemporary distinctions in the literature of wisdom psychology: virtue (socially valued behaviour), goodness (personally desirable states or conditions) and cognitive excellence.[12]

A life that is morally, psychologically and intellectually wise – the life of the sage – is arduous, unpopular and unachievable in any complete sense. This points to another set of aims for wisdom-oriented philosophy: to bring about the two ontological states that characterize the philo-sopher: *irony* – knowing that one's way of life is not, or not completely wise, and *eros* – longing for wisdom and being drawn to those who exhibit it to some extent.[13] Only as profound experiences and not merely as theoretical constructs do these states active the willingness to change one's life, and so constitute aims of wisdom-oriented philosophy.

The unique methods philosophers have used to reach these aims con-stitute further distinguishing characteristics of wisdom-oriented phil-osophy. We will describe three categories of these methods: intellectual, contemplative and active,[14] each of which includes a number of techniques. Intellectual wisdom practices include study and inquiry. Historically, one of the most important practices of philosophical study was pedagogical dialogue with a philosopher who could tailor the dialogue to the particu-lar questions and existential attitudes of the students,[15] and could form a loving relationship with them.[16] Pedagogical dialogue, as well as the study of wisdom literature and the lives of eminent philosophers, is meant to the-oretically inform students, but more importantly, to transform their way of life.[17] Philosophical *inquiry* as a wisdom practice applies methods such as observation, research and investigative dialogue to two primary objects: the nature of wisdom itself – what it means to live well – and a worldview that constitutes an explanatory context for one's wisdom practices. The production of knowledge as a means to the practice of good living[18] is a dis-tinguishing characteristic of wisdom-oriented philosophy recommended by some contemporary philosophers.[19]

Since ancient times the practice of inquiry dialogue – dialogue as a rigorous, collaborative search for truth or meaning – has been not only the most important method of wisdom-oriented philosophical inquiry, but the defining framework for all other methods. This is so because the dis-cursive nature of dialogue serves both rational and ethical functions, as Hadot explains:

> [N]either one of the interlocutors imposes his truth upon the other. On the contrary, dialogue teaches them to put themselves in each other's place and thereby transcend their own point of view. By dint of a sincere effort, the interlocutors discover by themselves, and within themselves, a truth which is independent of them . . . This *logos*, moreover, did not represent a kind of absolute knowledge; instead, it was equivalent to the agreement which is established between interlocutors who are brought to admit certain positions in common . . .[20]

Discursive rationality requires mutual exchange, questioning, critique and assistance, all voluntary and conducted within a framework of cooperative inquiry towards a *logos* of unconstrained agreement. This process requires a particular dialogical ethics, characterized by humility, respect for others and a regard for truth, making it a 'spiritual exercise,'[21] or wisdom prac-tice that stands in sharp contrast to the competitive, self-serving and often histrionic debates that typify political, courtroom, and even classroom discourse.

Contemplative wisdom practices include discursive practices like self-examination,[22] mutual exhortation,[23] contemplation of death[24] and of nature,[25] as well as non-discursive practices like meditation, present-moment mindfulness,[26] somatic awareness and attention to emotions, that deliberately disengage discursive thinking. Such practices often bring insight but their primary purpose is not intellectual, but rather to bring the philosopher to experience certain existential states associated with wisdom, such as autonomy, tranquility, inter-connectedness and compassion.

Active wisdom practices may be sub-divided into somatic disciplines, ceremonial practices and everyday conduct and comportment. Somatic discipline is both negative – the curbing of unhealthy cravings and habits – and positive – training in the direction of improved bodily function, form and feeling.[27] Performative exercises have to do with regulating one's actions and interactions to make them beautiful, honourable and satisfying experiences. The emphasis of the ancients on accomplishing one's duties[28] belongs to this category.

An important characteristic of wisdom-oriented philosophical practices in all three categories is the establishment of the philosophical community, which, Hadot observes, is integral to wisdom-oriented philosophical practice:

> [A]ncient philosophy was always a philosophy practiced in a group, whether in the case of the Pythagorean communities, Platonic love, Epicurean friendship, or Stoic spiritual direction. Ancient philosophy required a common effort, community of research, mutual assistance, and spiritual support.[29]

Philosophical community makes possible pedagogical and inquiry dialogue, as well as the practice of collaborative research and other forms of discursive rationality.[30] In addition, sharing meals and living in common facilitates the practices of mutual concern, care and correction, and thus of mutual example – since wisdom is a way of life – and the cultivation of intimate philosophical friendship, 'the spiritual exercise *par excellence*,'[31] that is both a means and an end of these practices.

Though academic philosophy has mostly deviated from these wisdom practices since the Middle Ages, two contemporary developments in philosophy are reorienting it toward the disciplined pursuit of wisdom. One is the rise within the academy in the popularity of schools of philosophy like pragmatism, feminism and continental philosophy which recognize the philosophical inquirer as an individual both embodied with desires and aversions, functions and malfunctions, and embedded in complex social, political, economic and ethnic contexts. The second is the development, mostly outside the academy, of what we are calling the applied turn in philosophy: the growth of philosophy cafes, philosophical counselling, business and medical ethics, philosophy with children, and other forms of philosophical practice. These programs have made philosophical concepts like justice, personhood, friendship, society, and the good, as well as methods of philosophical inquiry such as wondering, questioning, speculation, thought-experiments, hypothetical reasoning and logical analysis, more transparent and widely available. The result has been a renaissance of philosophy as a participatory activity that engages individuals in the search for meaning and wisdom. However, though gaining increasing support and momentum, these developments in philosophy have had a limited impact on schools and colleges.

Philosophy and education

The ways philosophy might help to turn education toward wisdom fall into three categories or spheres of influence. The first is the sphere of educational policy and curriculum standards, in which philosophers can contribute to professional and public understandings of the kinds of education appropriate to various aspects of human flourishing, and can criticize cultural phenomena that tend to turn education away from those ends. This was, in fact, the first way philosophers became involved with education: thinking philosophically about education's aims and methods, the nature of learning and thinking, the nature and status of knowledge, the educational responsibilities of students, parents, teachers and governments, and relationships between education and systematic theories of epistemology, ethics and social justice. Philosophers like Plato, Aristotle, Augustine, Montaigne, Rousseau, Kant, Dewey and Whitehead did not consider themselves philosophy of education specialists, but considered education to be intimately related to metaphysics, aesthetics, ethics, political theory and other areas of philosophical concern.

Unfortunately, this tradition has not continued to the present day. Since philosophy of education became a recognized academic field[32] philosophers of education have generally worked in colleges of education and been isolated from other philosophy faculty. Consequently, their discourse has been largely self-contained, with too little interest in, or participation from other philosophers – who worry that philosophy of education is not properly philosophical[33] – and from non-philosophical academics in education, who worry that philosophy's lack of a foundation in the social sciences makes it pedagogically irrelevant. In the 1950s analytic philosophers of education such as Paul Hirst, R. S. Peters, Denis Phillips and Israel Scheffler carved out a new role for their discipline: to overcome confusion, ambiguity and self-contradiction in educational theory and research by clarifying concepts and dispelling logical fallacies. This role had two components: the application of general philosophical theories such as freedom, punishment and authority to educational contexts and the development of educational terms such as 'knowledge,' 'indoctrination' and 'learning,' into philosophical theories. Analytic philosophy of education became a resource for the 'professionalization' of education, which, though beneficial to both disciplines, confirmed the judgment of mainstream philosophers that philosophy of education was not properly philosophical, for 'to apply philosophy is not thereby to do it'.[34] Also, the analytic preoccupation with logical and conceptual groundwork diverted philosophical attention away from such substantive issues as educational aims.

In spite of these historical setbacks, philosophers of education still have a role to play in steering educational aims and methods toward wisdom, as the work of Noddings and Sternberg demonstrate. This role includes addressing educational policy and standards directly, as John White recommends:

[T]he idea that education should equip pupils to lead flourishing lives and also help others to do so is, not surprisingly, very much to the fore. Where policy makers need help is in giving valid substance to this fine-sounding ideal, in detaching it from interpretations that fail to pass muster. This is where philosophy of education comes in.[35]

The role also includes wider cultural criticism: interrogating economic, social and political forces that make educational experiences repugnant and usurp them for ends that are undemocratic and otherwise unsuited to wellbeing.[36] The audience for such criticism is not limited to educational researchers and policy makers, but must include teachers, parents and often the entire community.

The second sphere in which philosophy might guide education toward wisdom is that of teaching, including curriculum design and pedagogy. The study of philosophy can guide teachers, teacher educators and

curriculum designers to engage students in critical and creative thinking and inquiry dialogue, and to find opportunities across school subjects to bring students' attention to ethical, aesthetic, political and other
areas of concern to human wellbeing.[37] The introduction of philosophy
of education coursework in teacher education was initiated in the U.S.
at the end of World War II, when the need for elementary and secondary teachers increased and programs of teacher education became more
disciplinarily informed.[38] England incorporated philosophy of education
into teacher education in the mid-1960s, and Australia followed suit in the
early 1970s.

Philosophical foundations courses typically introduce students to the
writings of canonical and contemporary philosophers relevant to education, with three major objectives: to show students how educational concepts like teaching and learning, addressed by psychology and the social
science, can also be approached philosophically; to introduce students to
philosophical methods of inquiry – especially textual exegesis, dialogue
and argumentative reasoning; and to call on students as future teachers
to conceive and articulate their own philosophies of education. These
objectives are eminently suited to teaching for wisdom, but this has neither
been the intent nor the result of these programs, for a number of reasons.
Philosophy of education typically disposes pre-service teachers to question
received knowledge by introducing them to a range of divergent traditions.
The result is that many students conclude that there are 'no right or wrong
answers' in philosophy and struggle to appreciate the discipline's relevance to education. Another problem is that, because pre-service teachers
typically have no background in philosophy and take no more than one or
two philosophy of education courses, their work in these courses is 'min-
imally philosophical'.[39] Pre-service teachers are usually not in a position
to asses the educational ideas of the philosophers they read – which often
strike them as antiquated or absurd – and find it difficult to discern the
relevance of philosophy to such contemporary issues as classroom management, inclusion, diversity and differentiated learning.

The decline of the analytic approach in the 1980s[40] became the catalyst
for two developments in philosophy of education that had ramifications
in teacher education. The first was an 'applied philosophy' approach to
education. Believing that philosophy of education 'should focus on practical problems of education',[41] many philosophers wrote position papers
and taught issues-based courses that explored educational policies like
zero-tolerance, the teaching of evolution and creationism, teacher sexual harassment of students and disability. Though useful in many ways,

this approach presents several obstacles to the orientation of education towards wisdom: its focus on practical problems often precludes consideration of wider concerns; the language and arguments are often highly technical; it is tailored for an audience of administrators, policy makers and other philosophers; and its emphasis on contemporary issues can result in short-lived solutions with few lasting insights.

The second post-analytic development was a shift in thrust of the work of many philosophers of education, from 'foundational' to 'anti-foundational', following the post-modern turn and the politicization of knowledge that occurred with Marxism, the Frankfurt School and feminist philosophy. The turn here was against not only the methods and claims, but in many cases against the aims of modern philosophy, to produce knowledge that is systematic, universal and certain – in a word, against the possibility of objectivity. Post-modern philosophers of education have taken part in a shift of emphasis in teacher education from reasoning to equity. Slowly but steadily, colleges of education have replaced critical thinking courses with courses in diversity, multi-culturalism and social justice. This trend has important advantages for philosophy's role in both the sphere of educational policy and standards, and the sphere of teaching and teacher education. Philosophers of education have returned to reckoning with education's implications in broad socio-political issues, with particular focus upon ethics and justice. This is a necessary development for the orientation of education toward wisdom. Furthermore, this work has been enriched by insights, concepts and methods of continental philosophy, feminism, critical theory, queer theory and race theory. Indeed, the field of educational theory has become much more multi-disciplinary, with particular advantage to the disciplines of English, sociology, history and political science. Teachers are being prepared to be more 'culturally responsive,' to beware of curriculum and pedagogy that is politically oppressive, and to prepare their students to be agents of social change.

Two inter-related disadvantages of anti-foundational philosophy of education are, first, that it can devolve into value relativism, and second that it often looses sight of the continued value of reasoning and other methods of inquiry that aim at some kind of objectivity. As Rene Arcilla explains, the quintessentially post-modern question, '*Whose values?*' compels individuals to 'adopt a polemical position' towards values that are not their own, proceeding from the recognition that they are in a struggle for limited resources.[42] In our experience, teachers often mistakenly assume that aiming for diversity, novelty and equity in their lessons is inconsistent with aiming for relevance, consistency, criticism, reliance on evidence and reasoned judgment; and that teaching for individual responsibility and self-governance is incompatible with teaching for collective responsibility and solidarity. In order for philosophers of education to underwrite the aim of wisdom, we must help prepare teachers to understand these sets of values as complimentary, and to construct curriculum and pedagogy that brings them together in a creative tension that informs the lives of their students.

Philosophy's third sphere of influence in education, the students themselves, is the one in which it has had the least influence, in spite of the fact that young people's engagement in certain kinds of philosophical practices constitutes the most direct approach to their education for wisdom. Historically, the most important endeavour of this kind has been the critical thinking movement – another post-analytic 'applied philosophy' approach to education. Beginning in the 1970s many educational foundations courses were required to focus on the teaching and learning of critical thinking, and philosophers argued that teaching thinking was within their domain of expertise because philosophy 'is the only discipline that has thinking as both its *subject* and its method of *inquiry*'.[43] Among the most influential figures in this movement were John Chafee, Robert Ennis, Matthew Lipman, Richard Paul, Harvey Siegel and Stephen Toulmin.[44] One of the most innovative aspects of the critical thinking movement was that it brought one aspect of philosophical practice not only to teachers, but also to children and adolescents. Taxonomies of critical thinking skills and dispositions were developed as curriculum objectives and reasoning became the 'fourth R' of education.[45] Interest in critical thinking spawned numerous educational conferences and teacher education textbooks, and changed the way school textbooks were written and classroom pedagogy was conducted. Importantly and somewhat ironically, critical thinking is the only movement initiated in the field of philosophy of education that was at once championed by non-philosophers – many of whom claimed critical thinking as part of their professional expertise – and influential in academic philosophy, as philosophy departments began to offer 'informal' logic courses patterned on, and even named as 'critical thinking,' as components of undergraduate general education programs.

By the 1990s, however, enthusiasm for critical thinking had begun to fade within education, due to a number of factors. There was residual scepticism within the philosophical community that children – in particular young children – could think critically. Also, academics in the arts and sciences joined a growing number of cognitive scientists in arguing that what constitutes critical thinking is so context-specific that it can only be taught within each discipline.[46] Further, the very ubiquity that marked the great success of the critical thinking movement contributed to its decline, as curriculum specialists, policy makers, text and test writers and teachers came to believe, rightly or wrongly, that they practice and promote critical thinking as a matter of course, without the need of further inquiry and practice – least of all under the supervision of philosophers. Finally, philosophy's post-modern turn in the 1980s and 1990s was partly a turn away from the epistemological commitments that define critical thinking: that certain methods of inquiry – e.g. deductive and inductive reasoning, seeking alternative views, maintaining relevance, accountability to peers, identifying fallacies, uncovering assumptions, evaluating evidence and self-correction – constitute certain kinds of objectivity. For many post-modernists, the very attempt to distinguish inquiry as a type of discourse that aims at certain kinds of objectivity, from other types of discourse such as persuasion and negotiation, was suspect.

Some philosophers of education responded to these criticisms by reconstructing analytic theories and methods of critical thinking. bell hooks articulated a theory of critical thinking as a collective liberatory practice, drawing on the work of Paolo Freire.[47] Matthew Lipman developed a tripartite conception of critical, creative and caring thinking.[48] Barbara Thayer-Bacon incorporated pragmatist, analytic and feminist epistemologies into her concept of 'constructive thinking'.[49] These post-analytic approaches view critical thinking not as a discrete set of universal and value-neutral skills and procedures, but as methods of discourse useful for certain, limited, culturally valued operations. Each of these approaches emphasizes dialogue as the ideal discursive format for the exercise of critical thinking, for its being tempered by other ways of knowing, for its contextualization in human concerns and projects, and for its being learned and habituated as modes of both inner and outer discourse. These developments underwrite the importance of the teaching of reasoning for wisdom-oriented education. Thinking that is both appropriately dispassionate and appropriately moved by the passions is necessary to human wellbeing, particularly in regard to questions about what constitutes one's wellbeing and how to pursue it.

Philosophy and education for wisdom

Education in critical and creative thinking, emotional perspicacity, dialogical prowess, democratic interaction and other procedures is necessary but not sufficient for children to become wise. They also need to study wisdom's content; to inquire directly into what makes a worthwhile life. As Sternberg has it, wisdom-based education involves students in the study of values, with the objective, 'not . . . to force-feed a set of values but to encourage students to reflectively develop their own.'[50] In other words, children themselves need to practice philosophy as the search for wisdom.

The longest-running, most globally widespread, and most age-diversified pre-college philosophy program is Philosophy for Children,[51] initiated by Matthew Lipman in the late 1960s. While this program involves only some of the practices mentioned above, it does so in ways that exemplify the third sphere of philosophy's role in education for wisdom. The program operates – with considerable variation in practice – according to a five-stage method[52] developed in the early 1970s by Lipman and Sharp for engaging children in philosophical inquiry:

1. Students read or enact a philosophical story together.
2. Students raise questions for discussion and organize them into an agenda.
3. Students dialogue about the questions as a *community of inquiry* facilitated by an adult with philosophical training. Discussion continues over subsequent philosophy sessions until the agenda for the reading is finished, or until the students agree to move on to next reading.
4. The philosophical facilitator introduces relevant activities to deepen and expand the students' inquiry.
5. The facilitator guides the students in conducting a self-assessment of their philosophy practice, and in applying their new understandings, e.g. in art or action projects.

The central practice of Philosophy for Children is the *community of inquiry*, a practice of collaborative dialogue that engages young people in clarifying terms, creating and testing hypotheses, giving and evaluating reasons, questioning assumptions, drawing inferences and other cognitive practices, as well as sharing perspectives, listening attentively, helping others make their point, challenging and building on other people's ideas and other social practices. These practices meet Sternberg's recommendation that wisdom-based education place particular emphasis 'on the development of dialectical thinking [which] involves thinkers understanding significant problems from multiple points of view and understanding how others legitimately could conceive of things in a way that is quite different from one's own'.[53] As Sharp explains, the community of philosophical inquiry instantiates the ethics of discursive rationality:

Participation in such a community fosters an ability to put one's ego in perspective [which] not only allows for children to be able to attend to each other's views, but also their needs (emotional, social and cognitive) and to learn the importance of being open to alternative possibilities . . . This ability is an outgrowth of the group work . . . Classroom communal inquiry can only foster wisdom if the participants can overcome a narcissism that blocks the ability to care for one another's thoughts and feelings, to seriously take each other's perspectives into account and to develop the capacity for empathy . . .[54]

The Philosophy for Children facilitator – typically the classroom teacher who has studied and practiced the method – neither leads the children to predetermined answers nor attempts to validate every opinion as equally sound. Instead, she models and prompts excellent cognitive and social dialogue moves, helps the students to see the structure that emerges in each dialogue, and encourages them to follow the inquiry where it leads, i.e. in the direction of the strongest arguments and evidence, including the evidence of their feelings and experiences. In this way the classroom teacher practices the kind of pedagogical dialogue developed in the ancient wisdom schools and recommended by Sternberg.[55]

The goal of the children's original inquiries in Philosophy for Children is for them to arrive at one or more *reasonable philosophical judgments*[56] regarding the issues and questions they have identified as most meaningful. In learning the rudiments of rigorous, open-ended and democratic dialogue, the students come to understand that arriving at judgments that are not only intellectually satisfying but personally meaningful and practically ameliorative will require each person to reconstruct or 'self-correct' the ideas and feelings with which she began at least partially. Sternberg concurs that 'Carried out over time, dialectical thinking involves thinkers' understanding that ideas and the paradigms under which they fall evolve and keep evolving, not only from the past to the present, but from the present to the future'.[57] This expectation of perpetual fallibilism is an important resurgence of Socratic *irony* and *eros* that constitute existential aims of wisdom-oriented philosophy.

The program's value orientation derives from the way it construes philosophy itself: as a yearning or wondering toward truth or meaningfulness, with implications for the students' everyday lives. The program materials (philosophical novels and supplementary dialogical exercises) occasionally focus on questions about what it means to live well, but additionally, questions having to do with ethics, aesthetics, epistemology, politics and other philosophical domains are also raised as issues consequential to children's experience.[58] Philosophy for Children relies on the Deweyan notion that these are aspects of most people's ordinary experience rather than remotely intellectual or esoteric subjects,[59] and on the awareness advanced by Lipman that children's experience is just as replete with these philosophical dimensions as is that of adults. Although the program has been utilized for educational objectives such as improved reasoning, creativity and social skills,[60] advocates of the program see these benefits as auxiliary to the benefit of children having the chance to conduct their own philosophical inquiry: to become aware of the aesthetic or the ethical in their own experience, to share their puzzlement and excitement, to inquire into the problematic, and to learn how to make sense of it all for themselves – to formulate their own judgments about what is what, and how things relate, and how their experiences could become more just, more beautiful, more meaningful. These objectives place Philosophy for Children in the tradition of philosophical wisdom practices. In an educational system that took wisdom as an indispensable aim, programs like this would be considered pinnacle experiences, for which other kinds of learning prepare students, rather than valued or not as instrumental or even supplemental to types of academic performances that have no necessary connection to students' immediate or future wellbeing.

Notes

1 Montaigne (1991), p. 183.
2 Hadot (2002), p. 59
3 Sternberg (1999).
4 'One of the purposes of education in a democratic society is to equip people for a flourishing life. As part of this aim they also become better qualified to make judgments about human flourishing.' White (2007), p. 25.
5 Noddings (2003a and 2003b).
6 Sternberg (1999), p. 62.
7 Pierre Hadot convincingly demonstrates that 'philosophy was conceived, from the Middle Ages onward, as a purely theoretical attitude.' (2002), p. 6.
8 Shusterman (1997), p. 3.
9 Ibid., p. 25.
10 Hadot summarizes these components as 'a complete transformation of his representations of the world, his inner climate, and his outer behavior.' 1995, 85–86. 'What is needed is the immediate transformation of our way of thinking, of acting, and of accepting events. We must think in accordance with truth, act in accordance with justice, and lovingly accept what comes to pass.' Ibid., p. 229.

11 '[T]he distinction between theory and practice is located within each of the parts of philosophy; there is a theoretical discourse concerning logic, physics and ethics, but there is also a practical or lived logic, a lived physics, and a lived ethics.' Arnold I. Davidson in introduction to Hadot (1995), p. i24.

12 Csikszentmihalyi, M. and Rathunde, K. (2003). The psychology of wisdom: An evolutionary interpretation. In R. J. Sternberg (ed.), *Wisdom: It's nature, origins and development* (pp. 25–51). New York: Cambridge University Press, cited in Sternberg (1999).

13 'Eros the *daimon* . . . embodies desire, for, like Socrates, he is aware that he is neither handsome nor wise. This is why he is a *philo-sopher* – a lover of wisdom. In other words, he desires to attain to the level of being of divine perfection . . . He suffers from being deprived of the plentitude of being, and he strives to attain it.' Hadot (1995), p. 162.

14 See Hadot (1995), p. 86.

15 'In oral discourse, there is the concrete presence of a living being. There is genuine dialogue, . . . and an exchange in which, as Plato says, discourse can respond to the questions asked of it and defend itself. Thus, dialogue is personalized: it is addressed to a specific person, and corresponds to his needs and possibilities.' Ibid., p. 163.

16 'Quite apart from the dialectical movement of the logos, the path traveled together by Socrates and his partner, and their common will to come to an agreement, are already a kind of love.' Ibid.

17 'He [Plato] did not aim to construct a theoretical system of reality, and then 'inform' his readers of it . . . Instead, his work consisted in 'forming' people – that is to say, in transforming individuals by making them experience . . . the demands of reason, and eventually the norm of the good.' Hadot (2002), p. 73.

18 Hadot observes that in antiquity 'people who developed an apparently philosophical discourse without trying to live their lives in accordance with their discourse, and without their discourse emanating from their life experience, were called "Sophists".' 2002, pp. 173–174.

19 Shusterman argues, 'If philosophy takes for its pragmatist goal not the grounding of knowledge but the production of better lived experience, then it need not be confined to the realm of discursive truth and the language-games of their justification. Philosophy can aim more directly at the practical end of improving experience by advocating and embodying practices which achieve this.' Shusterman(1997), p. 173.

20 Hadot (2002), p. 63.

21 '[T]he ethics of dialogue . . . for Plato is the spiritual exercise par excellence . . .' Ibid., p. 69.

22 '[E]ach time Marcus wrote down one of his *Meditations*, . . . he was exhorting himself to practice one of the disciplines: either that of desire, of action, or of assent. Hadot (1995), p. 201.

23 'In Epicurean communities, friendship also had its spiritual exercises . . . These include . . . mutual correction, carried out in a fraternal spirit; and examining one's conscience.' Ibid., p. 89.

24 'We can also see here the role played in Epicureanism by the thought of death . . . [I]t is precisely this exercise of becoming aware of life's finitude which reveals the

infinite value of the pleasure of existing within the present moment.' Ibid., pp. 225–226.

25 'Some [spiritual exercises], like the contemplation of nature as practiced in all philosophical schools, turned the soul toward the cosmos . . .' Ibid., p. 101.

26 '[T]he theme of the value of the present instant plays a fundamental role in all the philosophical schools. In short it is a consciousness of inner freedom. It can be summarized in a formula of this kind: you need only yourself in order immediately to find inner peace by ceasing to worry about the past and the future.' Ibid., p. 69.

27 Shusterman argues that 'the most radical and interesting way for philosophy to engage somatics is to integrate such bodily disciplines into the very practice of philosophy. This means practicing philosophy not simply as a discursive genre, a form of writing, but as a discipline of embodied life. One's philosophical work, one's search for truth and wisdom, would not be pursued only through texts but also through somatic exploration and experiment. By acute attention to the body and its nonverbal messages, by the practice of body disciplines which heighten somatic awareness and transform how one feels and functions, one discovers and expands self-knowledge by remaking one's self.' Shusterman (1997), p. 176.

28 Hadot (1995), p. 84.

29 Hadot (1995), p. 274. Elsewhere Hadot explains that 'There can never be a philosophy or philosophers outside a group, a community – in a word, a philosophical 'school' [which] corresponds, above all, to the choice of a certain way of life . . .' Hadot (2002), p. 3.

30 'Life in the Academy implied constant intellectual and spiritual exchange not only in dialogue, but also in scientific research. This community of philosophers was also a community of scholars, who practiced mathematics, astronomy, and political reflection. Even more than the Platonic school, the Aristotelian school was a community of scholars . . . It meant leading the life of a scholar and a contemplative, and undertaking research, often collective, on every aspect of human and cosmic reality . . .' Ibid., pp. 178–179.

31 Hadot (1995), p. 89.

32 Chambliss (1968) traces this development to the nineteenth century, whereas Kaminsky (1986) dates it with the inauguration of the John Dewey Society in 1935.

33 Pollack argues, for instance, that 'problems in education lack philosophical heaviness. There is nothing particularly metaphysical about them; neither are they especially epistemological, moral, or what have you in mien.' Pollack(2007), p. 245.

34 Pollack (2007), p. 246. His following sentence is: 'Application of philosophy is exogenous to philosophical activity itself; it comes after the fact.'

35 White (2007), p. 17.

36 Pollack argues: 'A philosophy of education can . . . be constructed around the purpose of laying bare the socio-philosophical assumptions underlying educational practice . . . Only thus will a clearer picture emerge of the forces at play in shaping our ongoing and evolving educational commitments . . . For the deeper beliefs underlying prevalent practice may turn out, on critical reflection, to be inept, incoherent, or otherwise ill-begotten and in need of revision, overhauling or adjustment. Pollack (2007), pp. 257 and 258.

37 Sternberg (1999) recommends, for instance, that 'students . . . be encouraged to think about how almost everything they study might be used for better or worse ends and to realize that the ends to which knowledge are put do matter,' (p. 80) and gives examples of how this might be done in history, science, literature and foreign language classes. (p. 81).

38 The Philosophy of Education Society formed in 1941 and in 1951, the John Dewey Society and the College of Education at the University of Illinois launched the journal, *Educational Theory.*

39 Peters (1983), p. 33.

40 Peters describes this decline as follows: 'The subject, so it now seems to me, was stimulated into life by this initial rush of philosophical blood to the head, and then its arteries began to harden. It settled down to a rather pedestrian period tidying up and trying to improve on existing analyses and arguments.' Peters, p. 33.

41 Siegel (1981a), p. 130.

42 Arcilla (1995), p. 141.

43 Beyer (1990), p. 55. Beyer further explains: 'Philosophical thinking is critical thinking, which means a willingness (indeed a predisposition) and an ability to scrutinize and evaluate thinking – one's own as well as others' – to determine truth, accuracy and worth and to construct logical arguments to justify claims or assertions.' Ibid.

44 See, e.g., Ennis (1989), Lipman (1988), and Paul (1987).

45 Harvey Siegel, 'The Future and Purpose of Philosophy of Education' *Educational Theory* (1981b) 31 (1), p. 11.

46 See, e.g. Willingham (2007).

47 See hooks (1994) and (2003).

48 See Lipman (2003), Chapters 11 and 12.

49 Thayer-Bacon (2000).

50 Sternberg (1999), p. 80.

51 The phrase 'Philosophy for Children' was coined by Matthew Lipman and Ann Margaret Sharp in the early 1970's. See *www.montclair.edu/iapc*, last accessed 5/5/08. Practitioners around the world today use phrases like 'Philosophy with Children,' '. . . with Children and Adolescents,' '. . . in Schools,' and '. . . for Young People,' to refer to their own work; however, in the literature these phrases are also often used to refer to any program that engages children in philosophical dialogue (as opposed, especially, to programs for teaching older children the history of philosophy). Unless otherwise indicated, we use the phrase 'Philosophy for Children,' in the latter sense, to refer not only to the materials and methods developed by Lipman and Sharp, but to similar programs, whether or not originally derived from Lipman and Sharp.

52 Lipman rearticulated the method in Lipman (2003), pp. 101–103.

53 Sternberg (1999), pp. 79–80.

54 Sharp (2007), pp. 5, 10 and 11.

55 'In a wisdom-based approach to teaching . . . teachers would . . . take a much more Socratic approach to teaching [in which] students take a more active role in constructing their learning [and] reconstruct knowledge from the point of view of others.' Sternberg (1999), p. 80.

56 See Gregory (2007), pp. 160–171.

[57] Sternberg (1999), p. 80.
[58] See Gregory (2007), pp. 2–6.
[59] Dewey writes, for instance, that 'the work of art develops and accentuates what is characteristically valuable in things of everyday enjoyment. The art product . . . issues[s] from the latter, when the full meaning of ordinary experience is expressed . . . A conception of fine art that sets out from its connection with discovered qualities of ordinary experience will be able to indicate the factors and forces that favor the normal development of common human activities into matters of artistic value.' Dewey 1989, p. 17.
[60] See Lipman, et al. (1980), Chapter 5, and the list of studies under the link 'Research on Philosophy for Children,' at the IAPC website *www.montclair.edu/ iapc,* last accessed 5/3/07.

References

Arcilla, R. V. (1995), *For the Love of Perfection: Richard Rorty and Liberal Learning.* New York and London: Routledge.

Chamblis, J. J. (1968), *The Origins of American Philosophy of Education: Its Development as a Distinct Discipline.* The Hague: Martinus Nijhoff.

Dewey, J. (1989), *The Later Works, 1925–1953, Vol. 10: 1934 Art as Experience.* Carbondale: Southern Illinois University Press (Jo Ann Boydston, series ed.).

Ennis, R. (1989), 'Critical Thinking and Subject Specificity: Clarification and Needed Research', *Educational Researcher,* 18 (3), pp. 4–10.

Gregory, M. (ed.) (2007), *Philosophy for Children Practitioner Handbook.* Montclair: Institute for the Advancement of Philosophy for Children.

Hadot, P. *What is Ancient Philosophy?* Cambridge: Harvard University Press.

—(1995), *Philosophy as a Way of Life: Spiritual Exercises from Socrates to Foucault;* ed. Arnold I. Davidson, trans. Michael Chase Malden: Blackwell Publishing.

hooks, b. (1994), *Teaching to Transgress: Education as the Practice of Freedom.* New York: Routledge.

—(2003), *Teaching Community: A Pedagogy of Hope.* Oxford: Taylor & Francis, Inc.

Kaminsky, J. S. (1986), 'The First 600 Months of Philosophy of Education – 1935–1985: A Deconstructionist History,' *Educational Philosophy and Theory,* 18 (2), 42–49.

Lipman, M. (2003). *Thinking in Education,* 2nd Edition. Cambridge: Cambridge University Press.

—(1988) 'Critical Thinking – What Can it Be?' *Educational Leadership,* 46 (1), 38–43.

Lipman, M., A. M. Sharp and F. S. Oscanyan. (1980): *Philosophy in the Classroom,* 2nd Edition. Philadelphia: Temple University Press.

Montaigne, M. de. (1991), *The Complete Essays,* trans. by M. A. Screec. New York: Penguin.

Noddings, N. (2003a), *Caring: A Feminine Approach to Ethics and Moral Education.* Berkeley: University of California Press.

—(2003b) *Happiness and Education.* Cambridge: Cambridge University Press.

Paul, R. (1987), 'Dialogical Thinking: Critical Thought Essential to the Acquisition of Rational Knowledge and Passions,' in J. Baron and R. Stenberg (eds.): *Teaching*

Thinking Skills Theory and Practice. New York: W. H. Freeman and Company, pp. 127–148.

Peters, R. S. (1983), 'Philosophy of Education' in Paul H. Hirst (ed.), *Educational Theory and its Foundations Disciplines.* Boston: Routledge.

Pollack, G. (2007), 'Philosophy of Education as Philosophy: A Metaphilosophical Inquiry,' *Educational Theory,* 57 (3), 239–260.

Shusterman, R. (1997), *Practicing Philosophy: Pragmatism and the Philosophical Life.* New York: Routledge.

Siegel, Harvey (1981a), 'How "Practical" Should Philosophy of Education Be?' *Educational Studies,* 12 (2), pp. 125–134.

—(1981b) 'The Future and Purpose of Philosophy of Education' *Educational Theory,* 31 (1), 11–15.

Sternberg, R. J. (1999), 'Schools Should Nurture Wisdom' in B. Z. Presseisen (ed.), *Teaching for intelligence.* Arlington Heights: Skylight Training and Publishing, pp. 55–82.

Thayer-Bacon, B. J. (2000), *Transforming Critical Thinking: Thinking Constructively.* New York: Teachers College Press.

White, J. (2007), 'Wellbeing and Education: Issues of Culture and Authority', *Journal of Philosophy of Education,* 41 (1), 17–28.

Willingham, D. T. (2007), 'Critical Thinking: Why is it so Hard to Teach?' *American Educator* (Summer 2007), 8–19.

Chapter 11

Pedagogy of Recovery

Maya Levanon

Introduction

My journey as a truth seeker, whether within the academic context or elsewhere, has brought me to participate in different group-settings, as a leader, a facilitator, participant or a guest. While I usually avoid categorizing experiences, knowing how the interdisciplinary quality blueprints our lives, I can still identify events, people or readings, that have been more influential than others. Generally speaking, I have been especially intrigued by constructivist epistemologies,[1] as these can be manifested in different realms, e.g. education and therapy, being epistemologies that in their subversive way have blurred the traditionalist boundaries between learning and healing, synergize both processes into a 'growing' one.

Throughout my ongoing endeavour with dialogical spaces I noticed that being fully engaged dissolves the separation between learning and recovering: When we genuinely learn, we partake in an ongoing recovery from the unexamined life, rescued from the asylum ignorantiae; by the same token, when we put ourselves completely in recovery, we learn who we are, what we want or what our limitations are.

While industrial capitalism trained us to approach life in terms of survival of the fittest, an alternative outlook teaches us to approach life as a form of art (Hadot, 1995; Nehamas, 1998). This path shows us how to construe and act within active yet cooperative, progressive and critical agencies. Mastering this art means seeing life's challenges as immense opportunities to leap forward, transforming from worriers to warriors.[2]

This transformation however requires a shift from solitary anxiety to comradeship, which is not to suggest failing to take responsibility or losing one's individuality.[3] Indeed we can identify a tension between the contemporary emphasis on individualism, that goes along with alienation and mistrust, and the innate longing to relate, manifested in the increasing numbers of socio-eco-architecture, international festivals, co-ops, support groups, the return to community-based religious values, even chat-rooms and instant messaging (Forman, 2004; Heelas, 1996; Heelas and Woodhead, 2005).

One interesting trend is the revisit of the Circles: a primeval setting, where members sit for conflict-resolution, learning, spiritual growth, even illumination. I call it 'the human mandala'. As a tool, the mandala facilitates understanding of our inner, archetypal world, where different rungs contribute different elements taken from our conceptualized experiences, and where the most significant aspect is situated in the centre. Likewise, in a circle of people set for the purpose of inquiry, each person represents a different angle and mode of thinking, while the centre remains empty, allowing it to be reloaded with communally constructed meanings. This structure emphasizing epistemological equality can be now found in educational, healing and casual settings.[4]

Despite their differences these circles share participants' motivations to transcend their present selves into more refined ones. In these circles there is a natural flow, and discursions are valued, as they reflect the different facets of human thinking and perennial concerns.

Quest Circles facilitate the development of new ways of thinking, communicating and knowing since they encourage participants to re-examine how presuppositions, beliefs and feelings control and shape their conduct. Following the constructivist approach, participants in Circles find new insights and build additional epistemologies by hearing new cognitive voices and ways of thinking, which they later implement in various contexts. Furthermore, although it is commonly argued that human development is stage-driven (e.g.: Erikson, 1980; Piaget, 1977), when we are fully aware of the process, and of those who surround us, development becomes an ongoing endeavour. Participating in the two forms of Circles discussed in this paper (i.e. Community of Inquiry, and Twelve-Step meetings) is a commitment to processes rather than to single events.

After briefly examining the history, characteristics and purposes of Community of Inquiry (Lipman, 2003), and of Twelve-Step meetings I will then explore the similarities and differences. I will argue that since their similarities are fundamental to their essence, for example the understanding that learning, growth and recovery are all ongoing processes, I will suggest practitioners on both sides should learn from the similar structures.

I employ critical self-narrative in addition to conceptual analysis as a methodology. In critical self-narrative the author speaks with a subjective, personal voice, revealing her mind-set and beliefs throughout the writing process (Carter and Doyle, 1996), and her personal experiences, as these resonate the issue inquired. Since both education and recovery platforms strive to ground theories in practice, I find this method of research especially appropriate.

Community of inquiry

The term 'community of inquiry' (henceforth CI) was imported to the educational realm by Dewey (1916/1968), whose pioneer implementation of democratic, constructivist principles in education emphasized the relevancy of lived experiences to learning. As a progressive, democratic pedagogy, CI invites students to participate in an invigorating learning process, based on the idea that taking an active role in an agenda rooted in students' interests, talents and narratives, does not only construe meaningful knowledge, but also improves students' thinking and social skills. Furthermore, by providing students with a genuine sense of ownership, they become empowered individuals with a healthy sense of self as related to others (Dewey, 1916/1968; Noddings, 1984).

My experience with CI started with Philosophy for Children, a program that aims at promoting philosophical thinking skills among children of different ages, while using CI as its pedagogy (Lipman, 2003). Additionally, I implemented this pedagogy in all of my philosophy courses, both at undergraduate and graduate levels, as well as with professional educators. It is important to understand though that for me, especially within the educational context, philosophy is not merely a sterile analytical body of knowledge, but a method of thinking, asking and inquiring; a method that encompasses and paves the path to further disciplinary inquiries. Another important premise in my educational philosophy, is that people are innately philosophical in that we ponder upon what traditionally has been associated with philosophy, yet we do not always have the time and place to explore these issues. In CI we are given this rare opportunity to wonder out aloud, hearing others doing the same, and by doing so continue an ancient dialogue. Inquiry is intrinsically a social act then, in that it is based on language and meaning, hence, practicing it in the agora way, advances the inquiry and the inquirers further. Additionally, and that is especially true for philosophical inquiry, is that as a dialectical endeavour we strive to see the whole picture. Exchanging different perspectives and inquiring together expands our epistemological references, i.e. our ways of knowing, asking and inquiring, and thereby reinforces the philosophical nature of the inquiry itself.

Though we can find numerous progressive pedagogies and curricula occupied with meta-cognition, CI is unique in that it marries critical ontology with holistic epistemology. Additionally, what makes CI stand out as a pedagogy is its aptitude to reach further, by celebrating different styles of thinking, knowing and being, given its premise of cooperative equity as opposed to liberal equality. While the latter stands for sterile aesthetic idealistic symmetry, equity lives within an imperfect reality while aspiring to meet students' different talents and needs, an idea that mirrors what we hope to find on the macro-level in an open-society,[5] where different voices and colours that fabricate the social quilt are recognized and embraced.

While liberal conceptualization of equality aims at classroom stability, CI, as a pragmatic manifestation of the dialectic, thrives on the *Dasein*, appearing as asymmetrical disequilibrium. As such it emphasizes the process over an explicit product. And so while its inquisitive *telos* prescribes an aspiration to arrive at a destination, whether having a clearer understanding or some answers, given its dialectic *ontos*, there is an awareness of the transient nature of things. Echoing our state of being, this special place of a cognitive un-ease enforces the inquisitive process, if simply because knowledge is the product of a healthy conflict (Dewey, 1916/1968; Palmer, 1987), which requires us to listen fairly, empathetically and actively; recognizing the other and her ideas. This is a very powerful transformative apparatus because not only does it enable us to be receptive, but in fact it reveals a whole new spectrum of possibilities that go beyond our limited cognitive habits. In this very place where dialogue transpires, ideas are being exchanged and synthesized, participants grow and so is the community as an organism.

This dynamic reminds us that 'dialogue' means that it is 'through words' that new ideas are born and entitled with meanings. This cooperative spirit is alien to modern ways. But perhaps now, when witnessing the expansion of corporate business culture into realms that are so intrinsically foreign to everything this 'culture' represents, e.g. education,[6] it is high time to emphasize alternative ways to the *homo homini lupus* mind-set, ways that understand that it takes a village to raise meaningful knowledge.

Whether CI decides on things based on consensus decision-making,[7] democratic procedures or a combination of both, the decision that has been made is always open to re-examination, similar to how the individuals in it are encouraged to reflect upon their personal views and positions. In other words, CI is an engagement that requires and provides opportunities to become reflective, humble and courageous. This introspection provides not only personal growth but also ongoing conciliation of ideas, thoughts, dreams and needs. Getting to a particular daily decision then, does not mean disregarding others; though a daily agenda can be promoted, minorities' rights are protected by the very nature of CI, which allows possibilities for change. Keeping this ideal in mind, CI allows participants, often for the first time, to hear other opinions and cognitive voices.

Earlier I argued that though we can find pedagogies and methods that advance the development of thinking skills, what makes CI different is that it celebrates differences, and thereby mediates not only the different community's voices but also those found within oneself. CI is like an entity with different organs that in order to function needs them all, while each maximizes its potential. Similar processes are essential for the individuals who constitute CI: to graduate from it is to synergize one's cognitions, emotions, social, political and spiritual skills.

As a nurturing pedagogy, CI brings together these intra-personhood aspects, respecting the individual and her particular needs, while recognizing that individuals are in turn part of a communal-social setting, hence the importance of nurturing inter-personal aspects as well. Within this public sphere participants are like citizens with rights and duties, and in that sense one of the CI's tasks is to enable participants to become active, confident, influential social agents.

Trying to encapsulate the essence of CI, I would suggest seeing it as a process of mutual dialogical learning, where following the Socratic tradition, participants tap into their inner wisdom and innate knowledge. CI is a channel that respects its participants as whole, reflective, ever-changing, active, talented, wise persons. By valuing participants' diverse talents, potentials and needs, we are logging into a classic tension, a tension between liberal and progressive education, and the tension between communal and individual needs in society in general. By facing this tension though, participants develop life-skills (e.g. active listening, suspending judgment, expressing emotions in public, healthy curiosity), while internalizing important values (e.g. tolerance, compassion, respect).

Although learners construe knowledge while using their personal biographies in CI, they are nevertheless asked to relate them to the agenda, when sharing experiences. Making those imperative connections can take place throughout the discussion itself, or by applying different opening activities, where participants bring the outside world into the circle in order to learn from each other, but also in order to become present. In my classroom, for example, we start by using rituals that signal us to bring our minds and hearts to the here and now, so we are ready to learn and discover.

Twelve-Step meetings – background

Originally developed by individuals who were seeking help in their journey toward sobriety, the Twelve-Step program (henceforth the 'Program') aims to provide guiding principles ('Steps' and 'Traditions') as well as mutual support in recovering from varied addictions and other compulsive behavioural problems. The Steps were first published in the late 1930s, in the first edition of *Alcoholics Anonymous*; since then more than 25 million copies have been printed globally. Participating in the Program includes admitting one's inability to control one's addiction/compulsion, recognizing a higher power that can provide strength, examining past mistakes with the help of a sponsor, making amends for these mistakes, learning to live with a new code of behaviour, and finally, helping others with similar issues.

Founders trace their initial inspiration to an American-based evangelical movement (The Oxford Group) back in the 1920s. The ethical premises of this group included honesty, purity, unselfishness and love, while emphasizing personal work done with other members, understanding that a shackled person cannot free himself. The autarkical body created was a hybrid between solitary work and searching for outside help.

The founders understood the importance of being non-denominational, open to anyone who seeks help. Though the Program acknowledges all three human dimensions (physical, mental and spiritual), and addiction as a symptom of disharmony in all three, it is considered spiritual since it emphasizes the importance of belief in a higher power, though it does not specify it.

In terms of practice, although the message of recovery has been translated to various addictions, and different groups run the meetings slightly differently, yet, generally speaking, meetings are restricted to particular addictions in order to avoid denial and distraction, and they normally open with sharing experiences, fears and ideas how to cope. Realizing they are not alone in their struggle, this practice infuses members with hope and encouragement. There is also a work with a sponsor, a veteran in the Program, who supports a newcomer throughout this challenging process.

Common threads

As stated earlier, it is my intention to draw upon the similarities between the two forms of gathering discussed here, namely CI and the Twelve-Step-meetings, as two forms of quest circles that although teleologically differ-ent, nevertheless share some fundamental attributes.

First, it is important to notice that both structures approach their engagements as ongoing journeys; furthermore, in both we can find a spiral movement from recovery – from substance abuse, ill-behaviour or ignorance – towards discovery, whether sobriety or knowledge. Both jour-neys, like any other, begin with one step, of self-acknowledgment. There is a sense of crisis, whether existential, essential to the addict in order to start looking for help, or epistemological, the Aporia, essential to begin-ning a shared inquiry.[8] Naturally, these crises may be interconnected, where in both the individual faces an abyss in front of which s/he has to learn how to build a new orientation that will become an immanent part of the process of allocating meanings.

In my discussion of CI, I argued that though it is a process-orientated practice, given its *telos*, participants do aspire to arrive at some destination. Yet, we find an ideological tension between these inquisitive and the dia-lectical natures. A similar tension can be found in the Program, where working the Program is understood as an ongoing life-endeavour, yet there is a clear understanding of destination (e.g. sobriety). Furthermore, as mentioned earlier, although the message of recovery has been translated to different addictions, meetings are limited to particular ones, in order to overcome distraction, similarly, while in CI there are digressions, an experienced group knows where and when to make a 'homerun' with the initial inquiry/question.

Another layer of that tension is that in the same way as 'understanding' and 'knowledge' are transient, the state of sobriety can be, which expresses itself in 'relapses'.[9] Relapse does not mean going back to square one, just like questioning one's knowledge does not; it is a dialectical movement that although frustrating, in fact forwards us in spiral movements, like in a dialogical inquiry (Vygotsky, 2002). Indeed the danger in both lays in an exceeding amount of frustration that can raise feelings of failure, anger and despair.[10] In other words, both CI and the Program provide an intro-spective platform and subsequently growth opportunities, yet, it is essen-tial to take this delicate journey with a guide, someone that will lend a hand in the more challenging moments, showing how to approach those challenges as breakthrough opportunities.

When working the Program, having a sponsor – and then sponsoring others – is essential. The sponsor is a veteran in the Program, who is familiar with the recovery process, and thus provides a newcomer with necessary support. Coming full circle, reaching the twelfth step means sponsoring a newcomer yourself. It is important to understand though that for many these relationships never end, as the need to attend meetings does not, yet, despite this core difference, the facilitator in the CI is an individual who has more experience and knowledge about the inquiry process and the journey towards knowledge. So we see that both the sponsor and the facilitator are not 'experts' but stewards.

In the Program we also find Tradition 8:[11] '(Alcoholic) Anonymous should remain forever non-professional, but our service centers may employ special workers'. CI is an answer to the culture of experts' hegemony, where students and facilitators cooperatively decide the daily agenda, having ownership over their learning process, knowing that their voices matter. In other words, there are no experts in the CI, as there are none on the Program.

This approach deconstructs the power structure usually found in groups (Aronowitz and Giroux, 1991; Foucault, 1980), bringing autonomy, empowerment and the inevitable responsibilities that come along. The relationships in both contexts are unique: though they are intimate, since closeness and trust are developed and eventually become immanent; they are different from counselling and friendship. The sponsor has a single purpose: to help those being sponsored to recover from behavioural problems; doing this advances the sponsor's recovery process as well; similarly, the facilitator's role is not about being the students' friend or counsellor; in fact, within the educational context this potentially violates some regulations. Instead, it is about building I-Thou relationships with each student individually, and with the CI as an entity, where the facilitator is a legitimate participant, genuine to the dialogue and to the Socratic learning process, where she merely 'midwifes' knowledge from within others and herself.

And if knowledge is innate, then in addition to working with a sponsor/facilitator, and attending group meetings/a classroom, there is a great emphasis on personal growth, resulting from personal work. Both in the Program and in the classroom setting, we know that everyone needs times alone as much as we need time in the togetherness. In the Program we find 'quiet time' for meditation, and in the CI we find time for solitary activities that advance reflection, much needed in order to question, process, synthesize and impersonalize new ideas we have just heard.

One of the most powerful solitary tools is journaling, which like 'journey' stems from the Latin for 'day', and taking these journeys is indeed about taking them one day at a time. Within the constructivist view of knowledge, where language is intertwined with one's sense of identity, journaling is especially relevant since it challenges our concept of this identity, which we often take for granted. Seeing identity as more liquid, allows us to envision our next evolutionary stage. In the Program, the journal is a personal safe heaven for exploration; in education new forms of qualitative research, often referred to as auto-ethnography, or simply 'autobiography' ('of a learner' 'of a teacher'), invite students to find their voices. My colleagues and I ask students to keep a journal, and to dedicate a section of their thesis to their-story; as constructivist educator, I want students to develop intimate relationships with knowledge and ways to access it, so it becomes immanent and meaningful. While tests and final papers examine one's knowledge, and perhaps even ability to think critically, inviting learners to be-in-the-process while reflecting on their present, promotes meta-reflection, which is necessary for a genuine growth. Both in recovery and learning then, journaling is a means for empowerment, where the writer sees her life as a story worth telling, where she is the hero and the author.

We see how important solitary work is for the processes of growth and recovery, but what about group-work? When individuals share personal past and present experiences, fears and hopes, forgotten/suppressed stories are brought to the surface, and can now be processed. In the Program commenting and reacting to others' stories is forbidden; it is like listening to oneself, and thus passive listening, where we can hear our stories in theirs. In CI, as a pedagogy that is strongly influenced by Dewey's philosophy of education, participants bring and share their personal experiences; connecting those with the subject at hand, they construe knowledge upon their stories. This can be done through the discussion itself, but also through an opening activity, whose purpose is that participants share tensions, worries and days full of experiences; since here commenting on each other is allowed and even encouraged, they either find solutions through their peers, or at least they are now able to leave what is un-necessary out of the 'sacred space.' I begin this centreing with chiming a Tibetan bell, its ancient sound signals everyone to bring our minds and hearts to where our bodies are to the circle. Not only does this bring our full awareness to the present, it also brings everyone together.

This dynamic between 'alone' and 'togetherness' echoes the tension found in the modern state, where we keep questioning what our priorities and obligations are: toward our personal growth, development and happiness; or is it towards the larger community? This tension stems from the understanding that indeed we need alone-time, yet, some fundamental human activities, behaviours and dispositions are shaped within the social matrix: different skills, though they may be innate in their raw form, become fully developed through social activities and practices (Vygotsky, 2002). This happens in the I-Thou, where my ideas are being expanded and fused with those of the other, with whom I conduct an open-ended[12] dialogue (Gadamer, 1993). In those unique moments we move from our intra-psychological phase toward the inter-psychological one; we further our capacity to solve problems alone by solving new, more complex problems with others. As a social activity, participants adopt roles, based on their opinions, beliefs and styles of thinking and communicating; yet, in an authentic dialogue, we are encouraged to examine new possibilities, expanding our epistemological spectrum as well as our ontological Being-in-the-world. While in a CI this process includes internalization of others' ideas and cognitive voices, so that later we can employ them to our personal future uses, in Twelve-Step meetings, although 'cross talk' is forbidden, as discussed earlier, expansion of one's sense of references occurs when hearing others' sharing.

For the I-Thou to take place, we need a place where we do not only feel not threatened or judged, but where we feel welcome for who we are, where our ideas and experiences are valued, where we can regain our voices and sense of self. We need a 'safe-space': a platform 'where it is safe for their [teacher] souls to show up and make a claim on the work they do' (Palmer, 2003, p. 380). Though 'safe-space' often has a primary purpose, it is not exclusive for sharing concrete concerns or particular issue; rather, these are places where participants, through a subtle balance between casual and profound ambience, grow as individuals who naturally have philosophical and spiritual questions. Having these questions at different stages in life, some are either afraid of dealing with them, or cannot afford the time and money to do so. Many of us need a local group that meets in a mundane context, where we realize we are not alone in our experiences, feelings and questions, which in itself has a calming and empowering effect. A few years ago, while keeping a teaching journal, I realized how often I was professionally confused simply because I had no one to share and compare my experiences and dilemmas with; I then understood the relevancy of 'safe-space'.

In my different professional contexts, I use different activities, from self-portrait collage, through journaling, to more philosophical thinking exercises (e.g.: 'what makes me "me?"' or self-interview) – all aim at self discovery. I often hear elevated sighs, and encouraging words, suggesting that professional adults who run 'ordinary' lives need this safe-space to explore and inquire without feeling threatened, where they can share and open up without feeling manipulated. We all need those spaces to relax, to let go, to connect. We live in such an alienated society; some of us live as strangers in our own homes, others literally live alone. In such reality, we often find it easier to open up in a more seemingly neutral environment.

Another dimension worth examining when speaking about the unique atmosphere that is essential for a successful establishment of the two forms of gathering, is their ethical foundations. The ethical foundations of the Twelve-Step Program are honesty, purity, unselfishness and love (though today, in some groups we might find a different discourse), aiming at replacing the addicts' destructive self-centredness with a moral conscious-ness and willingness to constructive behaviours. The same foundations are found in CI, even if we here employ a different terminology, e.g. instead of love we talk about caring and nurturing pedagogy, or instead of purity we talk about a genuine search for truth, or unselfish inquiry.

Another ethically related principle the two forms of gathering share is the way in which participants introduce themselves or are being introduced. In the Twelve-Step meetings individuals present themselves by their first names only, following one of the Traditions according to which principles come before personalities, while following the first Step which requires taking ownership of one's problem. In CI participants go through a seem-ingly similar process, when some practitioners put students' names next to their question. I will get back to this in the next section.

Nurturing pedagogy recognizes that though feelings and ideas may be individual, they are in fact initially developed and processed within the social matrix, and thus, a nurturing pedagogy strives to advance intra and inter-personal skills. In other words, one of the tasks of the CI is preparing students for the 'real world',[13] where they will function as influential, active citizens. In the Program we meet a similar idea, where the foundation of the work assumes whole-recovery, that is, the addict returns to her social context, including working, having sober friends and healthy relationships, managing one's financial affairs etc.[14]

Additionally, as mentioned earlier, the Program is strictly non-denominational, based on religious freedom, where everyone can grow spiritually by meeting herself through others, in a sacred space. CI, though democratic pedagogy, within the context of public school system in the US it has to avoid bringing religious beliefs to the table. Yet, in my integral educational view, doing so is artificial; hence, in my practice with adults, I challenge and question positions and beliefs, not for the sake of changing them, but rather, following the philosophical tradition, in order to be able to build knowledge from scratch. We have to remember that both in CI and in Twelve-Step meetings, participants are encouraged to examine the ways in which the collective presuppositions, beliefs and feelings in fact control and shape their interactions and reactions. Through a constructivist yet caring approach, they find insights through and with others. In other words, in both forms of the examined Circles, participants grow by meeting new skills and narratives, and slowly applying them to their personal conduct.

The differences

Though similar in many ways, we cannot expect two social institutions to be identical; and so is the case we have here. It is interesting to track those differences though, because they are the ones that can offer us insights regarding what and where we can make some changes and adaptation in each practice to keep it relevant.

The first difference that I would like to draw attention to is the fact that sponsorship relations are usually ongoing, which can be terminated once the two feel they fail to maintain healthy boundaries or cannot help each other anymore. In the educational context, relationships are by definition limited in duration. While this is due to the present education system, and may even hold some advantages, it is hard to build genuine I-Thou relations, that include mutual trust, respect and learning, when everyone is aware of an expiry date. In his discussion about learning-communities, Grinberg (2005) speaks about respect and trust as essential premises, but also as the result of acting within the informal space of camaraderie. We need time to build these important features, in order to dig deep into the relationships, which in turn will allow a deeper inquiry. Recently, I have accepted a new academic position, and the main reason for my choice was that it enabled me to work within such a format. In this unique interdisciplinary teacher education graduate program I work with a cohort for a period of two years for meetings as long as four hours or more on a weekly basis; this structure enables us to build camaraderie, trust and subsequently, it enables us to really build a community of deep inquiry.

Earlier, I mentioned how in Twelve-Step meetings individuals present themselves by first name only, and how in CI it is a common practice to add participants' first names next to their questions (Lipman, 2003). Although it appears to be a similar practice, there is a fundamental difference here; while in the first context identifying with one's first name only serves as a means for anonymity, putting students' names with their questions is an act of ownership and empowerment. In a CI, just like in the Program, participants ought to remember that principles/inquiry come first. Having said that, I and some other practitioners noticed how this practice may have unwanted outcomes, such as power and popularity games, and thus quit this practice altogether and instead developed methods of collecting students' questions in a way that only the instructor knows who sent which question. Using this method has assisted me to establish a healthier sense of trust and respect towards the act of learning itself.

Noticing the subtleness of power and ego in the classroom, and striving to deconstruct them for the sake of a deeper, more meaningful inquiry has brought me to notice yet another interesting difference between the two ideologies and practices. While CI theoreticians and practitioners tend to speak within the democratic discourse, Twelve-Step as a fellowship, though this is not explicitly spelled out, runs itself as an anarchist utopia: each group within each fellowship runs itself, rules are to be determined by members, roles rotate, and external statuses are left out once we enter the room. When I started working with CI theoreticians and practitioners, the first things I argued was that democracy is really not that great of a structure, but rather the lesser of existing evils. With my CI I strive to get as close as possible to positive anarchist structure within the limiting academic context. While I may be more knowledgeable on certain subjects than my students, as a group of graduate adults they teach me a lot about their professional context, which is so extremely challenging and complex. Also, as experienced teachers they can often facilitate a discussion, present a superb session and suggest readings. Additionally, I have recently presented my cohort with a 'manifesto' draft (see the Learning Circle Manifesto at the end of this paper), partially inspired by the Program, as well as by other alternative Circles.

Finally, earlier I argued that being a pragmatic manifestation of dialectics, dialogical CI values the process over a concrete destination. In the Program, on the other hand, there is a particular destination desired, that is to recover from a destructive behaviour or addiction. Nevertheless, members count anywhere from days to years of being sober or clean, marked by special medals and group's celebrations; furthermore, they also refer to themselves as 'addict' even 25 years into their sobriety, marking their awareness to how fragile and transient this state can in fact be. Moreover, although 'relapses' are not desired, they are immanent to the ongoing recovery process. Relapsing is like a dialectical rebound in one's line of argument, and in that sense, what at first appears as a fundamental difference is not necessarily so, and so perhaps these two journeys are more similar than I initially thought.

Conclusion

Whether it is for educational, religious, professional, social or therapeutic purposes, we find that humans gather if only because we long to connect with others, knowing intuitively that this is where we feel whole.

Nowadays, in addition to educational settings that practises pedagogies like CI, group therapy that celebrate peer dynamics, and other congregation formats whose increasing popularity has brought them from their previously underdog status deeply into the mainstream, we can find 'women circles,' 'drummers circles', 'Socratic Cafés' and more.

We gather in ongoing groups or ad hoc ones, using different formats, meeting in different locations, adapting different codes of behaviours. And although the individuals who gather often do not even know each other at the beginning, they all share the motivation to meet with other people for the purpose of getting stronger as individuals. In this paper I have examined two types of group-gathering, namely the pedagogy of Community of Inquiry (also known as CI), and the meetings of the different Twelve-Step fellowships.

Although these formats have their own unique characteristics, in both we can find that the individuals who join and actively participate in them wish to make some sort of transformation and growth, whether in themselves or in the subject of inquiry. In addition, we find that in both structures the process of inquiry and recovery are indeed determined as 'processes' rather than as 'events,' which is why, as mentioned earlier, I have decided to refer to both as Quest Circles.

As two practices where the maxim is 'working together in order to improve thy self,' they construe different structures, but follow similar codes of behaviour and goals. I believe that learning and even borrowing motifs from one another can benefit both.

While the Twelve-Step meetings are more conservative and follow certain structures, still we find how different groups run their meetings differently; while some stick to sharing and step-work, others borrow from different texts and even enable meditation and journal writing and sharing time in the meetings themselves. Within educational settings I believe, that we can find a greater freedom and range of actions. In my educational settings, with my students, I borrow – after some appropriate reconstruction – from the 'meeting' experience; as mentioned above. I begin a 3–4 hours sessions with a sharing circle, part of my evaluation requirements of my students is that they keep a journal of ongoing reflection, at times I even give them assignments that are strongly related to those that can be found in spiritual or recovery settings.

Indeed, it is my view that when it comes to constructivist 'spaces' we cannot distinguish learning from healing; as mentioned earlier, when we learn, we do not only recover from ignorance, we also learn the most challenging subject of all: thy Self, which although murky, is inevitable if we wish to recover from any kind of addictive or other destructive behaviour. Similarly, taking the journey toward spiritual and emotional recovery allows us to learn, often for the first time, who we are, and what our boundaries and limitations are, which consequently means, it allows others to enter our life and be part of it, for it is only through our relationships with others that we meet ourselves. Finally, though getting deep into the realm of philosophical counselling clearly takes me beyond the scope of this paper,[15] it is impossible to simply ignore it, since it is yet another form of learning philosophy as an art of living, learning how to lead a philosophical life, and how to solve life's dilemmas philosophically. In fact it may be one of the finest forms of learning and teaching philosophy. With that being said, if we are comfortable with group therapy, philosophical counselling and the classroom of CI, we could take the synergetic way and try to tie those practices together, which might become a new fascinating challenge that will be interesting to meet and examine in the near future.

Postscript: The learning circle manifesto[16]

When we enter the room, we transform.
Transformation needs to be charged.
Rituals are great battery chargers.
Meetings will open with rituals symbolizing our entrance to a sacred space of learning.
Sacred is centered.
Centered is connected, to ourselves and to each other.
Connected is the key to growth.
We want to grow as individuals, as professionals, as a community.
One ancient ritual is chiming a Tibetan bell.
Another is reading aloud text that puts us in the present.
Joke.
Poem.
Prayer.
I invite you to bring further centering rituals.
We are here now.

Let's share something from our past day, weekend or week.

Personal. Professional. Spiritual. Reflective. Anything.

Leaving all the worries behind.

Ready to learn.

We learn together.

As a community of learners.

We pose questions and discuss them together.

Discussion can get heated.

Respecting different views we avoid personal attacks.

We do not attack individuals, we criticize ideas thoughtfully.

Yet – when we notice someone made a logical fallacy, or contradicted herself, it is our responsibility as an inquiry group to let her know that.

Each person speaks for a limited time, allowing others to join the discussion.

The time-frame is determined by the group.

The facilitator can make changes if required.

If one takes over the discussion, the facilitator asks her to wrap it up.

The facilitator does so by indicating 'one minute' with the index finger.

This is not personal.

We do not interfere with someone's speaking.

From time to time we will run a 'consciousness parliament.'

This is time to share our feelings within the group.

In these meetings this manifesto will be re-evaluated.

After hours of discussion it is time to leave.

Time for closure.

We end an evening with different rituals.

We can go into the circle, each shares one's feeling right now.

One word can be powerful enough.

Leaving us with a week of wonder.

Until the next time.

Notes

[1] Within the context of this paper, by 'constructivism' I refer to knowledge that is based on one's experiences and then further developed by human interactions.

[2] Here 'warrior' refers to one who by mastering inner peace, personal freedom and a strong sense of self, doesn't need aggression or violence to ascend (see also: *Shambhala: The Sacred Path of the Warrior* (Shambhala Pocket Classics) by Chogyam Trungpa (1995), Boston: Shambhala Publications).

[3] The idea behind 'comradeship' is the understanding that one can be fully actualized as human through relationships.

⁴ Anything from support groups, Socratic cafés, women circles, knitting circles, drummer circles etc.

⁵ Recently I began using the term 'open-society' as I find it to reflect our multi-cultural, changing global reality, where due to immigration, media, etc. we witness a flow of cultures and ideas.

⁶ That is true if we distinguish between 'teaching' and 'educating'.

⁷ Consensus decision making is a method by which a whole-group strives to reach an agreement (*http://www.actupny.org/documents/CDdocuments/Consensus.html*, last viewed 28/05/2008). This process reflects perfectly the dialogical ideal of CI, where every voice is valued. This process enforces creative-critical skills when coming to synthesize diverse elements toward possible solutions.

⁸ In Plato's *Meno* we find a man who approaches Socrates with seemingly a very clear question: can virtue be taught? Socrates, being himself, responds with a ser-ies of questions, to which all of Meno's attempts to answer are rejected. Meno is ready for the Socratic journey only when he admits this ignorance.

⁹ Yet, while in CI perplexity is encouraged, when relapses occur, no one is being excommunicated, yet, this is not a desirable state.

¹⁰ After a classic Socratic manipulation, Meno finally surrenders, admitting his ignorance, yet, in his aggravation he is ready to throw it all out by bringing in his famous educational paradox.

¹¹ Traditions designed to keep members unified as a group and remember their cause.

¹² By 'open-ended' I mean entering an interaction willing to explore new territor-ies, allowing its natural flow, without giving it a pre-determined agenda, boundaries or deadlines.

¹³ Oddly enough, teachers' most common reaction toward dialogical pedagogy is usually questioning its relevance to the 'real world.'

¹⁴ In one of my guest-visit to an NA group I was bothered by how throughout the meeting, I repeatedly heard the fragmentizing paradigm: 'us' (those who used, and therefore 'marked' forever) and 'they' (those who never uses, and hence can never understand the 'us'); the overall subliminal message was that the 'world' out-there will never accept the addict as an equal member in the society (and mind you, this is also true for a graduate student who is using cocaine heavily, or a 'pot head'), something that personally I know to be untrue.

¹⁵ See the next chapter by Finn Hansen for an account of philosophical counselling.

¹⁶ This is how I introduce this style of learning and working together to my new classes. Each group then creates its own adaptation.

References

Aronowitz, S. and Giroux, H. (1991), *Postmodern education: politics, culture and social criticism*. Minneapolis: University of Minnesota Press.

Carter, K. and Doyle, W. (1996), 'Personal narratives and life history in learning to teach.' In J. Sikula, T. J. Buttery, and E. Guyton (Eds.), *Handbook of research on teacher education,* (2nd ed., pp. 120–142). New York: Simon & Schuster Macmillan.

Dewey, J. ([1916]1968), *Democracy and education: an introduction to the philosophy of education.* New York: Dover.

Erikson, E. H. (1980), *Identity and the life cycle.* New York: W. W. Norton & Company, Inc. (Original work published 1959).

Forman, R. K. C. (2004), *Grassroots spirituality – what it is, why it is here, where it is going.* Charlottesville: Imprint Academic.

Foucault, M. (1980), *Power/knowledge: selected interviews and other writings, 1972–1977* (C. Gordon, Trans. and Ed.). New York: Pantheon Books.

Gadamer, H. G. (1993), *Truth and method.* New York: Continuum.

Grinberg, J. G. A. (2005), 'Teaching like that': *The beginning of teacher education at Bank Street.* New York: Peter Lang.

Hadot, P. (1995), *Philosophy as a way of life: spiritual exercises from Socrates to Foucault* (M. Chase, Trans., A. I. Davidson, Ed.). Malden: Blackwell. (Original work published 1987).

Heelas, P. (1996), *New age movement: religion, culture and society in the age of post modernity.* Oxford: Blackwell.

Heelas, P., and Woodhead L. (2005), *The spiritual revolution: Why religion is giving way to spirituality.* Oxford: Blackwell.

Lipman, M. (2003), *Thinking in education* (2nd Ed.). New York: Cambridge University.

Nehamas, A. (1998), *The art of living: Socratic reflections from Plato to Foucault.* Berkeley: University of California Press.

Noddings, N. (1984), *Caring: A feminine approach to ethics and moral education.* Berkeley: University of California Press.

Palmer, P. J. (1987), 'Community, conflict and ways of knowing: ways to deepen our educational agenda' [Electronic version]. *Change,* 19(5), 20–25.

—(2003), 'Teaching with heart and soul: Reflections on spirituality in teacher education'. *Journal of Teacher Education,* 54(5), 376–385.

Piaget, J. (1977), *The development of thought: Equilibration of cognitive structures.* New York: Viking.

Plato, (1976), *Meno* (G. M. A. Grube, Trans.). Indianapolis : Hackett Publishing.

Trungpa, C. (1995), *Shambhala: The Sacred Path of the Warrior.* Boston: Shambhala Publications.

Vygotsky, L. (2002), *Thought and language* (A. Kozulin Ed.). Cambridge: The MIT Press.

Chapter 12

Philosophical Praxis as a Community of Wonder in Education and Professional Guidance

Finn Thorbjørn Hansen[1]

Introduction

In this relatively short article I shall present some thoughts and experiences I have been gathering during my many years as both an Associated Professor teaching philosophy of education and counselling theory but also as a philosophical counsellor.

I start by making this distinction because there is a huge difference between on the one hand talking and theorizing *about* philosophy and education and teaching teachers, nurses or counsellors of different sorts in those subject matters through *applying* these philosophical and educational theories *to* the practice of the teacher, nurse or counsellor – and on the other hand to take our departure from the lived experience of the teacher, nurse or counsellor to find and extract or 'deliver' the *lived* philosophical or educational theory *in* their concrete practice.

Especially when we deal with MA students, who arrive at the university at a mature age with lots of work experiences, I have found it necessary to use a different approach from when I teach young students who have just arrived from college.

In fact I think that one can facilitate even deeper processes of learning, and understanding in MA classes *if* we fundamentally take our departure from the lived experiences of our MA students and then go on using phenomenological and hermeneutic approaches to tear out the more universal and general aspects and dimensions of their lived experiences. This kind of learning process is a very complex and delicate one, which in fact would be better described as a *Bildung*-process, that is, as a liberal education or self-cultivation.[2] It is a process, where the student is encouraged to dwell upon and wonder about her own relation to the subject matter and her own implicit 'personal philosophy of education' and 'personal view on life', which indeed always is also at stake even in the most professional activities – and to combine this personal self-knowledge with the curriculum and professional knowledge and value horizons, she is embedded in as a professional practitioner in a more general manner.

In the next section I shall point to the existential and phronetic dimension of the professional by using a rather simple model made by the nursing theorist Barbara Carper (1978), which I have found inspiring. Then I will turn to what it might mean to philosophize and *to be* in a state of wonder, and why this being in a state of fundamental wonder can strengthen the professional in her judgment, her *phronesis*. I end the article with some practical descriptions of the way to a 'Community of Wonder' in the classroom or counselling setting and point to what I call the Seven Socratic Virtues as hallmarks for this movement. For a more elaborate description of philosophical counselling and Socratic Dialogue Group (which I gather under the term *Philosophical Praxis*) I must refer to my latest book *At stå i det åbne. Dannelse gennem filosofisk undren og nærvær* [To Stand in the Openness. Bildung through Philosophical Wonder and Presence] (2008a) or other recent articles in English (Hansen, 2007a, 2007b, 2008b).

The four dimensions within professional practice and reflection

Hanne is a nurse in a hospice in Denmark. She is taking care of one of her patients today, a 61-year-old man who has a severe and advanced form of cancer. In fact, the cancer has spread so much that this man might only have a month or a week to live. It is not possible to say exactly how long he has got, because he has lucid moments when he can walk and talk without great pain. At lunch the son and only child of this man calls the hospice. He wants to take his father out in his car to go fishing at a special lake they both know very well in the North of Denmark. The drive would take several hours. From a medical point of view that would in fact not be a responsible act to allow, so the nurse immediately advises the son not to do so. A car trip and a fishing tour like this might easily aggravate his father's health condition. It would be too hard on him, she tells him. He might even die on the way to the lake. But the son, who has many good childhood memories of his father and himself going fishing, insists on his wish to take his father to the lake. Hanne is touched by the insistence of the son and understands why this is important to both the son and his father. So she goes to her colleagues to discuss the request. After a long conversation with the head of the department of nurses they decide to say 'Yes' to the son. The reason of their judgement stems, one could say, not from a medical paradigm of the professional nurses but rather from their main care of their patient – from what I would term their 'existential paradigm of quality of life.' It might be that the father will die on his way to the lake or when sitting with his son fishing – but might that not be a more joyful and dignified way of dying than dying in the hospice where the son might not even be there with him at that moment?

This example shows, of course, that nurses and health professionals (but I would also say professionals as such because every professional act has also an ethical and existential dimension connected to it) are not only driven by scientific and technological rationales and professional knowledge and methods. They are also directed by an attitude of care and practical wisdom, where more ethical and existential considerations and judgments are exercised.

The American nursing theorist Barbara Carper (1978) captured many years ago these different ways of being a professional nurse by a four-level model. She points out that the body of knowledge that serves as the rationale for nursing practice has patterns, forms and structures that serve as horizons of expectations and exemplify characteristic ways of thinking about phenomena. She identifies four fundamental patterns of knowing, which I would say can also be used in a broad sense for professionals as such, for those who are working with people and human relations (teachers, counsellors, social workers, etc.).

The first pattern of knowing (the *empirical-scientific level and knowledge*) derives from the 'nursing science' and medical science, which is of course first of all based on the empirical-analytical and objective research traditions. Here we are, as she says, '. . . almost lead to believe that the only valid and reliable knowledge is that which is empirical, factual, objectively descriptive and generalizable' (Carper, 1978, p. 16). This is the knowledge and the methods (which Aristotle would call the *episteme* and *techne* of the nursing practice), which can give the nurse a professional and objective attitude.

But people, as we know, are not just objects to be observed and treated as if they were broken machines. The patient – this concrete human being in front of this concrete nurse – is indeed a unique being, and every moment and every relation is – so the experienced and open-minded nurse learns – charged with the unpredictable and unexpected. To really sense, see and *be* with this unique person the nurse has in some way to start all over again, to put her many models, professional methods and scientific theories with all its categories, solutions and definitions in brackets. Seen in this very open way every human being becomes a 'newcomer' and a 'mystery' – and not a 'latecomer' (something we already know precisely what it is) and a 'problem' (something we can solve if we just apply the right knowledge and techniques).

To see, to really see, the other person as if for the first time, that is, as a *mystery* and not as a *problem* (Marcel, 1950), is of course not quite possible. We will always arrive at a situation, a relation and a person with some kind of pre-understanding and assumptions (Gadamer, 1960). But the art, Barbara Carper tells us, is to be aware of (1) the unique mode of the situation and relation in the concrete meeting with the patient, (2) the personal tacit and philosophical assumptions, which the nurse inhabits both as a professional nurse and as a person, and (3) the ethical call of the situation and relation. That is, what the situation calls me to do, as seen from an ethical and moral perspective.

The second level in her model is therefore the *sensuous-aesthetic level or knowledge*. This is the knowledge of the unique – it is, as she formulates it, 'the knowing of a unique particular rather than an exemplary class' (Ibid., p. 18). To get this kind of 'sense for the particular' the nurse has to learn learning practices, which open her up to sensing and experiencing the world in more empathic, meditative and aesthetic ways through felt and lived experiences. This level is hard to describe and systemize because it seems very subjective, concrete and bound to the contextual situation, or as Carper writes:

> An esthetical experience involves the creation and/or appreciation of a singular, particular, subjective expression of imagined possibilities or equivalent realities, which "resists" projection into the discursive form of language. (Ibid., p. 16)

So, it demands other research traditions than the empirical-analytical, and these other research traditions are phenomenology and qualitative research methods (Van Manen, 1990, Martinsen, 1993; Dahlberg et al., 2008).

The third level is the *personal-existential level or knowledge*. This is the knowledge that the nurse must turn to in order to (1) understand better her own psychological and cultural rationales, actions and behaviour, and (2) understand better her personal philosophical assumptions and reflect on existential questions and themes. This is the level where the nurses investigate how they interact with and encounter their patients at a psychological as well as at an existential level. And this has indeed to do with self-knowledge. As Carper writes:

> Personal knowledge is concerned with the knowing, encountering and actualizing of the concrete, individual self. One does not know about the self; one strives simply to know the self. This knowing is a standing in relation to another human being and confronting that human being as a person. This "I-Thou" encounter is unmediated by conceptual categories or particulars abstracted from complex organic wholes. The relation is one of reciprocity, a state of being that cannot be described or even experienced – it can only be actualized. (Ibid., p. 18)

She refers to the philosopher Martin Buber (1958), who makes a fundamental distinction between being in an I-Thou relation and an I-It relation. When the nurse is approaching the patient as something 'to treat' with clear ideas of methods and techniques and a detached attitude, the patient is transformed from a living and authentic whole human being into an object. Their relation has become an I-It relation. To arrive in an I-Thou relation requires another kind of 'knowing that promotes wholeness and integrity in the personal encounter, the achievement of engagement rather than detachment; and it denies the manipulative, impersonal orientation' (Ibid., p. 20).

The goal of the I-Thou relation is in other words to actualize an authentic personal *symmetric* relationship between two persons who meet in their common engagement with the same subject matter or phenomena. This is a relation, which cannot be captured only through a psychological understanding but first of all through an existential and philosophical understanding.

The last level in Carper's model is the *moral-ethical level or knowledge*. It is – especially when it comes to the ethical dimension – closely connected to the aesthetic and existential level. At this fourth level the focus is either related to the norms and ethical codes of the discipline and the nurse profession or practical community within which this profession is embedded (the moral dimension). Or, the focus is related to the ethical dilemmas and personal ethical questions with which the nurse is confronted *in* the concrete situation and relation with the patient or health situation (the ethical dimension).

Ethical knowledge and judgment in this perspective is a question of an ability or readiness to listen to the call (the 'ethical demand' as the Danish philosopher K. E. Løgstrup (1997, 2007) would say – see also Andersen and Niekerk (2007)), of the situation and judge and act upon that sense of call.

This is also in the nursing research described as the phronetic dimension referring to Aristotle's concept of *phronesis*, which means practical wisdom (Aristotle, 2002). Here both the explicitly articulated theoretical knowledge and reflection on what the good life could be and how one should act, and insights into different philosophical ethical positions, are required. But in addition to this – and even more important – for the concrete ethical judgment by the nurse an awareness is required of the nurse's own view of the good life which implicitly can be found *in* her lived experience (her *lived philosophy* of the good life). In fact, if she only followed the ethical code of her profession or only judge on the basis of her theoretical knowledge and understanding of different philosophical and ethical positions – she might easily end up with unethical judgements and actions because *she* would not judge from her own presence, her own being in *this* concrete situation with *this* particular human being (Martinsen, 1993).

The last two levels in Carper's model will, at the research level, first and foremost be dealt with through the philosophical hermeneutic research tradition of scholars such as Gadamer, Arendt, Ricoeur, Løgstrup and Levinas.

My point now is that Carper's four levels are still meaningful to use today, especially when we want to understand *where* philosophy can help the professional to become more aware of the phronetic and existential dimension of her work and life.

I have experienced in my work of philosophical counselling of nurses, teachers and counsellors that these four levels make sense in their contexts. But I have also discovered that these four levels also make sense in trying to understand what philosophical counselling is and what is going on when it is practised.

But before I turn to a description of the philosophical counselling process, I want to examine a little bit closer the relationship between doing philosophy (being in a state of wonder) and strengthening the professional's practical wisdom (*phronesis*).

The spiritual and ethical dimension of philosophizing

The Danish philosopher Søren Kierkegaard once wrote in his diary the following passage:

How true and how Socratic was this Socratic principle: to understand, truly to understand, is to be. For us more ordinary men this divides and becomes twofold: It is one thing to understand and another to be. Socrates is so elevated that he does away with this distinction. (JP, 4:4301)

Kierkegaard also says the same in another way by saying that, one thing is to understand what one is saying and doing, but quite another thing is to understand oneself *in* what is said and done! Kierkegaard (1846) points to Socrates as the ideal of what he describe as an 'existing thinker'(*en existerende Tænker*), that is, the thinker who is *not* just occupied with abstract and theoretical and systematic reflection and speculations in the strive for a more and more objective truth. What the existing thinker instead is engaged in is exactly to think *from* his existence, from his lived experiences and being-in-the-world here-and-now. What he (and Socrates if we are to follow Kierkegaard's reading of Plato) does is to move into to a 'double reflection', which consists of two movements. First there is the movement into the concrete lived experience (the 'primitive' as Kierkegaard named it). This is what we in human science, in phenomenology and hermeneutics, would call the 'phenomenological seeing'. To find your way into the story, into the lived experience and to feel the landscape of this concrete experience is not an easy task to do. It requires a lot of slowness and humility in our thoughts and an openness and a 'being touched' (one has to be touched and to think from this 'touchedness' if we are to be allowed into the concrete phenomena we are at wonder about), which make us sensible for the 'tone' of impressions of life or phenomena that want to be articulated and thought (see also Heidegger, 1968; Lindseth, 2005).

The second move in Kierkegaard's double reflection is to listen to the eternal in the temporal, the unconditional in the conditional, the universal in the particular and concrete experience. This is what we in human science call 'the hermeneutic awareness' (Gadamer, 1960). Here we are driven to listen out for the deeper meaning of the concrete life expression through first of all a fundamental state of wonder and love of wisdom. If we are not listening to the phenomena in a Socratic not-knowing state of mind, if we are not in a fundamental wonder and longing to understand what might not be understandable through our concepts and discursive thoughts – if we only try to examine and clarify through different systematic and analytical reflections in the hope of gathering more information and knowledge (this is what normal scientists are supposed to do in the spirit of objectivity) – then we will not be able to hear and encounter the phenomena as they speak *to us*. This is a fundamental phenomenological-hermeneutical insight and, as we shall see, also an insight which is paramount for the practice of the philosophical counsellor.

Kierkegaard summarizes his thoughts on this subject by saying that to get close to this insight we have to transform our selves. And to do so is indeed an art of life. As he says, to exist is an art of life:

> The subjective thinker is not a scientist – he is an artist. To exist is an art. The subjective thinker is aesthetical enough to make the content of his life aesthetical, ethical enough to regulate it, and dialectical enough to master it. (Kierkegaard, 1846, p. 341, my translation)

Thus, we see that the Art of Existence is in the eyes of Kierkegaard a combination of three dimensions or levels: an aesthetical, a dialectical and an ethical dimension. By 'dialectical' he means that human beings attempt to display that, which cannot be grasped by direct communication but only through indirect communication through the *logos*, the discursive language and dialectical and negating movements in this language . And this indirect communication is lead or inspired by the more aesthetical and ethical attitudes and modes of life. To be in an existential reflection, to philosophize in this way, one has to reflect all those three levels as a whole in the thinking act.

The French philosopher Michel Foucault was, as Arnold Davidson tells us in his foreword to Foucault's *The Hermeneutics of the Subject* (Foucault, 2005) a great admirer of Kierkegaard although he did not explicitly write about him. One of the things that Foucault and Kierkegaard had in common was their ambivalent love for Socrates. In Foucault's later writings Socrates more or less becomes a hero or ideal for being a 'parrhêsiast' (a truth teller). But here 'truth' is not to be confused with a systematic, collected and discursive truth and knowledge. 'Truth' in Foucault's sense should more be understood in line with Heidegger's 'Wahrsagen' or Kierkegaard's 'existential truth'. To take care of the truth is in a way to let go of our utilitarian attempts to master and control our selves and our surroundings. It is – as the ancient Greek would say – to protect or save the phenomena from our attempt to control it through categories, definitions and answers and problem-solving. To take care of the truth is trying *to be* in the phenomena you want to understand. Or as Kierkegaard said: to understand, to really understand, is to be.

Foucault makes a clear distinction (inspired by his colleague Pierre Hadot (1995)) between 'philosophy as a discourse' and 'philosophy as a life form' or an 'art of life'. It was philosophy as an art of life that he was fascinated by in his later writings. Foucault also describes this kind of philosophizing – where the person who philosophizes has to move into a

kind of self-transformation in order to be closer to (or hear) and understand the phenomena – as a 'spiritual exercise'. By spirituality he meant:

> We will call 'spirituality' then the set of researches, practices, and experi-
> ences, which may be purifications, ascetic exercises, renunciations, con-
> versions of looking, modifications of existence, etc., which are, not
> knowledge but for the subject, for the subject's very being, the price to be
> paid for access to the truth. (Foucault, 2005, p. 15).

Spirituality in Foucault's sense of the word postulates that the truth is not
given to the subject by a simple act of knowledge. The truth is, as he continues, only given to the subject at a price that brings the subject's being
into play. So it follows from this point of view that there can be no truth
without a conversion or transformation of the subject. Foucault also calls for
this philosophical self-transformation 'the movement of *Eros* (love)', that is,
the Socratic *Eros* which meant the love or longing for wisdom and beauty.
So, one might make a distinction between philosophy in its more modern
understanding, and then *philo-sophia* in its more original Greek sense, which
was more a kind of spiritual exercise. Or as Foucault writes:

> We will call 'philosophy' the form of thought that asks what it is that
> enables the subject to have access to the truth and which attempts to
> determine the conditions and limits of the subject's access to the truth.
> If we call this 'philosophy', then I think we could call 'spirituality' the
> search, practice, and experience through which the subject carries out
> the necessary transformations on himself in order to have access to the
> truth. (Ibid.)

One could, of course, wonder how or whether 'philosophy' in fact can give
knowledge and understanding about what it is, which gives the subject
access to the truth. *If* the philosopher himself is not in the middle of a
spiritual search and practice and experience, how would he know? Maybe
this is why it is wise to insist, that the existential reflection must be a double
reflection as Kierkegaard did.

There is a remarkable similarity between Foucault's way of talking about
'the aesthetics of existence' and Kierkegaard's 'art of existence'. As the
Foucault scholar Thomas Flynn (1985, 1988) has showed in his studies on
the writings of the later Foucault, Foucault also talks about the importance
of a harmony between on the one hand the dialectical and discursive view
of life of the philosophical practitioner (*logos*), and the lived experience

3. **Existence** (ethics, *ethos*)

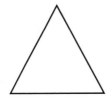

1. **Bildung** (dialectics, *logos*)   2. **Authenticity** (aesthetics, *bios*)

FIGURE 1   The three hallmarks for the Philosophical Praxis

and philosophy (*bios*) of the practitioner on the other hand. And this combination of *logos* (philosophy *about* life) and *bios* (philosophizing *from* life) has to be balanced by what Foucault calls *ethos*. A person's *ethos* is the person's whole way of being and acting in respect for 'the ethical care of the self' and the culture and human relations he or she is embedded in (Foucault, 1988a, 1988b).

So we see, and this I have elaborated much more in other writings (Hansen, 2003, 2008), a kind of triangle within which this 'Art of Life' and 'Existential Reflection' is brought to life (Figure 1).

Let me now take a last step with one of the other great philosophers before I turn to the practice of philosophical counselling. This step will be taken with Hannah Arendt (1978). She would agree with Kierkegaard, that we have to be moved into a double reflection in order to be in wonder and experience what it means to 'philosophize'. Especially in *Life of the Mind* (1978) she asks, what it is that makes us think, and where we are when we think. When we are truly philosophizing we are, according to her understanding, in 'another place' – a place she so beautifully describes as the 'non-time space in the very heart of time' (Arendt, 1978, p. 210). This might also – one could presume – be what Kierkegaard calls the eternal movement *in* time ('Evigheden i Øjeblikket'), where we in a way leave the 'World of Appearance' to be engaged in Being as such.

Professional philosophers in our modern age do not think in this way, she proclaims. They do not have a sense for the spiritual 'Being-dimension' in philosophy. As she writes:

> The question, when asked by the professional [philosopher], does not arise out of his own experiences while engaged in thinking. It is asked from outside – whether that outside is constituted by his professional interests as a thinker or by the common sense in himself that makes him question an activity that is out of order in ordinary living. (Arendt, 1978, p. 166)

But, as she develops further in *Life of the Mind*, if we as philosophers and teachers of philosophy do not ask questions that arise from our own and students' experiences while engaging in thinking, we will not strengthen our and our students' abilities to make ethical judgments. From her perspective there is a close relation between 'thinking' and 'ethical judgment'. It is through thinking in the existential sense that we prepare the way for the good judgment. Thinking in Arendt's eyes is about our readiness to wonder. And wonder makes us very present and mindful about the particular situation and relation we are engaged in. She even describes this thinking as a process of the Socratic *Eros*. In that way, one could say that the Socratic *Eros* is a pre-condition for *phronesis*.[3]

These thoughts by Kierkegaard, Foucault and Arendt could of course and should be elaborated much more but for the purpose of this article, this is enough to point to the necessity of another kind of teaching and practising philosophy in the classroom and guidance practice, if we are to help students and professionals in their understanding of not just, what they say and do, but also *where* they are in what they are saying and doing. To practice this kind of existential or 'spiritual' reflection philosophical counselling and Socratic dialogue Groups seem to offer some suggestions on how to do that.

Philosophical praxis as a community of wonder

The main idea behind philosophical counselling and Socratic Dialogue groups[4] is not to help solving some specific personal or professional problems. It is rather to investigate at first the hidden assumptions (the coordinates) of the problem setting: What are we taking for granted in our whole way of looking at the problem and the life where this problem seems to emerge? What is the lived philosophy, which is assumed behind all the attempts the person has made to 'solve' or escape the problem? And what are the ideals and values that seem to direct the professional in her interests and view on 'successful criteria' for solving the problem or living a 'good successful life'?

This approach might be a first and natural step to take because people often arrive in the classroom or counselling session with some very specific problems or interests they want to solve or follow. But the philosophical counsellor and Socratic facilitator want to do more than that. They want to shift from a philosophical *practice* (where philosophy is used as a tool for something else – a utilitarian approach) to a philosophical *praxis* (where *philo-sophy* gets into play and where *praxis* in the Aristotelian sense means doing something which is a value in itself). When philosophy becomes a *praxis* we are not *doing* something with philosophy. It is rather philosophy which does something *with us* provided that we engage ourselves with it (Heidegger, 2000, p. 13)!

Now, to be engaged in philosophical praxis is the whole purpose of philosophical counselling and Socratic Dialogue Groups. One of the first problems of getting people into that state of mind or 'spirit' is to make them critically investigate their own secure meanings and conventional norms. To be able to philosophize in this sense, one has to have the courage and openness and longing for 'standing in the openness', or as Arendt would say, to think with out banisters. One has, again in her words, to 'unfreeze' our daily words and concepts and understandings in order to find out the original and living meaning of the word or concept. But this is a very difficult and delicate thing to do, because we as Socratic facilitators or Philosophical Counsellors are, of course, also caught up in frozen thoughts and ideas of what a human being or good life is and so on. When facilitating a philosophical counselling session or Socratic Dialogue Group the facilitator, of course, knows 'something' that the visitors do not know. But this is knowledge which is only like the warming up bands before the real star of the night shows up on the scene. What we as Socratic facilitators have a better sense of than the visitor and some competence in doing, is, what I have termed 'phronetic musicality' and a sense of the importance of thinking *from* the lived experience, and to wonder about it.

The latter – *to be* in a state of wonder – is not something that the facilitator can manufacture and control. It is rather something that happens to the visitor and at best to all (including the facilitator!). What he or she can do though, is to bring the visitor(s) to the doorstep of the state of wonder. He or she can – in the spirit of Socrates – tease and provoke (like a gadfly) the confidence of the other person's cocksure knowledge and personal meanings. And when the visitor gets puzzled and unsure and is in a state of *aporia* (perplexity) then a shift of scene will occur. Then the facilitator will walk *with* the visitor in a dialectical movement where they together try to find a new footing, a third place which goes beyond the previous understanding of both the visitor *and* the Socratic facilitator. It is important to note that in the eyes of Kierkegaard, Foucault and Arendt this Socratic midwifery and art of dialogue was not a *pedagogical* attempt to move the visitor to a special pre-determined truth which Socrates already knew about. The only direction he wanted to push/guide his visitor was in the direction of wonder and the love of wisdom. To be in this state of wonder about and love and search for the truth, good and the beauty in life was for Socrates a great value in itself (maybe the greatest value a human being can ever hope for – only the Gods, Socrates would say, would be able to find and possess the truth, good and the beauty, not human beings).

So one could say, that in the beginning – which by the way normally takes most of the time in a normal Socratic Dialogue Group or philosophical counselling session – the Socratic facilitator is guiding and displaying an asymmetric relation, because he or she has some knowledge and methods to provoke the visitor out into the open. Yet he or she also has, but more on a intuitive level, learned from his or her lived experiences being out in the open and the 'unknown' in former 'Communities of Wonder' and thus has a sense (or philosophical musicality[5]) of when they or the visitors are or are not in a state of wonder. But again, the facilitator can only lead and guide to the doorstep of wonder. Then the event of philosophy takes over by itself more or less like a jazz musician describes what happens when he on the high peaks of his performance improvises and jams with other musicians. In those moments there are no methods to follow – only the call of the situation and the subject matter in itself (zu den Sachen selbst – Gadamer, 1960).

One of the movements, one can make to get closer to this doorstep, is also to reflect starting from the more aesthetic aspects of one's experience of the subject matter, which one tries to understand.

I sometimes make a distinction (after the stage of *aporia* in the Socratic dialogue) between *Dialectics 1* and *Dialectics 2*.

Dialectics 1 is driven by good logical arguments and counter-arguments and a discursive reflection and language. But this kind of reflection will in the end lead us to an even deeper puzzlement, which the Ancient Greeks call *thaumazein*, that is, a fundamentally felt experience of 'admiring wonder' (Arendt, 1978). In this kind of wonder we experience ourselves as much more embedded *in* the world, in our existence, and a sense of confidence, gratitude, awe and wonder about this world, and the whole universe we are a part of, emerges. If we reach some new insights (what the Greek called *nous*) then those insights must be seen as events, something that happens *to* us – like an unexpected gift.

Dialectics 2 has another motivation and movement. This dialectical movement and search is now more driven by a 'being touched' and questions such as: What in all those thoughts and ideas we have been discussing and reflecting upon makes an impression on you? Which 'voices of life' do you hear when you get silent and try to contemplate and meditate from the lived experience and on the experience of wonder? It makes a difference in my experience to ask such questions. It creates a much more profound and sincere dialogue and reflection ('thinking' in the sense of Arendt, and 'existential reflection' in the sense of Kierkegaard).

I have somewhere else (Hansen, 2008a) described this Socratic *Bildung* process much closer in '12 steps' from *doxa* and *aporia* to *thaumazein*, *silence* and *nous* and further on to *phronesis* and *hexis*, where the new insights through an ethical care of the self will be lived out in daily life and changed life habits and life forms.

Here I just want to present the 'Seven Socratic Virtues', which I have found, are very fruitful to be aware of and think from, when we want to engage in philosophical praxis. At the end of the day – when we are getting nearer the Community of Wonder – to learn how to philosophize is not so much a question of possessing certain professional philosophical knowledge or methods but rather to exercise certain virtues that can bring us out into the 'winds of thoughts' (Arendt), which can overwhelm us and move us (philosophy as a pathos) when we are in a philosophical praxis.

From my many years as a Socratic facilitator and with the inspiration from the understanding of Socrates and the Socratic Midwifery by Kierkegaard, Foucault and Arendt, I have come to the seven virtues as listed in Figure 2.

The first and most important Socratic virtue is with no doubt *love*. This can be understood and practiced both in the Greek sense of *Eros*, or the Christian sense of *agape* or *caritas*. Both aspects of the human striving for and desiring of the divine wisdom on the one hand, and on the other hand the aspect of giving space to something in life, which is bigger than human life and human enterprises, which we must try to be receptive and humble enough to receive, all this is at stake in philosophy.

The second Socratic virtue is *silence*. When we are to reflect upon our deepest values and articulate what we find, and have experiences by ourselves, as the most important things in life – then we are stocked with silence (Socrates describe it as being paralysed by an electric ray). These important things – as Plato also points at in his famous *Seventh Letter* (see Rhodes, 2003) – are

---

1. Love (*Eros, agape, caritas*)
2. Silence
3. Ontological humility
4. Humour
5. Courage
6. Discipline (ethical care of the self, to *live* a philosophical life)
7. Friendship (*philos*)

FIGURE 2   The Seven Socratic Virtues

connected to the unsayable domain of life but can be reached through silence (see also Carafa, 2004). Or as Arendt says: 'The abode of thinking is the place of silence'.

The third Socratic virtue I call – with an inspiration from the French philosopher Gabriel Marcel (1950) – *ontological humility*. This is a kind of intellectual chastity and embarrassment, because the human thought – how sharp and gloriously it ever might be – seems nevertheless always to 'run into the border of human language' when people are dealing with existential life phenomena.

Those three virtues are a kind of contemplative virtue connected to the single person's encounter with the big questions of life and the grand existential life experiences.

But the person must also – so to speak – return to the cave of Plato, after having been out in some more spiritual seeings and hearings, to live a human life with his or her fellow men again. The question now is how to keep the 'small fire'(*nous*) alive in the midst of human affairs – what also is described as *phronesis*. The next four Socratic virtues are connected to the social life of human beings.

The fourth virtue is *humour*. Not humour like the good joke but humour as an attitude to life. This is indeed a complex concept and attitude to explain in few words. But it has to do with our ability to see the grand things in the small elementary things in life, and the littleness in what human beings consider to be the grand things in life. It is an existential balance between the tragedy of life and the comical in life, that one can find in Søren Kierkegaard's concept of humour (see Hansen, 2002b, 2003).

The fifth virtue I name *courage*. This is because it is one thing to understand something, and maybe also to understand oneself in what is said, but it is another thing to act upon this understanding. To live out the thoughts we think – or to dare to think those thoughts that we in fact live. Again and again in Socratic Dialogue Groups I experience the need for this courage to bring oneself into play. To stand in the openness requires courage.

The sixth virtue is *discipline*. It demands a lot 'of work and self-discipline to try to live a philosophical life, a life with ethical care for oneself and one's fellow human beings. Really to change bad habits, which make us 'spiritually lazy', demands that we fight against a consumer culture and hasty age, where it is almost impossible to strive in daily life for wisdom, beauty and meaningfulness.

The seventh virtue might be the second most important virtue (the most important being the love of the world). That virtue is *friendship*. The German philosopher Karl Jaspers once said, that 'truth begins when two people are together'(Jaspers, 1954). We all know how important a 'soul companion' can be and how sincere and profound a conversation can develop if we experience a friendship with all its trust, acceptance, respect, open-heartedness, playfulness and loyalty. Aristotle among others also points to friendship as a fundamental condition for philosophizing. To create or hope for a friendly, playful and sincere atmosphere among the participants in a Socratic Dialogue Group – where we dare and are encouraged *to be* ourselves - might seem very difficult. Especially if nobody really knows each other from the start. But the wonderful and strange thing is, as I have experienced so many times, that this cheerful, trusting, friendly, playful and sincere mode among participants does happen. Maybe it is because people here experience a 'free space' away from daily problem-orientated, strategic and utilitarian approaches. That is, a place where they are allowed to be with and reflect from those things in life that matter most of all to them. I believe so, because coming back to those experiences and values, and to have an open-minded and engaged dialogue and wonder with other people about those values and experiences, is like going from a very cramped and stuffy room out into a beautiful big piece of landscape. These kinds of events or experiences of expansions of horizons will normally create a kind of 'philosophical companionship'.

Conclusion

Philosophy – at its best – is a practical exercise in presence. It is, as Kierkegaard, Foucault and Arendt describe in different ways a spiritual experience and activity, which can bring the person closer to her own being-in-the-world. To understand, to really understand one's profession and oneself in this profession – as a student, teacher, nurse or counsellor – requires that the student or professional practitioner understands herself *in* what she is saying and doing. It is argued that it is only when one is related to and aware of one's presence in the situation and relation, that one can authentically 'see' the other person and act with ethical judgment. As professionals working with people and human relations, this '*Bildung* process' seems paramount. To do the right thing at the right moment in a wise way is also described as practical wisdom (*phronesis*) in the literature of professional practices. The big question of course is how we can train students and professionals in this *Bildung* process and in *phronesis*.

Philosophy as a spiritual exercise can invite us into this process. In this article I have, however, in different ways pointed at the importance of making a sharp distinction between *practice* and *praxis*, between being on the one hand in a theoretical and abstract approach or utilitarian and problem-solving approach and on the other hand to be in an existential and Being-oriented approach. Most relations in professional work (as well as in traditional philosophy teaching) are either guided by a scientific (*episteme*) or instrumental and therapeutic relation (*techne*).

When we want to strengthen the phronetic dimension of the professional he or she has to step into another kind of relation with their clients or patients. In fact in those authentic and existential moments it would be wrong to describe them as clients or patients. In those moments they are met and perceived as unique human beings. They are then rather to be understood as 'visitors' or 'guests' in their conversations and practices.

Philosophy understood as a philosophical praxis can – so the postulate goes and here I have to refer to my research in other places (Hansen, 2003, 2007a and b, 2008a and b) – invite you to an I-Thou relation, where the philosophical counsellor and his visitor enters a Community of Wonder. The way to such a community is not a straight way of logical argumentation and counter-arguments. The way to a deeper existential wonder (*thaumazein*) requires a three-dimensional approach. That is an aesthetical, dialectical and an ethical approach. We have in this article seen these dimensions described in different ways. And in every case Kierkegaard, Foucault and Arendt argue that it is not enough to approach either philosophy or the professional curriculum from a traditional academic (theory *about* practice) or application approach (applied theory *on* practice). If we want to learn how to philosophize and to understand the professional practice in a deeper sense, then we have to take our departure from the lived experience (see the theory *in* practice) and from there on we need to reflect and wonder about this lived experience and our relation to it. By sharing our wonder, by being silent, slow and mindful in thought, so that we can 'hear' what the phenomena of life have to tell us, and by trying in companionship with others to articulate those impressions and wonders, we move into what Arendt so beautifully calls 'the small non-time space in the very heart of time'. In those moments there is a symmetry in the relation and a kind of 'philosophical companionship'. Philosophical counselling and Socratic Dialogue Groups are suggested as philosophical praxis where these kinds of spiritual and self-transformative moments can happen. Arriving at a Community of Wonder through a philosophical counselling session or Socratic Dialogue Group, and to be trained in these kinds of Socratic *Bildung* processes, is not first of all a question of having learned and processed the right knowledge or methods (what the professional philosopher primary aims at). It is a question of attitude. The seven Socratic virtues are offered as a possible way to arrive to the doorstep of the Community of Wonder.

These virtues might also be a way of opening the eyes of the professional philosopher and the traditional philosophy teacher for the existential and phronetic dimension of philosophy. And maybe then in fact they will begin to philosophize in the ancient Greek and spiritual sense of the word.

Notes

[1] Dr. Finn T. Hansen is an Associated Professor at the Danish School of Education, Aarhus University where he for over ten years has been researching in Socratic Dialogue Groups and Philosophical Counselling in connection to Existential Pedagogy. He is also chairman of the Danish Society of Philosophical Practice and his Ph.D. dissertation had the title 'The Philosophical Life – An edification Ideal for Existential Pedagogy' (2003). He runs MA courses in Philosophical Counselling at his university for teachers, nurses and counsellors, and workshops for social workers outside university.

[2] For a discussion of the concept of 'Bildung' see Løvlie et al. (2003) and Bauer (2003).

[3] I have elaborated on this topic in Hansen, 2003, 2007b, 2008a and b.

[4] For more detailed information about the tradition and methods behind Philosophical Counselling and Socratic Dialogue Group I will refer to Achenbach (1987); Lahav and Tillmann (1995); Raabe (2001); Herrestad et al. (2002); Kessels (2004), Saran and Neisser (2004); Lindseth (2005), Hansen (2000, 2002a and b, 2003, 2005, 2007a and b, 2008a and b).

[5] Some might see the term ' philosophical musicality' as an 'elitist argument'. They may ask: 'Does it suggest we need a given talent to do philosophy? As regards music, some people are just tone-deaf and have no talent at all, so are there people who never get very far in philosophy because of their natural disposition?' This is not the case *at all* when Arendt is talking about 'thinking'. Every human being is able to think (to do *philo-sophia*), we are all 'thinking human beings' as she says in *Life of the Mind*, but we might get so caught up in cognitive (intellectual) reflections and utilitarian considerations that we forget or overlook the way of thinking and existential reflection that Arendt and Kierkegaard talk about. Especially highly intelligent people who are used to systematize and 'use' knowledge and who have a firm belief in cognitive rational judgements and common sense can be at risk of becoming temporally 'tone deaf' in hearing and seeing the mysteries in our ordinary daily living. To hear and be lead by wonder we have, as I have described above, to take our departure from our lived experiences while engaging in thinking. Sometimes a very experienced nurse will have easier access to this kind of thinking than an educated MA or Ph.D. student in philosophy (or a professional philosopher) because the latter primarily reflect from a paradigm of *episteme* and *techne* whereas the experienced nurse thinks and acts from her lived experience and what Aristotle terms as *phronesis*.

References

Achenbach, G. (1987). *Philosophische Praxis*. Köln: Verlag für Philosophie Jürgen Dinter.

Andersen, S. and K. V. Knoten Niekerk (2007). *Concern for the other. Perspectives on the ethics of K.E. Løgstrup*. Indiana: University of Notre Dame Press.

Arendt, H. (1978): *Life of the Mind*. London: Harcourt, Inc.

Aristotle (2002). *The Nicomachean Ethics*. Oxford: Oxford University Press.

Bauer, W. (ed.) (2003). *Educational Philosophy and Theory*, 35 (2), April 2003.

Buber, M. (1958). *I and Thou*. (trans. Ronald Gregor Smith). New York: Charles Scribner's Sons.

Carafa, A. (2004). 'Silence as the foundation of learning'. *Educational Theory*, 54 (2).

Carper, B. (1978). 'Fundamental Patterns of knowing in Nursing', *Advances of Nursing Science*, 1, 13–23.

Dahlberg, K., Dahlberg, H. and Nyström, M. (2008). *Reflective Lifeworld Research*. Sweden: Studenterlitteratur.

Flynn, T. (1985). 'Truth and subjectivation in the later Foucault'. *The Journal of Philosophy*, LXXXII, Jan.–Dec. 1988.

—(1988). 'Foucault as parrhesiast: his last course at the Collège de France'. In: *The Final Foucault* (eds. J. Bernauer and D. Rasmussen). Cambridge: MIT Press.

Foucault, M. (1988a). 'Selvomsorgens etik som frihedspraksis'. In *UNDR. Nyt Nordisk Forum*, No. 55.

—(1988b). *Technologies of the Self*. (ed. Luther H. Martin, H. Gutman, and P. H. Hutton.). London: Tavistock.

—(2005). *The Hermeneutics of the Subject. Lectures at the College de France 1981–1982*. New York: Palgrave Macmillan.

Gadamer, H.-G. (1960). *Truth and Method*. (trans. in 1975. 2nd Revised Edition). New York: Seabury Press, 1989.

Hadot, P. (1995). *Philosophy as a Way of Life - Spiritual Exercises from Socrates to Foucault*. Oxford: Blackwell Publishing.

Hansen, F. T. (2000). *Den sokratiske dialoggruppe* [The Socratic Dialogue Group]. Copenhagen: Gyldendal.

—(2002a). 'The use of philosophical practice in lifelong and self-directed learning'. Herrestad, H., A. Holt and; H. Svare (eds). *Philosophy in Society*. Oslo: Unipubforlag.

—(2002b). *Why the Ethic behind Philosophical Counselling must be Humorists in a Kierkegaardian Sense*. Paper presented at The North American Conference in Philosophical Counselling, 1, November 2002, Saint Paul University. *www.ustpaul. ca/Philosophy/revue/pdf/2004_hansen.pdf*, last viewed 28/05/2008

—(2003). *Det filosofiske liv – et dannelsesideal for eksistenspædagogikken* [The Philosophical Life – as an edifying ideal for existential pegagogy. Copenhagen: Hans Reitzels forlag.

—(2005). 'The existential dimension in training and vocational guidance – when guidance counselling becomes a philosophical practice'. *European journal on Vocational training*, Thessaloniki, 2005, January-April 2005/I, N°34.

—(2007a). 'Philosophical Counselling. A hermeneutical-dialogical approach to career counselling'. In P. Plant (ed.). *Ways – On Career Guidance*. Copenhagen: Danmarks Pædagogiske Universitets forlag.

—(2007b). 'Eros, Authenticity and Bildung as keywords for philosophical practice in teacher training'. *Paideusis – Journal of Canadian Philosophy of Education* (ed. H. Bai), December 2007.

—(2008a). *At stå i det åbne. Dannelse gennem filosofisk undren og nærvær.* [To Stand in the Openness. Liberal Education through Philosophical Wonder and Presence]. Copehagen: Hans Reitzels forlag.

—(2008b). 'Phronesis and Eros – the existential dimension of phronesis and clinical supervision of nurses'. In: Chris Johns (ed.). *Creating Phronesis.*

Heidegger, M. (1968). *What is called Thinking?* New York: Harper & Row, Publishers, (a translation of *Was Heisst Denken?* (1954) by J. Glenn Gray).

—(2000). *Introduction to Metaphysics.* New Haven and London: Yale University Press.

Herrestad, H., A. Holt and H. Svare (ed.) (2002). *Philosophy in Society.* Oslo: Unipubforlag.

Jaspers, K. (1954). *Way to Wisdom: An Introduction to Philosophy* (trans. by Ralph Manheim). New Haven: Yale University Press.

Kessels, J., Boers, E. and Morstert, P. (2004). *Free Space. Philosophy in Organisations.* Amsterdam: Boom.

Kierkegaard, S. (1846). *Afsluttende Uvidenskabelig Efterskrift.* Søren Kierkegaard Skrifter, Vol. 7, Gad forlag, Copenhagen. See also *Concluding unscientific postscript to Philosophical fragments.* Princeton University Press, 1992.

—(1975). *Søren Kierkegaard´s Journals and Papers* (Vol. 4). Seven volumes, edited and translated by Howard V. and Edna H. Hong. London: Indiana University Press.

Lahav, R. and Tillman (ed.) (1995). *Essays on Philosophical Counselling.* Lanham: University Press of America.

Lindseth, A. (2005). *Zur Sache der Philosophischen Praxis.* Freiburg/München: Verlag Karl Alber.

Løgstrup, K. E. (1997). *The Ethical Demand.* Indiana: University of Notre Dame Press.

Løgstrup, K. E. (2007). *Beyond the Ethical Demand. Introduction with Kees Van Kooten Niekerk.* Indiana: University of Notre Dame Press.

Løvlie, L. K., L. Mortensen and S. E. Nordenbo (eds) (2003). 'Educating Humanity. Bildung in postmodernity'. *Journal of Philosophy of Education,* May 2003.

Marcel, G. (1950). *The Mystery of Being I & II.* London: The Harvill Press.

Martinsen, K. (1993). *Fra Marx til Løgstrup. Om moral, samfundskritik og sanselighet i sykepleien.* Oslo: TANO.

Raabe, P. (2001). *Philosophical Counselling. Theory and Practice.* London: Praeger.

Rhodes, J. (2003). *Eros, Wisdom and Silence – Plato's Erotic Dialogues.* London: University of Missouri Press.

Saran, R. and Neisser, B. (2004). *Enquiring Minds. Socratic dialogue in education.* London: Trentham Books.

Van Manen, M. (1990). *Researching Lived Experience. Human Science for an Action Sensitive Pedagogy.* New York: State University of New York Press.

Select Bibliography

All philosophers can be read under the aspect of education as the contributors show by drawing on a wide variety of philosophers from Adorno to Wittgenstein. The select bibliography aims only to provide a starting point for those who wish to reflect further on their teaching. It is by no means meant to be exhaustive.

Journals that publish a wide variety of articles related to teaching philosophy

Discourse: Learning and Teaching in Philosophical and Religious Studies
Educational Philosophy and Theory
Journal of Philosophy of Education
Teaching Philosophy

Useful websites

www.philosophyteachers.org (American Association of Philosophy Teachers), last viewed on 10/06/2008.
www.prs.heacademy.ac.uk (The Higher Education Academy Subject Centre for Philosophical and Religious Studies), last viewed on 10/06/2008.
www.pdcnet.org (Philosophy Documentation Centre), last viewed on 10/06/2008.

A selection of books

Bresler, L. (ed.) (2004), *Knowing Bodies, Moving Minds: Towards Embodied Teaching and Learning.* Dordrecht: Kluwer.
Burbules, N. (1993), *Dialogue in Teaching: Theory and Practice.* New York and London: Teachers College Press.
Crews, R. J. (2002), *Higher Education Service-Learning Sourcebook.* Westport: Oryx Press.
Curren, R. (ed.) (2007), *Philosophy of Education. An Anthology.* Oxford: Blackwell.
Dewey, J. (1964), *Democracy and Education.* New York: Free Press/Macmillan.
—(1997), *Experience and Education.* New York: Touchstone.
Gil, A., Perez Lancho, B. and Manzano, M. (eds) (2006), *Proceedings of the Second International Congress on Tools for Teaching Logic.* Salamanca: University of Salamanca.

Grimes, P. and Uliana, R. L. (1998), *Philosophical Midwifery: A New Paradigm for Understanding Human Problems with its Validation*. Costa Mesa: Hyparxis.

Hadot, P. (1995), *Philosophy as a Way of Life – Spiritual Exercises from Socrates to Foucault*. Malden: Blackwell Publishing.

Howe, K. (ed.)(2005), *Philosophy of Education*. Urbana: Philosophy of Education Society.

Howie, G. and Tauchert, A. (eds) (2002), *Gender, Teaching and Research: Challenges for the 21ˢᵗ Century*. London: Ashgate.

Langford, G. (1985), *Education, Persons and Society: A Philosophical Enquiry*. London: Macmillan.

Leder, D. (1998), *Games for the Soul: 40 Playful Ways to Find Fun and Fulfilment in a Stressful World*. New York: Hyperion.

Lipman, M. (2003), *Thinking in Education* (2nd ed.). New York: Cambridge University.

Lisman, C. D. and Harvey, I. E. (eds) (2000), *Beyond the Tower: Concepts and Models for Service-Learning in Philosophy*. Washington, DC: AAHE (American Association for Higher Education Series on Service-Learning in the Disciplines).

Lucas, C. J. (1969), *What is Philosophy of Education?* London: The Macmillan Company.

Noddings, N. (1998), *Philosophy of Education*. Boulder: Westview Press.

Noddings, N. (2003), *Caring: A Feminine Approach to Ethics and Moral Education*. Berkeley: University of California Press.

Poole, S. (2006), *Unspeak: How Words Become Weapons, Weapons Become a Message, and How That Message Becomes Reality*. New York: Grove Press.

Preston, C. (2003), *Grounding Knowledge: Environmental Philosophy, Epistemology, and Place*. Athens: University of Georgia Press.

Raabe, P. (2001), *Philosophical Counselling. Theory and Practice*. London: Praeger.

Read, R. (2007), *Philosophy for Life*. London: Continuum (ed. Lavery).

Shusterman, R. (1997), *Practicing Philosophy: Pragmatism and the Philosophical Life* New York: Routledge.

—(2008), *Body Consciousness. A Philosophy of Mindfulness and Somaesthetics*. Cambridge: Cambridge University Press.

Yancy, G. (2007) (ed.), *Philosophy in Multiple Voices*. Lanham: Rowman & Littlefield.

—(2002) (ed.), *The Philosophical I: Personal Reflections on Life in Philosophy*. Lanham: Rowman & Littlefield.

Index